Macroeconomics Demystified

Demystified Series

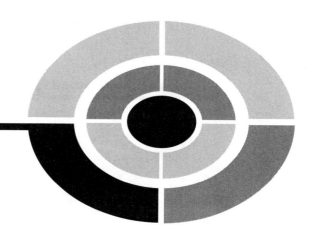

Macroeconomics Demystified

AUGUST SWANENBERG

McGRAW-HILL

New York   Chicago   San Francisco   Lisbon   London
Madrid   Mexico City   Milan   New Delhi   San Juan
Seoul   Singapore   Sydney   Toronto

3 4 5 6 7 8 9 0 DOC/DOC 0 9 8 7

ISBN 0-07-145511-6

McGraw-Hill books are available at special quantity discounts to use as premiums and sales promotions, or for use in corporate training programs. For more information, please write to the Director of Special Sales, McGraw-Hill Professional, Two Penn Plaza, New York, NY 10121-2298. Or contact your local bookstore.

Library of Congress Cataloging-in-Publication Data

Swanenberg, August.
   Macroeconomics demystified / by August Swanenberg.
      p.   cm.
   Includes index.
   ISBN 0-07-145511-6 (pbk. : alk. paper)
   1. Macroeconomics. I. Title.
   HB172.5.S93 2005

  339—dc22   2005004074

To all those who have questions about our global economy.

CONTENTS

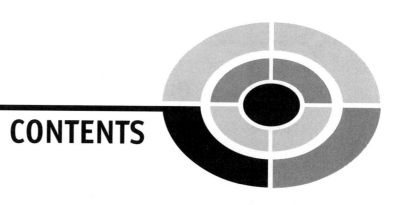

Contents

             14.1   Introduction   202
             14.2   The Goals of Monetary Policy   203
             14.3   Monetary Policy Rules   204
             14.4   Effective Policy   205
             14.5   The Mix of Monetary and Fiscal
                    Policy   206
             14.6   Global Economics and Monetary
                    Policy   208
             14.7   Hints   211
             Quiz and Answers   212

APPENDIX 1   **The Elasticity of Supply and Demand**   **217**

APPENDIX 2   **Measuring GDP, the Expenditure and
             the Income Methods**   **222**

APPENDIX 3   **A Brief History of Economic Models**   **224**

             Final Test 1 Questions   **231**

             Final Test 1 Answers   **247**

             Final Test 2 Questions   **259**

             Final Test 2 Answers   **274**

             Sources   **285**

             Glossary   **287**

             Index   **313**

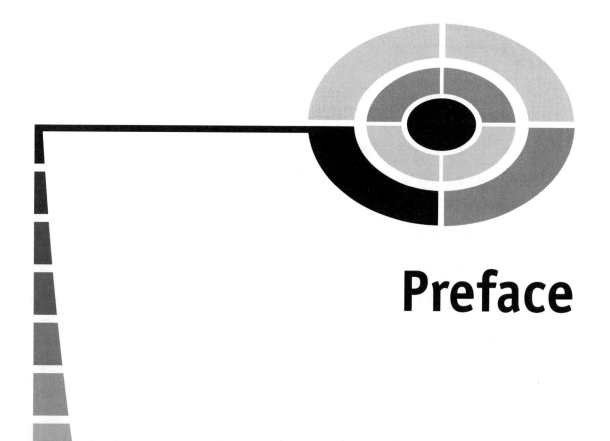

Preface

Macroeconomics touches our lives in many ways: through the income we earn in the labor market, the interest rate on our mortgage, the rates on our credit cards, and the fluctuations in the stock market, to name just a few.

In addition, the media surround us with daily headlines such as "jobless recovery," "declining dollar," and "widening trade deficit," as well as with commentary about federal fiscal and monetary policies and their impact on topics such as inflation, unemployment, Social Security, and health care.

Historically, the impact of macroeconomics has also been profound.

For example, the discussions about central banking in George Washington's first administration accelerated the development of our national political parties. Thomas Jefferson and the Democratic-Republicans, who argued that the central bank violated states' rights and was therefore unconstitutional, vehemently opposed "federal" banking, strongly advocated by Alexander Hamilton and the Federalist party.

Another example is the Great Depression (1929–1939), a traumatic experience for the United States and the western world, which led to the active policy involvement of the federal government in the pursuit of low inflation, full employment, and robust economic growth.

Yet despite its importance, there remains something mysterious about economics. Why? I believe there are two important reasons:

- **"Economics" language.** Just listen to the economics experts who use "foreign" words (cost-push inflationary pressures?) mixed with comments such as "this economy desperately needs confidence-boosting measures." Economics has a language of its own and, like any foreign language, we need to practice it to become fluent. Fortunately, the number of "foreign" words is limited and we can learn this language more quickly than, for example, French or Japanese.

  In this book, to help the student, we have used straightforward, yet precise, definitions of macroeconomic terms. Special examples of current and historic events related to macroeconomics illustrate the significance of key concepts. We hope this will greatly assist students in learning the "foreign" economics language.

  Key terms are highlighted throughout the text for easy lookup. A comprehensive glossary of macroeconomic terms and definitions is provided for quick and easy cross-referencing.

  For a thorough professional guide to microeconomic and macroeconomic terms, *The Economist: Dictionary of Economics*, 4th ed. (Graham Bannock, Ron Baxter, and Evan Davis, Bloomberg Press, 2003) is a highly valuable and authoritative reference.

- **"Economics" math.** Many people believe that a lot of math is required to understand economics. This is not true. No higher math is needed for basic economics. It is true that charts are used in economics, mostly to illustrate a theory. The good news is that one chart (i.e., supply and demand) covers so much of economics that, if you understand this chart, you are well on your way. We added a special section "Getting Started: Using Charts in Economics" that includes a discussion of the basic supply and demand graph.

I wrote this book for all those who have questions about macroeconomics—especially after reading an article or watching TV—and want them answered. *Macroeconomics Demystified* offers a unique approach to learning about macroeconomics:

- Global economics is treated as a core topic (in many macroeconomics books it is relegated to the last chapter), and global issues are included in chapters about U.S. policy. Examples of current global topics, varying from China's central banking policy to the European Central Bank, are highlighted throughout the text.
- Historical examples (e.g., the "South Sea Bubble" of 1720, the 1970s oil crisis) illustrate the recurring challenge of maintaining economic growth.
- Chapters are always followed by a quiz—including answers with explanations—to provide immediate feedback to the reader about his or her progress in understanding the material.

Preface

- Two final comprehensive tests (120 questions in total) include all major topics covered in introductory college courses in macroeconomics. Extensive answer-explanations are provided for in-depth understanding.
- A comprehensive glossary is provided for the quick and easy lookup of macroeconomic terms and their usage throughout the text.

Good luck "demystifying" macroeconomics!

Acknowledgments

I am grateful to my wife, Julie, and my daughters, Irene and Audrey, for being great sports while I kept tapping the keyboard for months. I am especially indebted to Irene who, fresh from her AP Macroeconomics exam, contributed many valuable insights. Also, kudos for Spencer, our Labrador retriever, who quietly and wisely kept his distance from the project.

I want to thank my sponsoring editors, Lisa O'Connor and Stephen Isaacs at McGrawHill. In the initial phase of the project, Lisa provided continuous encouragement and excellent feedback while demonstrating her keen grasp of macroeconomics.

Pattie Amoroso, senior editior, was a wonderful guide through the maze of revisions and editing that ultimately produced this book. Thank you for all your help.

I also want to thank copyeditor Alice Manning, production supervisor Maureen Harper, proofreader Roberta Mantus, and Westchester Book Group who did the book composition.

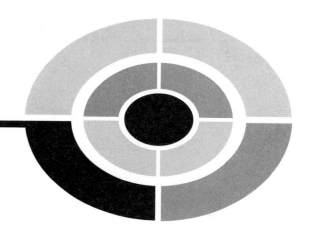

Getting Started: Using Charts in Economics

A Note to the Reader

Some of you may not be familiar with charts or may have forgotten your math lessons from long ago. This chapter is for you.

We also suggest that those of you who are familiar with charts still browse this introductory chapter, because we included a special section about supply and demand charts that will be very helpful in future chapters.

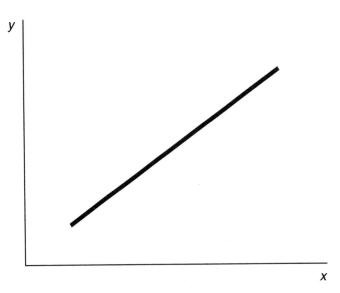

Figure I-1. A positive relationship between *x* and *y*.

Charts

We use *charts* in economics because they help to illustrate how markets and economies work. They also clarify the differences between economic theories without requiring lengthy explanations and equations. Charts are therefore valuable tools in studying economics.

Basic charts in economics have a *horizontal scale line (x axis)* and a *vertical scale line (y axis)*; the intersection of the two lines is called the *origin*. Price and quantities are the most important variables in economics. Because both are (usually) positive, we look only at that part of the scales where *x* and *y* are positive, (or zero) (see Fig. I-1).

In economics, there are three important relationships between variables:

- *Positive relationship.* The variables move in the same direction: When *x* increases, *y* also goes up (see Fig. I-1).
- *Negative relationship.* The variables move in opposite directions: When *x* increases, *y* goes down (see Fig. I-2).
- *Unrelated.* When one of the variables changes, the other does not. This means that the line is either vertical or horizontal (see Fig. I-3).

The *slope* of a relationship is the change in the value of the variable (e.g., price) on the *y* axis divided by the change in the value of the variable on the *x*

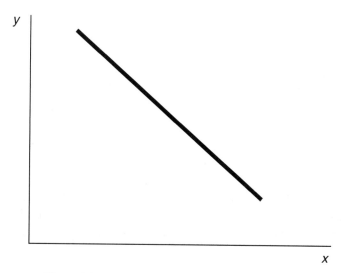

Figure I-2. A negative relationship between *x* and *y*.

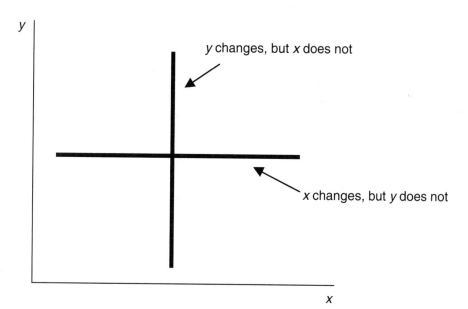

Figure I-3. No relationship between *x* and *y*. Vertical and horizontal lines indicate no relationship.

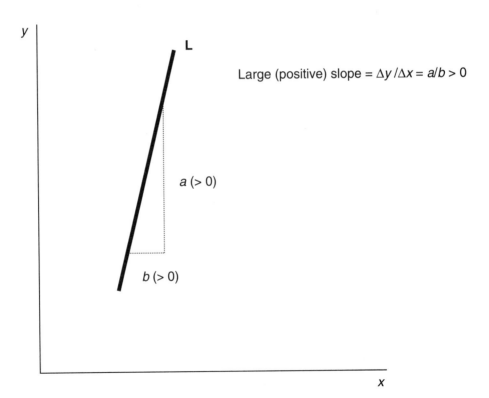

axis (e.g., quantity). The formula for the slope of the relationship between x and y is sometimes written as $\Delta y/\Delta x$, with the symbol Δ meaning "change in." This means that

The slope of the relationship between x and $y =$ change in y/change in $x = \Delta y/\Delta x$

A positive relationship is also called *upward-sloping* because its slope is positive. A negative relationship is called *downward-sloping*. A *straight line* (or *linear* relationship) has a constant slope, while a *curved line* (or *nonlinear* relationship) has a slope that varies, depending on the value of x.

The slope is a shorthand way to indicate the kind of relationship between variables x and y. For example, straight lines have different slopes, depending on the type of relationship (positive, negative, or no relationship) and on how "vertical" or how "horizontal" the lines are. Line L in Fig. I-4 has a large, positive slope a/b

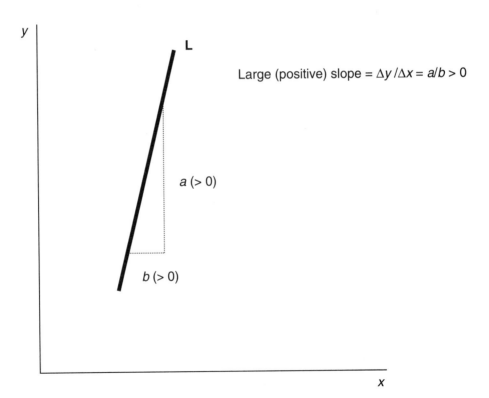

Figure I-4. Straight line L with large positive slope.

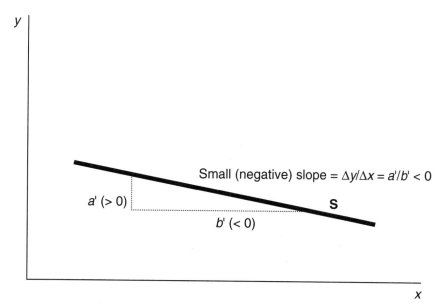

Figure I-5. Straight line S with small negative slope.

(highly vertical, positive relationship), while line S in Fig. I-5 has a small, negative slope a'/b' (highly horizontal, negative relationship).

The slope is important because it helps to answer questions about what the change in one variable will mean to the other variable. For example, how much does the quantity demanded of a product change when the price of the product goes up by 10 percent? In Fig. I-4 (line L), a small change in x has a large, positive impact on y. In Fig. I-5 (line S) a large change in x has a small, negative impact on y.

An important assumption is used to understand the relationships between more than two variables, for example, the relationships between price, quantity demanded, and consumer income. These kinds of relationships can be analyzed by holding the value of one or more variables constant while charting the relationship between the two remaining variables. For example, we can chart the relationship between price and quantity demanded, while assuming that consumer income is constant (e.g., income = $50,000). The assumption of holding one or more variables in a relationship constant is called *ceteris paribus* (Latin for "all other things held the same"). It allows us to chart the relationship between price and quantity demanded, while keeping in mind that income is at a certain level. If we change consumer income (e.g., from $50,000 to $60,000), then the price-quantity curve will shift, as illustrated in Fig. I-6.

Income is held constant at \$50,000 for demand curve D_1, which describes the relationship between price and quantity demanded. The demand curve shifts to the right from D_1 to D_2 if income increases from \$50,000 to \$60,000. This leads to a higher quantity demanded (Q_2 instead of Q_1) for the same price P.

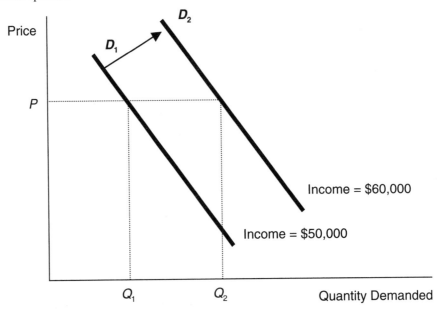

Figure I-6. The *ceteris paribus* assumption.

Charting Supply and Demand

The *ceteris paribus* assumption is very helpful for charting supply and demand. For example, in studying the quantity demanded of a brand of automobile, we want to first understand how price affects quantity demanded, while holding all other relevant factors, such as the prices of other brands, preferences, income, and so on, constant. It makes sense to assume that the higher the price for a car, the less the quantity demanded will be. This means that demanded quantity Q goes down as price P goes up. In other words, there is a negative relationship between P and Q. The *ceteris paribus* condition means that the quantity demanded is assumed to depend on the price level only, while other variables are assumed to be held constant (consumer preferences, income, and so on).

In economics, the convention is that price is on the y axis and quantity on the x axis. A linear demand curve is illustrated in Fig. I-7.

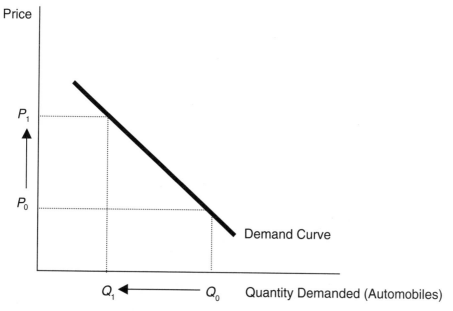

Figure I-7. Quantity demanded goes down from Q_0 to Q_1 as price (of automobiles) increases from P_0 to P_1.

Next, we want to understand how the supply of automobiles is affected by the price (while holding other factors, such as input prices and production technology constant). We assume that the higher the price for a car, the more likely it is that producers will supply more, because they can increase their revenues. So the quantity supplied Q goes up as price P increases (see Fig. I-8).

When we combine the demand curve and the supply curve in one chart, the intersection of the curves yields the market-clearing price P^* where quantity demanded and supplied Q^* are in balance (see Fig. I-9).

Assume that consumer income increases (a factor we held constant so far) from INC to INC$^+$. As a result the demand curve D will shift to the right (to D') because the quantity demanded at a given price goes up because of the income increase, provided the good is not inferior (see Chapter 2, "Microeconomics"). The result is a higher market price P' and higher market quantity Q' (see Fig. I-10).

We are now able to understand the impact of a variable (e.g., consumer income) on the outcome in the market. A similar demand analysis for change in preferences, prices of other products, and so on can be done. Also, we can analyze supply by first looking at price and quantity and then varying factors such as

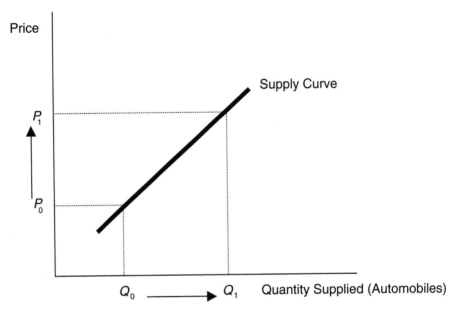

Figure I-8. Quantity supplied goes up from Q_0 to Q_1 when the price of automobiles increases from P_0 to P_1.

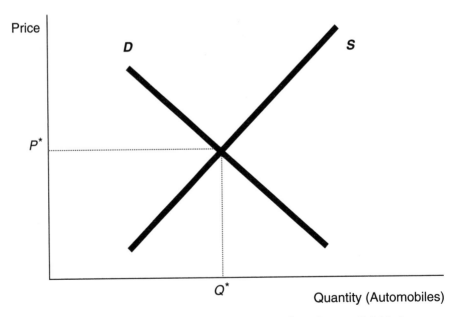

Figure I-9. The intersection of demand curve D and supply curve S yields the market-clearing outcome (Q^*, P^*).

The shift in the demand curve from D to D' (caused by an increase in consumer income from INC to INC$^+$) moves the market outcome from (Q^*, P^*) to (Q', P'): the higher income INC$^+$ leads to a higher market quantity and higher market price.

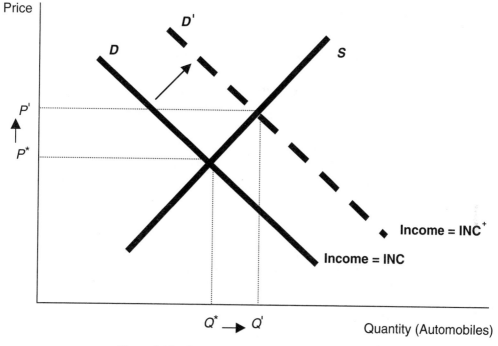

Figure I-10. Impact of a change in consumer income.

technology. This kind of supply and demand analysis is very important in economics and is used throughout the book.

Hints

HI.1 Economists use charts to simplify analysis. Charts can be very illustrative in demonstrating the impact of a change in income or a change in technology by a simple shift of a line. In addition, it can be very insightful to illustrate an economic theory (e.g., Keynesian theory) by using a chart.

HI.2 Charts are very helpful in describing statistical results, such as the yearly rate of inflation over the last 20 years. This kind of analysis is called a *time series*.

Mini-Quiz

True or False? Explain.

1. A horizontal line means that x and y are related.
2. If the relationship between two variables x and y is a vertical line, then x and y are not related.
3. The slope of a negative relationship is positive.
4. The slope of a straight line is a constant.
5. It is not possible to chart things that are not related.

Mini-Quiz Answers

1. False. A horizontal line means that y does not change, no matter what the value of x. This implies that x and y are not related.
2. True. The vertical line means that x does not change at all, no matter what the value of y is.
3. False. The slope of a negative relationship is negative, not positive.
4. True. The slope of a straight line (or linear relationship) does not change; it is a constant.
5. False. Vertical and horizontal lines indicate that no relation exists between x and y.

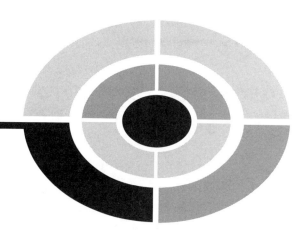

Macroeconomics: A Quick Self-Test

This self-test is a quick way to test your current knowledge of macroeconomics. Do the test again after you have finished the book. You *will* be able to tell the difference. Good luck!

Please indicate T for true and F for false in the statements that follow.

1. If a nation maintains a high economic growth rate, then structural unemployment will be low.   T   F
2. Money is an important economic resource.   T   F
3. The higher the GDP, the better off everybody is.   T   F
4. Full employment means that unemployment is zero.   T   F
5. The average recession lasts about the same amount of time as the average expansion.   T   F
6. Inflation hurts everyone.   T   F
7. The money we use has intrinsic value.   T   F
8. Tariffs are sometimes needed to protect our standard of living from cheap foreign labor.   T   F
9. The Federal Reserve's main task is to insure the deposits of bank customers.   T   F
10. The U.S. economy is an unguided free-market economy.   T   F

Note: Answers to Self-Test on next page.

Answers to the Macroeconomics Quick Self-Test

All answers are *False*.

1. Structural unemployment results from new technology that replaces workers (e.g., the use of robotics in manufacturing). Advances in technology support a high economic growth rate, and therefore structural unemployment may be a result of economic growth. This requires that workers be retrained to obtain the necessary skills to be successful participants in the labor market.

2. Money is not considered an economic resource (also called a *factor of production*). The economic resources are land, labor, capital, and entrepreneurship.

3. A higher GDP does not imply the equitable distribution of income. There may be people who are worse off, even when the GDP grows.

4. Full employment is the sum of frictional unemployment (people who are temporarily unemployed because they are in transition from one job to another) and structural unemployment (unemployment caused by technology advances and lack of training or education). The U.S. rate of full employment is estimated to be between 3.5 and 4.0 percent.

5. The average expansion lasts about four years; the average recession, about one year.

6. Those who borrowed money in the past are the immediate beneficiaries of inflation because the "old" amount of money they are required to pay back has decreased in value as a result of inflation. For example, the bank will be repaid for the $1,000 it lent several years ago, but the $1,000 now buys less than it did several years ago; that is, the borrower wins and the bank loses. The example assumes that no special "inflation" or "cost-of-living" indexing or adjustment rule applies to the originally negotiated loan.

7. Modern economies use fiduciary money with practically no intrinsic value; that is, the coins and paper themselves are almost worthless. The use of money is based on trust (i.e., the government has officially declared the money to be the legal means of payment). In contrast, the use of money in less developed economies may involve silver and gold coins with immediate, inherent value (i.e., intrinsic value).

8. The use of tariffs leads to higher costs of products and will not protect the standard of living. Free trade is a powerful source of economic growth, and protectionist measures may benefit some groups (e.g., domestic producers protected by the tariff) but not the whole economy.

9. The Federal Reserve is responsible for U.S. monetary policy, with the major goal of achieving price stability by influencing the supply of money. The insurance of bank deposits is provided by the Federal Deposit Insurance Corporation (FDIC), created by Congress in 1933.

10. The U.S. economy, although primarily a free-market economy, is guided by the government's (and the Federal Reserve's) policies to achieve major macroeconomic goals, including economic growth, full employment, and price stability.

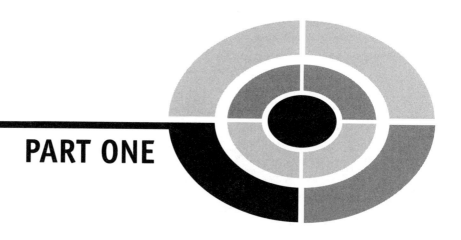

PART ONE

Setting the Stage

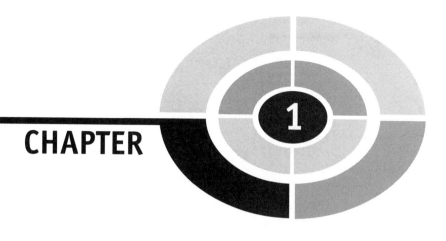

CHAPTER 1

Introduction to Economics

The main premise of economics is simple enough: "You can't have everything you want." But who gets what? Why? And is it the best we can do?
And on a larger scale, how does our national economy work? What are "good" results? What are "not so good" results? Is our economy efficient, or could it do better? Can we change the outcome?
These are essential questions in economics. Let's look for answers.

1.1   Scarcity

Scarcity is a situation in which the needs and wants of an individual (or a group of individuals) for economic goods exceed the resources available to satisfy them. Because of scarcity, the available resources have to be rationed, either through price or through an organized distribution mechanism. The objective of economics

is to explain the way in which the production, distribution, exchange, and consumption of goods and services take place.

Because of scarcity, economic decisions will always involve a form of *trade-off*, that is, consuming (or producing) more of one good or service means consuming (or producing) less of another. For example, if we decide to buy a book for $25, we also decide to not use the amount for something else, such as putting it in a savings account.

Microeconomics is the study of economics focusing on the behavior of individual units or groups of units, such as households, corporations, or industry sectors. *Macroeconomics* is the study of the economics of very large entities, such as a national economy.

1.2   Economic Systems

An *economic system* is the organization of production, distribution, exchange, and consumption of goods and services used by people to achieve a certain *standard of living*.

Economic systems may have different degrees of central control and private ownership and different exchange mechanisms. There are four general types of economic systems:

- The *free-market economic system* uses private ownership, individual economic freedom, competition, the profit motive, and the market price system to achieve economic goals. Encouraging the pursuit of individual economic self-interest in free markets is expected to provide efficient and productive outcomes that are in the best interest of society as a whole. The government is not expected to intervene to change the outcome. The U.S. economy in the nineteenth century and the early twentieth century is an example of this kind of system.

- The *centralized economic system* uses public ownership and centralized control of the means of production. A central authority controls economic plans, and individual decision making plays a limited role in determining economic policy. North Korea, Cuba, and the former U.S.S.R. are examples of this kind of system. China used to be another example of a fully centralized system, but it has recently moved toward a mixed centralized/free-market system.

- The *mixed economic system* has elements of both the free market and a centralized system. The U.S. economy was historically a free-market system, but government (and the Federal Reserve) has played an increasingly important role in the last hundred years. Western European economies traditionally have provided a stronger central role for government than the U.S. economy, although they are still essentially free-market economic systems. China and Russia, with historically centralized systems, are developing free-market approaches in their respective economies.

- The *traditional economic system* is based on customs and habits, relying mostly on relatively simple technologies. Developing nations (e.g., certain nations in Africa) are examples of traditional systems. Very traditional systems (e.g., those in rural areas in developing nations) may (partly) rely on a *barter economy*, that is the acquisition of goods and services by exchanging other goods and services for them. Recently, barter deals involving surplus products and credits have developed in modern economies, for example, TV advertising time.

Modern economic systems in Western nations are primarily free-market systems with a significant guiding role for the government. In the remainder of this book, we will limit ourselves to the guided free-market economic system for the allocation of scarce resources. Within this context, an *economic good* is any physical object or service rendered that could command a price in a market.

Free-market systems allow people to pursue their self-interest: Consumers buy goods according to their preferences, and firms are required to produce what consumers desire if they want to stay in business. This is called *consumer sovereignty*.

Because of competition from other businesses, firms have the incentive to produce high-quality products in an efficient, low-cost manner. Firms may decide on the type of organization that best suits their objectives. Three basic types of organization used by firms are

- *Sole proprietor.* The owner and the business are legally treated as one entity, and the individual recognizes profits as income.
- *Partnership.* More than one owner is involved, and profits are recognized as income and divided among the owners through some form of sharing. Individuals and company are, legally, combined entities.
- *Corporation.* The business is a separate entity for legal purposes. The income of the business is not recognized as the individual owners' income. The owners are stockholders, and the corporation continues independently from the individuals who founded it.

The factors of production are owned by individuals in a free-market economy, unlike centralized economies, where the state holds ownership. Therefore *property rights* are critical in the free-market economy, for producers as well as consumers.

For example, imagine buying a house in a system that does not fully protect individual ownership or a person's right of exclusive usage.

1.3 Economic Models

Models are simplified representations of complex objects, such as geographic maps. Some models are better suited to represent an object than others. For example, a flat map in an atlas is good enough to measure distances within a U.S. state, but we will need a globe to measure very large distances (e.g., from the Netherlands to New Zealand).

Models can provide insights about real-world economic events. Economists try to find the model that—they believe—best describes economic reality and study the implications of that model for economic policy. *Economic policy* is the deliberate course of action taken by government to influence the outcome of the economy (e.g., lowering personal taxes to stimulate the economy). *Economic reasoning* is the logical application of model assumptions and the analysis of the consequences.

To simplify the analysis of relationships among three (or more) variables, economists use the *ceteris paribus* ("all other factors held constant") condition. For example, the *demand curve* is the relationship between price and quantity demanded, with other factors such as income and preferences held constant (see also "Getting Started"). If either income or preferences change, the demand curve will shift.

1.4 Opportunity Cost

Opportunity cost is a central concept in economics. It is a key to understanding individual choice in microeconomics, and it is also of fundamental importance in macroeconomics (e.g., international trade).

Scarcity implies that a trade-off exists between wants that can be satisfied and those that cannot be. If we have $25 and we spend it to buy a book, we have made a choice that has a trade-off: We gave up doing something else with the $25, such as buying a restaurant meal, gas for the car, or movie tickets, or depositing the money in a savings account.

A person's opportunity cost of an action is that person's next highest-valued alternative given up as a result of the action. For example, Person A who buys the book may consider the restaurant meal the next-best alternative. This means that Person A's opportunity cost of buying the book is the restaurant meal. Person B

values saving the money as the next-best alternative, and therefore Person B's opportunity cost of buying the book is depositing the money in a savings account. The example demonstrates that the opportunity cost of the book purchase is not the same for every person and depends on each person's preferences.

1.5   Production Possibilities Curve

The *production possibilities curve (PPC)* is the graphical representation of the opportunity cost of using scarce resources to produce one good (or service) instead of another good (or service). We assume that resources can always be shifted from one product to the other.

Assume that the economy (see Fig. 1-1) is currently producing 20 units of good B and 0 units of Good A. The opportunity cost of increasing production of Good A from 0 units to 1 unit is giving up 1 unit of Good B (i.e., going from 20 units to 19 units). The opportunity cost of increasing production of Good A from 1 unit to 2 units is giving up 3 units (i.e., 19 units – 16 units) of Good B. Finally, the opportunity cost of increasing production of Good A from 2 units to 3 units is giving up 16 units (i.e., 16 units – 0 units) of Good B.

This demonstrates that the *"bowed out" (concave)* production possibilities curve implies increasing opportunity costs as production of one good or service rather

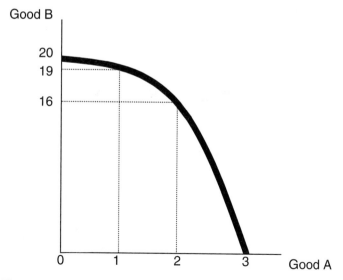

Figure 1-1.   The concave ("bowed out") production possibilities curve.

than another continues to increase. This reflects the increasing lack of skilled or specialized resources as production of a specific good or service goes up. For example, if Good A represents hospitals and Good B office buildings, then the increasing construction of hospitals will put a strain on the number of people specialized in hospital construction, increasing the opportunity cost of building ever more hospitals.

The previous PPC example refers to relatively small-scale, microeconomic cases involving production of two specific goods or services, A and B. The following PPC example applies to macroeconomic situations, and the production possibilities represent the output (and capacity) of an entire national economy.

The PPC of an entire economy is determined by the availability of its factors of production. *Factors of production* (or inputs) are the economic resources available to an economy to produce goods and services. They are

- *Land* (all natural resources, including the sea and outer space)
- *Labor* (the people available for, or engaged in, the production of goods and services, including their physical and intellectuals skills and effort)
- *Capital* (machines, plant, and buildings that make production possible, excluding raw materials, land, and labor)
- *Entrepreneurship* (the ability and will to efficiently and creatively organize resources for production)

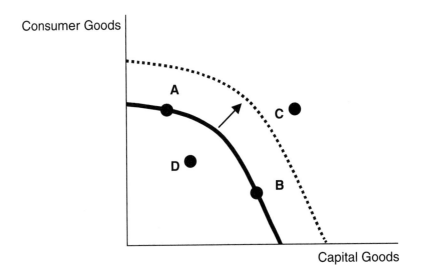

Figure 1-2.   The economy's production possibilities curve (PPC).

Efficient production requires firms to operate on the production possibilities curve (the "frontier"), not at some point inside the curve. In Fig. 1-2, point D is inefficient because resources are underutilized, while point C is not attainable with current levels of resources and technology. Points A and B on the curve are efficient because they use all available resources. Point A indicates the production of a relatively high number of consumer goods, while point B indicates the production of a relatively high number of capital goods. Point D indicates unemployment of the labor force and underutilization of capital: The economy is not operating efficiently and is in a (short-run) recession or depression.

When more capital goods are produced, the larger capital stock (e.g., factories and equipment) will allow the economy to increase its *economic growth*. In addition, increases in labor, natural resources, or technology may shift the production possibilities curve to the right (see the dotted curve in Fig. 1-2).

1.6 Comparative Advantage

The production possibilities curve can also be used for applications in international trade. Assume that Countries A and B produce beer and orange juice and that their PPCs are given in Fig. 1-3.

Country A can produce both more beer (9 million gallons) and more orange juice (3 million gallons) than Country B. This means that Country A has an *absolute advantage* in the production of both items (assuming their resources are equal).

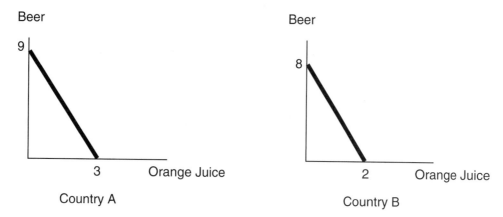

Figure 1-3. PPCs for Countries A and B (in millions of gallons).

The opportunity cost is the given-up good (or service) that cannot be produced if a country decides to produce an alternative good or service. The country with the lowest opportunity cost has a *comparative advantage* and should specialize in the production of that good or service.

Country A's opportunity cost to produce 1 gallon of beer is giving up 1/3 gallon of orange juice (i.e., 3 divided by 9), while Country B's opportunity cost to produce 1 gallon of beer is 1/4 gallon of orange juice (i.e., 2 divided by 8). Therefore, Country B has a comparative advantage in producing beer because its opportunity cost (0.25 gallon of given-up orange juice) is less than Country A's opportunity cost (0.33 gallon of given-up orange juice). Conversely, Country A's opportunity cost to produce 1 gallon of orange juice (3 gallons of given-up beer) is smaller than Country B's opportunity cost (4 gallons of given-up beer), so Country A has a comparative advantage in orange juice production.

The countries combine production by Country A specializing in orange juice and Country B specializing in beer. To make trade beneficial, a country must receive an amount for its production greater than its opportunity cost. In this example, Country A must get more than 3 gallons of beer for each gallon of orange juice traded, and Country B must get more than 1/4 gallon of orange juice for every gallon of beer traded.

NOTE N1.6A

A Short History of International Free Trade

Before 1800, the scope of international free trade was limited, and countries pursued narrow domestic economic goals.

In the sixteenth and seventeenth centuries, the so-called *mercantilists* emphasized the power of the national economy, favoring state intervention to maximize wealth by building huge export surpluses. In the late eighteenth and early nineteenth centuries, *classical economists* condemned mercantilism as inefficient. The classical school favored free trade between nations, based on comparative advantage and without government interference. Although the classical view has been refined in the last two centuries, it essentially remains the dominant theory of international free trade.

The 1948 *General Agreement on Tariffs and Trade (GATT)* was the first comprehensive framework to establish worldwide free trade based on a commitment by nations to remove special protective tariffs and trade arrangements. The GATT framework culminated in the *World Trade Organization (WTO),* a global organization dedicated to multilateral trade with a minimum of trade barriers.

For example, the WTO spearheaded the worldwide removal of global quotas on textile products by 2005.

Recently, there has been significant progress in the development of free-trade areas. They include the North American Free Trade Agreement (NAFTA), the European Union (EU), the Association of South East Asian Nations (ASEAN), and Mercosur (the "Southern Common Market," a customs union of a group of South American nations). The objective of these organizations is the reduction of internal import tariffs and quotas and the abolition of preferential trade agreements.

NOTE N1.6B

David Ricardo and International Trade

Comparative advantage and opportunity cost are the driving forces behind international trade. Curiously, Adam Smith (1723–1790), who is considered the founder of classical economics, missed this crucial point. David Ricardo (1772– 1823) was the first person to recognize the importance of a country's relative advantage (*not* its absolute advantage) as the key source of benefits from international trade.

1.7   Hints

H1.1   It is important not to confuse money with economic resources. Money is a medium of exchange, while economic resources are factors of production. For example, the word *capital* refers to goods used in the production process, such as factories and equipment. It is not financial capital, which is the money used to purchase factories and equipment.

H1.2   The example in Fig. 1-3 shows two countries with linear production possibilities curves. This means that the opportunity cost is constant at each level of production, unlike the increasing opportunity cost of the "bowed out" or concave PPC in Fig. 1-4.

H1.3   There are two quick ways to determine which country, A or B, has a comparative advantage for Product X when both countries have linear PPCs.

Input Method (for example, see Fig. 1-4)

For both countries, divide the inputs required for 1 unit of Product X by the inputs required for 1 unit of Product Y.

Figure 1-4.   Comparative advantage, input method.

Input Method

Hours Needed to Produce 1,000 Bushels	*Country A*	*Country B*
Wheat	12 hours	10 hours
Barley	6 hours	10 hours

Opportunity cost for wheat: 12 hours/6 hours = 2.0   **10 hours/10 hours = 1.0**

Opportunity cost for barley: **6 hours/12 hours = 0.5**   10 hours/10 hours = 1.0

Country B has a comparative advantage (lowest opportunity cost) for wheat; Country A has a comparative advantage for barley.

Figure 1-5.   Comparative advantage, output method.

Output Method

Output in Bushels with 120 Hours of Input	*Country A*	*Country B*
Wheat	10,000	12,000
Barley	20,000	12,000

Opportunity cost for wheat: 20,000/10,000 = 2.0   **12,000/12,000 = 1.0**

Opportunity cost for barley: **10,000/20,000 = 0.5**   12,000/12,000 = 1.0

Country B has a comparative advantage (lowest opportunity cost) for wheat; Country A has a comparative advantage for barley.

The country with the lowest ratio (or opportunity cost of producing X) has a comparative advantage for Product X. The other country will have a comparative advantage for Product Y.
Output Method (for example, Fig. 1-5)
For both countries, divide output for Product Y by output for product X. (Note: This is the reverse of the input method.)

The country with the lowest ratio (or opportunity cost of producing X) has a comparative advantage for Product X. The other country will have a comparative advantage for Product Y.

H1.4   Economics is not necessarily restricted to material welfare only. A more general definition may be that "economics studies human behavior as a relationship between ends and scarce means that have alternative uses." Borderline areas between economics and fields such as psychology, sociology, history, accounting, and geography are hard to define precisely. In addition, the mutual impact of politics and economics is significant and points to the subjective nature of economics, despite its scientific aspects.

Quiz

Choose the one best answer for each question.

Q1.1   Opportunity cost is
   (a) paid for by society.
   (b) the cost of producing a good or service.
   (c) the highest-valued alternative given up by making a choice.
   (d) all the alternatives given up by making a choice.
   (e) giving up an opportunity because it's not important.

Q1.2   Which of the following is a macroeconomic topic?
   (a) How does a rise in the crude oil price affect gas refinery prices?
   (b) How do new gas mileage regulations affect sales of SUVs?
   (c) Why are desktop computers so cheap?
   (d) What factors determine the nation's inflation rate?
   (e) How does recent growth in the food manufacturing industry affect the grocery industry?

Q1.3   *Ceteris paribus* means
   (a) theory is composed of assumptions and hypotheses.
   (b) what is true for the whole must be true for the parts.
   (c) all other factors are held constant.
   (d) models leading to positive conclusions are faulty.
   (e) people's free will makes prediction impossible.

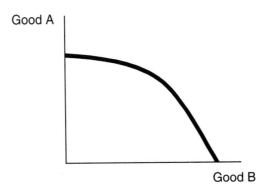

Figure 1-6. Concave ("bowed out") production possibilities curve.

Q1.4 Which of the following is true if the production possibilities curve is concave to the origin (see Fig. 1-6)?
(a) Marginal costs are decreasing.
(b) Opportunity costs are increasing.
(c) Resources are perfectly substitutable.
(d) There are increasing returns to scale.
(e) Both products satisfy consumer wants in the same way.

Q1.5 Which of the following is *not* an economic resource?
(a) Land
(b) Labor
(c) Capital
(d) Money
(e) Entrepreneurship

Q1.6 For a product or service to be scarce, it must be
   I. available for free.
  II. something people want.
 III. limited in supply.

(a) I only
(b) I and II only
(c) II and III only
(d) I and III only
(e) I, II, and III

Q1.7 The fundamental problem of economics is
(a) developing a price mechanism to resolve scarcity.
(b) reducing unemployment.

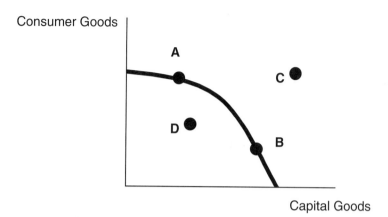

Figure 1-7. The economy's production possibilities curve.

(c) establishing a fair tax system.
(d) providing social goods and services.
(e) allocating scarce productive resources to satisfy
      wants.

Q1.8 Keeping all other factors the same, which point in Fig. 1-7 describes the
       situation in which the economy can produce more consumer goods with
       the same number of capital goods?
       (a) Point A (on the PPC)
       (b) Point B (on the PPC)
       (c) Point C (outside the PPC)
       (d) Point D (inside the PPC)
       (e) None of the above

Q1.9 Which of the following would cause a leftward shift of the economy's
       production possibilities curve?
       (a) A decrease in consumer demand
       (b) A decrease in the total population of available
            workers
       (c) A increase in unemployment
       (d) An increase in the productivity of technology
       (e) An increase in capital

Q1.10 See Fig. 1-8. What kind of advantage exists in the production of wine
        and beer between Countries A and B, and what kind of specialization
        and trade will occur?

Figure 1-8.   Input requirements for wine and beer production in Countries A and B.

Labor Input Required to Produce 100 Gallons	*Country A*	*Country B*
Wine	10 hours	7 hours
Beer	6 hours	7 hours

(a) Country A has an absolute advantage in the production of both wine and beer; no specialization or trade between countries will occur.

(b) Country B has an absolute advantage in the production of both wine and beer; no specialization or trade between countries will occur.

(c) Country B has a comparative advantage in the production of beer and will specialize in beer production, trading beer for wine from Country A, which will specialize in wine.

(d) Country A has a comparative advantage in the production of beer, and will specialize in beer production, trading beer for wine from Country B, which will specialize in wine.

(e) Country A has a comparative advantage in the production of beer, and no specialization or trade will occur.

Q1.11 Private ownership of resources and the market price system are characteristic of what kind of economic system?

(a) Traditional

(b) Mix of centralized and free market

(c) Centralized

(d) Free market

(e) Traditional, rural areas

Q1.12 If more capital goods (e.g., factories and equipment) are produced in a free-market economy, then

(a) unemployment goes up.

(b) it leads to inefficient production.

(c) economic growth increases.
(d) opportunity costs go up.
(e) it leads to less private ownership.

Quiz Answers

Q1.1 (c). Opportunity costs result from scarcity, which requires choice; the opportunity cost represents the trade-off (the next-best alternative or the highest-valued good or service *not* chosen). For example, activities that take time usually have an opportunity cost because scarce time could have been spent on other valued activities. People's opportunity costs may be different; that is, even if they select the same product, their next-best alternative may be different because of personal preferences.

Q1.2 (d). Macroeconomic topics deal with the economy as a whole, as opposed to specific products (e.g., oil, food, or computers) or specific sectors (e.g., food manufacturing or retail). A nation's inflation rate is a typical macroeconomic topic; it refers to overall price levels in a national economy.

Q1.3 (c). *Ceteris paribus* is Latin for "all other things held constant," a common simplifying assumption in economics. For example, the aggregate demand and aggregate supply curves depend on the price level, *ceteris paribus*. This means that a specific quantity-price curve results, provided all other variables are held constant (e.g., preferences and technology).

Q1.4 (b). The concave production possibilities curve reflects the fact that it is increasingly hard to find resources, for example, skilled labor, to produce more and more of the one product at the expense of the other product. This is the principle of increasing opportunity costs.

Q1.5 (d). Money is a medium of exchange; it is not an economic resource (or factor of production).

Q1.6 (c). Scarcity results when the needs and wants of an individual (or group) exceed the resources available to satisfy them. Consequently, the available resources have to be rationed, either through price or through some central distribution system.

Q1.7 (e). Economics is about the problem of allocating scarce resources. It does not need to be through price that resources are allocated (instead, it could be through a central distribution system). Although the other answers

Figure 1-9. Opportunity costs for Countries A and B.

Opportunity Cost	Country A	Country B
Wine (100 gallons)	167 gallons beer	100 gallons beer
Beer (100 gallons)	60 gallons wine	100 gallons wine

represent worthwhile objectives, they are not the fundamental problem of economics.

Q1.8 (d). Points A and B are on the production possibilities curve, which means that the economy cannot produce more consumer goods without giving up capital goods (points on the curve are on the economy's efficient frontier). Point C is outside of the PPC and therefore cannot be produced by the economy; it exceeds the available economic resources. Point D, inside the PPC, allows the economy to move up vertically (i.e., produce more consumer goods) while maintaining the same number of capital goods.

Q1.9 (b). The production possibilities curve represents the efficient frontier for an economy, based on that economy's factors of production (land, labor, capital, and entrepreneurship). The curve will shift left (indicating a decreased capacity to produce) if the availability of one of these factors decreases. A decrease in the worker population decreases the availability of labor as a factor and consequently decreases the capacity of the economy (*ceteris paribus*, i.e., all other things being equal). Answer (c) refers to a temporary issue and is therefore not related to the economy's capacity.

Q1.10 (d). Neither country has an absolute advantage in both products. The country with the lowest opportunity cost for Product X has a comparative advantage, will specialize in the production of X, and will trade Product X for the other product, the "specialty" of the second country. The opportunity cost for Country A of producing 100 gallons of beer (6 hours) is the forgone production of wine, i.e., 60 gallons (the amount of wine Country A *could have* produced within 6 hours). We calculate the opportunity costs as indicated in Fig. 1-9.

Country A has a comparative advantage in beer and will specialize in beer, trading for wine with Country B, which has a comparative advantage in wine production.

Q1.11 (d). Private ownership and the market price system are hallmarks of the free-market system. They may occur in (a), (b), or (e), but they are *the* characteristic of (d). Please note that answer (c) is incorrect.

Q1.12 (c). Production of more capital goods increases the capital stock of an economy and increases its productive capacity. Therefore, it enhances economic growth by moving the production possibilities frontier outward.

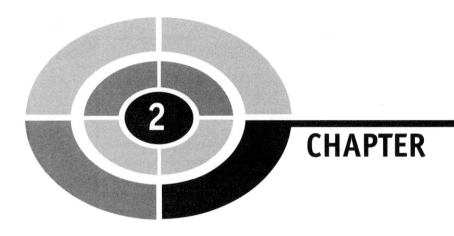

CHAPTER 2

Microeconomics

Potential buyers need potential sellers (and vice versa).
Potential buyers and sellers meet in marketplaces, for example, the garage sale next door, classified ads, eBay, or the New York Stock Exchange.
When potential buyers and sellers agree on a price, the actual exchange of goods and services for money takes place.
The market equilibrium, when potential demand and supply are balanced, is the intersection of the demand curve and the supply curve.

2.1   Markets

A *market* is any organization of contacts between potential sellers and potential buyers based on a mutually accepted means of exchange. This definition covers a wide variety of markets, from sophisticated electronic financial markets to traditional street markets. In the 1990s, the Internet created novel types of exchanges for consumers (e.g., online ordering and eBay), and for businesses (e.g., e-procurement and business-to-business online auctions).

For a successful market to develop, the participants' confidence in the exchange mechanism is required. Without the inherent trust of potential buyers and sellers, a market would not be able to function (see Note N2.1 on eBay's feedback score).

NOTE N2.1

eBay's Feedback Score

eBay, a major online auction Web site, provides services that are unique and impossible to duplicate by old economy ("brick-and-mortar") companies. In fact, eBay's job is to connect people rather than to sell them things. Therefore, eBay is a novel market in the purest sense: a new type of organization that allows potential demand and supply to exchange. All eBay participants receive a "feedback score" based on their previous buying and selling participation, quality of product offered, timing of delivery, and so on. This way, potential buyers or sellers can evaluate specific potential partners in an exchange to assess their reliability. Also, they build their own feedback score ("reputation") by participating in transactions.

Demand is the quantity of goods and services that consumers are willing to buy at different prices, while *supply* is the quantity of goods or services that producers are willing to sell at different prices.

The *Law of Demand* states that the quantity demanded increases as the price goes down, and the amount that consumers are willing and able to purchase decreases when prices go up. This law holds provided everything else remains the same (the *ceteris paribus* assumption). The factors held constant include income, prices of substitutes and complementary goods, and consumer preferences (see the section "Getting Started" for an example of *ceteris paribus*).

The *Law of Supply* states that the quantity supplied increases as the price goes up, and the quantity producers are willing to produce decreases when prices go down. This law holds provided everything else remains the same (the *ceteris paribus* assumption). The factors held constant include technology, the cost of inputs, and the prices of other goods.

2.2   Demand Curve

The *demand curve* is a graphic representation of price (on the *y* axis) and quantity demanded (on the *x* axis), based on a schedule of potential demand. For simplicity, we assume that the demand curve is a straight line. It has a negative slope (i.e., it runs downward from top left to bottom right) because of the Law of Demand.

Figure 2-1.   Schedules for demand curves D_1 and D_2.

Price (P)	Quantity Demanded (D_1-Curve)	Quantity Demanded (D_2-Curve)
10.00	20	30
9.00	30	40
8.00	40	50
7.00	50	60
6.50	55	65
6.00	60	70
5.50	65	75
5.00	70	80
4.00	80	90
3.00	90	100
2.00	100	110

Please note:

- The movements *along* the demand curve are changes in demand caused by price changes, i.e., the first and second columns (for the D_1 curve) or the first and third columns (for the D_2 curve).
- The movement *of* the demand curve (caused by variations in factors other than price, e.g., income) is represented by the second and third columns (shift from the D_1 curve to the D_2 curve). The D_2 curve is identical to the D_1 curve with an additional quantity of 10 added for each given price. Going from D_1 to D_2 is a rightward shift of the demand curve, perhaps as a result of higher consumer income.

The schedules for demand curves D_1 and D_2 are given in Fig. 2-1. The graphic representation of these two demand schedules is given in Fig. 2-2.

Both curves are linear relationships (or straight lines; see "Getting Started"), and curve D_2 represents a shift of $+10$ in quantity demanded at any given price (relative to curve D_1).

Note the critical difference between the two types of movement:

- Movement *along* the demand curve results from changes in price that cause changes in quantity demanded; for example, movements along curve D_1 (with all other factors held constant).

Figure 2-2.   Demand curves D_1 and D_2.

- Movement *of* the demand curve—for example, from curve D_1 to curve D_2 is a result of variations in factors other than price.

  A variety of factors can cause the consumer's demand curve to shift.

INCOME

A higher income typically increases the quantity demanded of *normal goods.* In the case of *inferior goods*, however, a higher income can lead to a decrease in the quantity demanded. For example, hamburger meat is an inferior good. As income rises, consumers replace hamburger with steak, and so demand for hamburger goes down as income rises.

There is also the impact that other goods have on the demand curve.

SUBSTITUTES

A *substitute* for Good A is a Good B that at least partly satisfies the same needs of consumers. In this case, an increase in the price of Good A will increase the demand for Good B because Good B becomes relatively cheaper. For example, if a commuter has the choice of commuting by car or commuting by train, the two forms of transportation are substitutes. If the price of gas goes up, commuting by train may become preferable to commuting by car. Similarly, an increase in oil prices may prompt higher demand for hybrid cars, solar panels, and alternative energy solutions.

COMPLEMENTARY GOODS

Good B is *complementary* to Good A if their consumption is interdependent, such as coffee and cream, saucers and cups, or a car and gasoline. An increase in the price of (complementary) Good B will decrease demand for Good B and, because of the complementarity, also decrease demand for Good A.

CONSUMER EXPECTATIONS

Expectations may influence current buying behavior; for example, if the price of fresh fruits (e.g., oranges from Florida) is expected to increase, people will tend to buy more now.

TASTES AND PREFERENCES

Consumers' desire for a product may increase because of the sudden popularity of an item (e.g., MP3 players) or because a product enters the mainstream (e.g., cellular phones) after the early adoption period.

2.3   Supply Curve

The *supply curve* is a graphic representation of price (on the y axis) and quantity supplied (on the x axis). Please note that potential quantity supplied at a given price is *not* necessarily the same as the potential quantity demanded at that same price. For example, at very high prices, the quantity supplied is probably much larger than the quantity demanded.

Because of the Law of Supply, supply curves always have a positive slope (it runs upward from bottom left to top right). As price goes up, quantity supplied increases, and vice versa. An example of two supply schedules is given in Fig. 2-3. The graphs for the two schedules are given in Fig. 2-4.

Figure 2-3. Schedules for supply curves S_1 and S_2.

Price (P)	Quantity Supplied (S_1 Curve)	Quantity Supplied (S_2 Curve)
10.00	100	110
9.00	90	100
8.00	80	90
7.00	70	80
6.50	65	75
6.00	60	70
5.50	55	65
5.00	50	60
4.00	40	50
3.00	30	40
2.00	20	30

Please note:

- The movements *along* the supply curve are changes in supply caused by price changes, i.e., the first and second columns (for the S_1 curve) or the first and third columns (for the S_2 curve).
- The movement *of* the supply curve (caused by variations in factors other than price, e.g., production technology) is represented by the second and third columns (shift from the S_1 curve to the S_2 curve). The S_2 curve is identical to the S_1 curve with an additional quantity of 10 added for each given price. Going from S_1 to S_2 is a rightward shift of the supply curve, perhaps as a result of improved production technology.

Changes in supply may occur when product prices change, but there may also be reasons for changes in the supply curve itself, that is, a shift in the amounts of goods and services that a producer is willing and able to supply. Some of these factors, independent from product price changes, are discussed here.

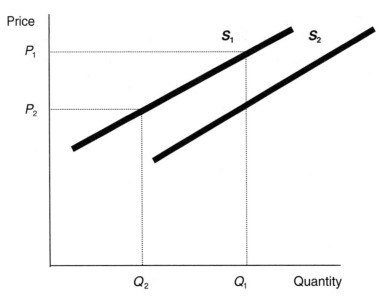

Figure 2-4. Supply curves S_1 and S_2.

TECHNOLOGY

New technology has the capacity to increase productivity (more output per person-hour). This makes it less expensive to produce at each level of output, shifting the supply curve to the right.

INPUT PRICES

Land, labor, capital, and entrepreneurship are the factors of production. If the price of those factors increases, costs of production go up and the firm will produce less at each given product (output) price. The same holds if the price of intermediate goods increases.

PRICES OF OTHER GOODS

If a producer manufactures Products A and B and the relative price of Product A goes up as a result of increased demand, the manufacturer could decide to increase the amount of Product A supplied and decrease the amount of Product B.

PRODUCER EXPECTATIONS

Producers who anticipate increases in factor costs will tend to accelerate production, and so the supply curve will shift to the right (increase in supply).

GOVERNMENT POLICY

Government can influence the supply through taxes, subsidies, and quotas, For example, excise taxes on a product make that product more costly to produce, and quantity supplied will go down. A subsidy by government lowers costs per unit, thus increasing supply. Quotas restrict the number of products a foreign firm can bring into the market and thus decrease the supply.

2.4   Market Equilibrium

Buyers and sellers exchange goods and services in a marketplace for a price. *Market equilibrium* results when price, quantity demanded, and quantity supplied are such that neither buyers nor sellers have an incentive to change. This happens when the demand curve and the supply curve intersect at the *equilibrium price P** and the *equilibrium quantity Q**. This represents a stable market outcome. At prices below the equilibrium price, a shortage exists and the price goes up. At prices above the equilibrium price, a surplus exists and the price falls. The corresponding equilibrium price *P** is also called the *market-clearing price*.

EXAMPLE: Equilibrium Price and Quantity

Using the demand and supply curves introduced in Sections 2.2 and 2.3, we can now determine the equilibrium in four different market situations.

The first equilibrium (D_1 and S_1) occurs at $P = 6.00$, $Q = 60$ (see Fig. 2-5).

In the second situation, the equilibrium price goes up from 6.00 to 6.50 and the equilibrium quantity increases from 60 to 65 when the demand curve shifts (D_1 to D_2) to the right, perhaps because of higher consumer income. This means that prices are increasing as a result of higher demand (see Fig. 2-6).

In the third situation, the supply curve shifts to the right (S_1 to S_2), perhaps because of improved production technology. This decreases the equilibrium price from 6.00 to 5.50, while the equilibrium quantity goes up from 60 to 65 (see Fig. 2-7).

Figure 2-5.   Market equilibrium: demand curve D_1 and supply curve S_1.

Equilibrium occurs when quantity demanded equals quantity supplied, i.e., equilibrium price = 6.00 and equilibrium quantity = 60.

Price (P)	Quantity Demanded (D_1-Curve)	Quantity Supplied (S_1-Curve)
10.00	20	100
9.00	30	90
8.00	40	80
7.00	50	70
6.50	55	65
6.00	**60**	**60**
5.50	65	55
5.00	70	50
4.00	80	40
3.00	90	30
2.00	100	20

Please note that the equilibrium price of 6.00 is a special price. For any price above 6.00, the quantity supplied will be higher than the quantity demanded. Because of this surplus, the price will fall. For any price below 6.00, the quantity demanded will be higher than the quantity supplied. Because of this shortage, the price will go up.

Finally, in the fourth situation (see Fig. 2-8), both the demand curve (D_1 to D_2) and the supply curve (S_1 to S_2) shift to the right, leading to the original price level of 6.00 but a higher quantity (70). The price decrease resulting from improved production technology cancels out the price increase resulting from higher demand. The quantity level has increased from 60 to 70 (from the first, original equilibrium).

The equilibrium concept is critical in economics because it provides a predictable market outcome for given demand and supply curves. In addition, it allows

Figure 2-6. Market equilibrium: demand curve D_2 and supply curve S_1.

Equilibrium occurs when quantity demanded equals quantity supplied, i.e., equilibrium price = 6.50 and equilibrium quantity = 65.

Price (P)	Quantity Demanded (D_2-Curve)	Quantity Supplied (S_1-Curve)
10.00	30	100
9.00	40	90
8.00	50	80
7.00	60	70
6.50	**65**	**65**
6.00	70	60
5.50	75	55
5.00	80	50
4.00	90	40
3.00	100	30
2.00	110	20

Please note that the equilibrium price of 6.50 is a special price. For any price above 6.50, the quantity supplied will be higher than the quantity demanded. Because of this surplus, the price will fall. For any price below 6.50, the quantity demanded will be higher than the quantity supplied. Because of this shortage, the price will go up.

us to predict changes in price and quantity when one (or both) of the curves shifts. In macroeconomics, the demand and supply equilibrium approach is used for the economy's aggregate demand and supply, money demand and supply, labor demand and supply, dollar demand and supply, and so on.

The word *equilibrium* comes from a Latin word meaning "even-balanced," and it describes a situation in which all acting influences are canceled by others, resulting in a stable system. In traditional economics, a market has a single prevailing price for commodities of uniform quality. This is called the *Law of One Price.*

Figure 2-7.   Market equilibrium: demand curve D_1 and supply curve S_2.

Equilibrium occurs when quantity demanded equals quantity supplied, i.e., equilibrium price = 5.50 and equilibrium quantity = 65.

Price (P)	Quantity Demanded (D_1-Curve)	Quantity Supplied (S_2-Curve)
10.00	20	110
9.00	30	100
8.00	40	90
7.00	50	80
6.50	55	75
6.00	60	70
5.50	**65**	**65**
5.00	70	60
4.00	80	50
3.00	90	40
2.00	100	30

Please note that the equilibrium price of 5.50 is a special price. For any price above 5.50, the quantity supplied will be higher than the quantity demanded. Because of this surplus, the price will fall. For any price below 5.50, the quantity demanded will be higher than the quantity supplied. Because of this shortage, the price will go up.

NOTE N2.4

William Stanley Jevons (1835–1882)

Jevons was one of the first economists to recognize the Law of One Price in markets. If different prices were to exist in one market for products of uniform quality, then arbitrage trading would quickly take care of any differences. Jevons was one of the founders of the discipline of econometrics, or using statistical and

Figure 2-8.   Market equilibrium: demand curve D_2 and supply curve S_2.

Equilibrium occurs when quantity demanded equals quantity supplied, i.e., equilibrium price $= 6.00$ and equilibrium quantity $= 70$.

Price (P)	Quantity Demanded (D_2-Curve)	Quantity Supplied (S_2-Curve)
10.00	30	110
9.00	40	100
8.00	50	90
7.00	60	80
6.50	65	75
6.00	**70**	**70**
5.50	75	65
5.00	80	60
4.00	90	50
3.00	100	40
2.00	110	30

Please note that the equilibrium price of 6.00 is a special price. For any price above 6.00, the quantity supplied will be higher than the quantity demanded. Because of this surplus, the price will fall. For any price below 6.00, the quantity demanded will be higher than the quantity supplied. Because of this shortage, the price will go up.

mathematical applications in economics. He invented moving averages and also proposed a theory of the business cycle based on sunspots, boosting the study of statistics in economic empirical work.

The specific examples of supply and demand equilibrium can be summarized in a general market equilibrium chart to show how the market equilibrium results from the intersection of the demand and supply curves (see Fig. 2-9).

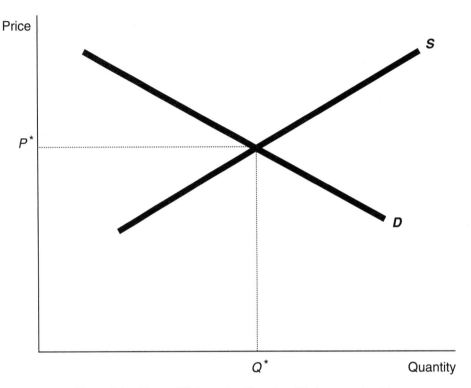

Figure 2-9. The equilibrium price P^* and equilibrium quantity Q^*.

As demonstrated in the examples, we can assess the impact of shifts in the supply and demand curves on the market's equilibrium results (see Fig. 2-10).

Supply and demand equilibrium analysis is the foundation for understanding key results in economics. It is used throughout the book because it is indispensable for better understanding

- Specific market dynamics (e.g., goods and services, labor, capital and investment, money, and foreign exchange)
- The impact of economic policies

2.5 Hints

H2.1 Don't confuse quantity demanded with demand. A change in the price of the product will cause a change in the *quantity demanded*, while a change

Figure 2-10.   The impact of shifts in upward-sloping supply curves and downward-sloping demand curves on the market's equilibrium price and quantity.

Demand	Supply	Price	Quantity
Increase	Increase	Indeterminate	Increase
Increase	Decrease	Increase	Indeterminate
Decrease	Increase	Decrease	Indeterminate
Decrease	Decrease	Indeterminate	Decrease

in one of the other factors (income, preferences, and so on) will change the *demand*, shifting the demand curve.

H2.2   An individual's demand curve is the schedule of the individual's quantity demanded at each price. The *microeconomic market demand* is the horizontal (i.e., for a given price) summation of individuals' demand curves, or the sum of quantity demanded for all individuals at a given price.

H2.3   Please note that *macroeconomic (or aggregate) demand* will be defined differently from microeconomic demand. Macroeconomic demand is the value of aggregate demand (e.g., consumption and investment), and this measure is related to the aggregate price level in the economy to derive a macroeconomic aggregate demand curve.

Macroeconomic demand and supply is *not* the horizontal summation of individual demand or supply curves because total demand in the economy goes across industry sectors, and therefore the sum of quantity demanded is not meaningful ("adding apples and oranges").

Quiz

Choose the one best answer for each question.

Q2.1   The demand curve and its inverse relationship between price and quantity demanded is based on the assumption of
(a) all other things held constant.
(b) changing expectations.
(c) complementary goods.

(d) increasing marginal utility.

(e) all of the above.

Q2.2   If there is an increase in demand for a good, what will most likely happen to the price and quantity of the good exchanged?

	Price	Quantity
(a)	Increase	Increase
(b)	Increase	Decrease
(c)	Decrease	Decrease
(d)	Decrease	Increase
(e)	No change	No change

Q2.3   Which of the following factors cause(s) a shift in the supply curve?
   I. Consumers deciding to buy more of the product
   II. Higher wages paid to workers
   III. A decrease in the number of suppliers

(a) I only

(b) II only

(c) I and II

(d) I and III

(e) II and III

Q2.4   If two goods are substitutes for each other, an increase in the price of one will necessarily

(a) not decrease the demand for the other.

(b) increase the demand for the other.

(c) decrease the quantity demanded of the other.

(d) increase the quantity demanded of the other.

(e) do none of the above.

Q2.5   The Law of One Price states that

(a) all products in the same market have identical prices.

(b) every consumer buys the same quality product in the market.

(c) legally, only one price can be charged for a uniform product.

(d) there is a single price in the same market for products of uniform quality.

(e) every producer sells the same quality product in the market.

Q2.6   How does an unusually cold winter affect the equilibrium price and equilibrium quantity of antifreeze?
(a) It lowers the price and decreases the quantity.
(b) It lowers the price and increases the quantity.
(c) It doesn't change price and increases the quantity.
(d) It raises the price and increases the quantity.
(e) It raises the price and decreases the quantity.

Q2.7   What happens to the demand or supply of books if there is an increase in the price of the paper used in the books? The increase shifts
(a) the supply curve to the left.
(b) the supply curve to the right.
(c) the demand curve to the left.
(d) the demand curve to the right.
(e) none of the above.

Q2.8   If a product is a normal good and people's income goes up, the new equilibrium quantity is _____ the initial equilibrium quantity.
(a) equal to
(b) greater than
(c) less than
(d) could be (a) or (b), depending on suppliers' reaction
(e) could be (a) or (c), depending on suppliers' reaction

Q2.9   In the market for oil, the development of a new deep sea drilling technology _____ the demand curve for oil and _____ the supply curve of oil.
(a) shifts leftward; shifts leftward
(b) shifts rightward; shifts rightward
(c) does not shift; shifts rightward
(d) does not shift; shifts leftward
(e) does not shift; does not shift

Q2.10   Movement *along* the demand curve means that
(a) changes in price cause changes in quantity demanded.
(b) changes in price cause a shift of the demand curve.
(c) changes in income cause a shift of the demand curve.
(d) changes in price cause the demand curve to shift.
(e) changes in price cause the demand curve to become horizontal.

Q2.11   The equilibrium price does not go up when a negatively sloped demand curve shifts to the right if
(a) the supply curve is vertical.
(b) quantity supplied goes up as price goes up.
(c) income goes down and the product is normal (i.e., not inferior).
(d) the price of substitutes goes down.
(e) the supply curve is horizontal.

Q2.12   If producers anticipate declining wage rates in the future, what will happen to the supply curve?
(a) It shifts to the right.
(b) It becomes horizontal.
(c) It becomes vertical.
(d) It shifts to the left.
(e) It doesn't change.

Quiz Answers

Q2.1 (a). The demand curve is the relationship between price and quantity demanded, assuming that other things (e.g., consumer income) do not vary (*ceteris paribus*).

Q2.2 (a). The increase in demand implies a shift to the right of the demand curve. Assuming that the supply curve remains the same (*ceteris paribus*), the equilibrium price and quantity will increase.

Q2.3 (e). Higher wages (increasing factor costs for suppliers) and a decrease in the number of suppliers cause supply to decrease (shift of the supply curve). Changes in consumer preferences cause a shift in the demand curve, not the supply curve.

Q2.4 (b). A substitute is a product that (partly) satisfies the same needs of consumers. Substitutes are defined by positive cross-price effects: A product is a substitute for another if its quantity demanded increases when the other product's price goes up.

Q2.5 (d). The Law of One Price states that uniform products in the same market command identical prices.

Q2.6 (d). As consumers increase their demand for antifreeze, the demand curve shifts rightward. The supply curve does not shift. Therefore, the equilibrium price rises and the equilibrium quantity increases.

Q2.7 (a). Paper is a resource used to manufacture books; if paper becomes more expensive, the quantity supplied (at a given price) will be less. Therefore, the supply curve shifts to the left.

Q2.8 (b). Because the product is a normal good, the increased income leads to increased demand at any given price. This means that the demand curve shifts to the left while the supply curve remains the same, and, consequently, the equilibrium quantity increases.

Q2.9 (c). The new technology for deep sea drilling, enhancing oil production, will increase the quantity supplied at any given price and therefore will shift the supply curve to the right. The demand curve does not shift as a consequence of new production technology.

Q2.10 (a). A movement *along* the demand curve means a movement within the schedule of a specific demand curve; therefore, it means the effect on quantity demanded of the change in price.

Q2.11 (e). Demand curves for normal goods shift to the right if income increases, eliminating answer (c). If the price of substitutes goes down, it leads to less demand (the curve shifts to the left), ruling out (d). If quantity supplied goes up as price goes up, this means that the supply curve is positively sloped; this causes the price to rise if the (negatively sloped) demand curve shifts to the right. This eliminates (b). A vertical supply curve causes a strong positive change in price as the demand curve shifts to the right, ruling out (a). Only a horizontal supply curve will lead to an unchanged price after a rightward shift of the demand curve.

Q2.12 (d). The anticipation of declining wage rates will cause firms to produce less now (at relatively high rates) and delay production until the expected wage rate declines occur. The decision to produce less now causes the supply curve to shift to the left.

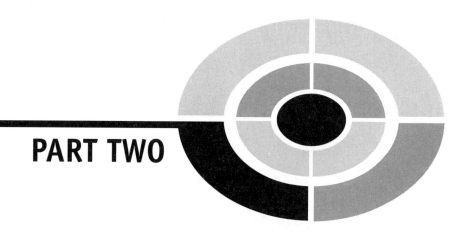

PART TWO

The Basics of Macroeconomics

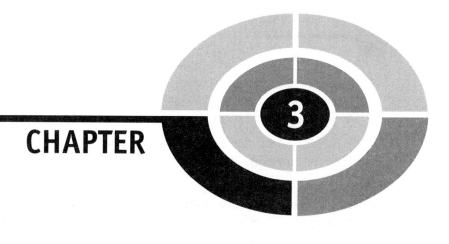

CHAPTER 3

Introduction to Macroeconomics

How does the U.S. national economy work?
What is the role and influence of the major sectors: households, firms, government, and foreign? How do resources and money flow across sectors?
What should we measure? How should we measure it?
What are considered "good" results for a national economy, and what goals should be pursued?

3.1   The Circular Flow Model

Macroeconomics is the study of national economies and the determination of national income. It involves the major sectors of the national economy, that is, households, firms, government, and the foreign sector. A straightforward model of the flows of resources and money moving across the sectors of the national economy is a major tool for the analysis of the economy's performance.

The *circular flow* of income is a model of the economy that describes the movement of resources across the sectors of the economy. In a simple economy (one with no foreign or government sector), the money flows in the circular model consist of

- Wages and salaries paid by firms to households.
- Money spent by households and received by firms.

Corresponding to money outflows are resources received in return, that is, labor provided by households to firms, and goods and services provided by firms to households. There is a complete symmetry between the two sectors, with each providing a real resource, receiving cash in return, and spending the cash on the supplies of the other sector.

The circular flow in a domestic economy (including the government sector but excluding the foreign sector) is depicted in Fig. 3-1.

In this example of a circular flow, you can notice the symmetry of the flows mentioned earlier. This symmetry is used at a later stage to identify basic relationships between national income and national expenditures, which are of critical importance in macroeconomics.

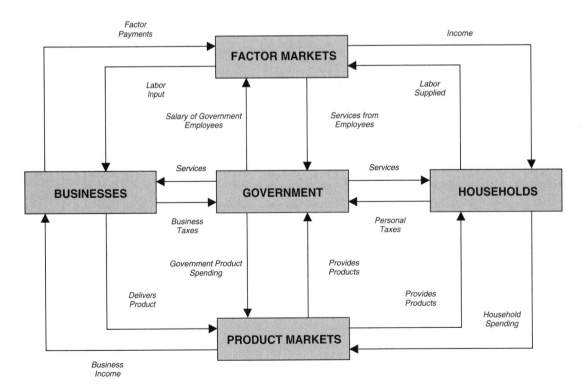

Figure 3-1.   The circular flow of macroeconomics in a domestic economy.

Because of the basic symmetry in the circular flow, we derive two fundamental equalities:

- The aggregate income earned through the supply of factors of production is equal to the national income.
- The national income is equal to the aggregate expenditures made, based on the income.

National income is also called *real Gross Domestic Product (real GDP)*. A definition of GDP follows in Section 3.3.

National income accounting is the estimation of the output or income for a nation as a whole. *Output* and *income* are interchangeable because a nation's domestic output and its income are identical. The value of output equals total expenditures for that output, and these expenditures are also the income for those who produced the output. Therefore, we can use both the expenditure method and the income method to calculate GDP. The expenditure method is used throughout the book. Both methods are discussed in Appendix 2.

3.2 Macroeconomic Goals

Until the 1920s, a large number of economists believed that flexible prices would adjust in the long run to provide full unemployment. Unemployment would be temporary, lasting only until workers were willing to accept lower wages and producers rehired those workers, thus eliminating unemployment. Consequently, government did not need to follow special policies to achieve full employment.

The Great Depression (1929–1939), a decade of high unemployment and stagnation, cast severe doubt on this point of view. The revolutionary Keynesian theory of the 1930s indicated that government policy could help achieve full employment. This new perspective transformed government from a passive observer to an active policy maker. The 1930s are therefore considered the beginning of the modern study of macroeconomics.

After World War II, laws were enacted to explicitly recognize the goals and responsibilities of the federal government. In 1946, Congress passed the Employment Act, stating that "it was the policy and responsibility of the federal government to use all practical means to promote maximum employment, production, and purchasing power." In 1978, Congress passed the Full Employment and Balanced Growth (Humphrey-Hawkins) Act, which established two specific goals: an unemployment rate of 4 percent and a 0 percent inflation rate.

The federal government pursues three major macroeconomic goals: economic growth, price stability, and full employment. Therefore, the U.S. economy can be considered a guided market economy, with fiscal policy (the federal budget) and monetary policy (the Federal Reserve System) as the main tools that guide the economy to the major macroeconomic goals.

3.3   Gross Domestic Product

U.S. Gross Domestic Product (GDP) is the dollar value of all final goods or services bought by the final user during the given time period.

- Nonproduction transactions are excluded from GDP. Therefore, financial transactions and sales of items produced in previous periods are excluded.
- Intermediary products, or components of final goods and services, are excluded to avoid double counting. Note that the value of intermediary products is already represented in the value of the final products.
- GDP is measured in dollar terms (not in physical units).

Nominal GDP equals the value of GDP expressed in current price levels. *Real GDP* (GDP expressed in real terms or at constant prices) equals the value of nominal GDP adjusted for changes in prices. For example, nominal U.S. GDP in 2003 was $10.8 trillion.

The difference between nominal and real GDP can be illustrated by the following example. Assume that nominal GDP grows by 12 percent and nominal consumption also increases by 12 percent. If consumer prices go up by 8 percent, then "real" growth in consumption is only 4 percent (i.e., at constant prices, corrected for the change in prices). In order to compute values in real terms (or at constant prices), deflation of (current-price) nominal values using the appropriate index (e.g., the Consumer Price Index or Producer Price Index) is required.

There are two major constant-price methods to value real GDP:

- The base-year price method values GDP in a given year using the base-year prices.
- The chain-weighted output index uses the prices of two adjacent years to determine the GDP growth rate.

The recent growth rates of U.S. real GDP are shown in Fig. 3-2.

Potential GDP is the amount of goods and services that could be produced if all of the economy's factors of production were fully and efficiently employed.

% Change from year ago

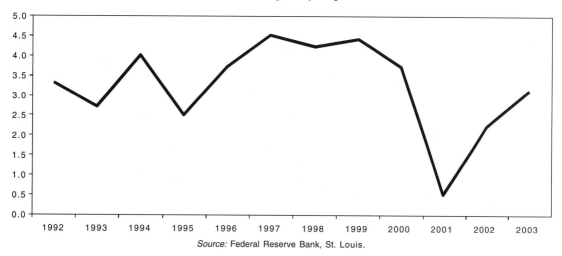

Source: Federal Reserve Bank, St. Louis.

Figure 3-2. U.S. real GDP growth, 1992–2003.

Potential GDP is also called real GDP at full-employment level. This value of GDP represents a point on the edge (the frontier) of the nation's production possibilities curve (PPC).

Real GDP is a narrow measure of well-being, and some people believe that GDP is not the appropriate way to measure progress.

GDP has several measurement imperfections. First, it overadjusts for inflation because many improvements in product quality are represented as price increases only. Second, GDP excludes the value of household-based services (e.g., homemakers), the underground economy (i.e., transactions hidden from government), leisure time, health and life expectancy, and environmental quality. Finally, the measure does not take political freedom and social justice into account.

The pattern of upward and downward movement of GDP over many years is called the *business cycle*. The business cycle, a well-observed economic occurrence, has a variable time span, but is typically around five years. Government policy tries to dampen the peaks and troughs of the cycle. The business cycle is caused by people's expectations, firms' planned and actual investment decisions, and also possibly monetary influences.

The business cycle has four main parts (see Fig. 3-3):

- Expansion (GDP increases)
- Peak (expansion ends, recession starts)

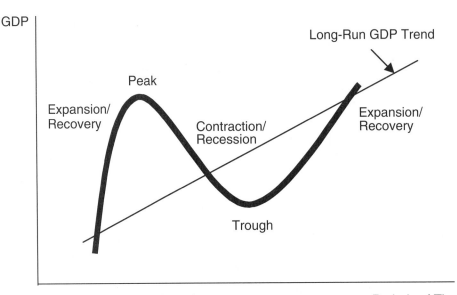

Figure 3-3. The business cycle: fluctuations in GDP.

- Recession (GDP decreases for at least two quarters in a row)
- Trough (recession ends, expansion starts)

3.4   Economic Growth

After a lengthy post–World War II debate about unemployment, macroeconomic theory turned its focus from relatively short-term issues (the heritage of the Great Depression) to the longer-term issue of economic growth.

Economic growth is the sustained increase in a nation's GDP (or its per capita GDP). *Technology* is defined to include new machinery and plants (i.e., physical capital) and also improved knowledge of efficient production methods. The classical *growth model* assumes that technology is predetermined (exogenous), and it is not considered to be part of the economic model. Therefore, in the classical model, technological advances occur in a random fashion, independent of economic variables. Endogenous growth models try to explain the development of technology as a part of the economic model. Early endogenous models emphasized investments in human and physical capital. Modern theory highlights education and research, stressing the need for innovation and studying the benefits of government subsidies. The latest focus, sustainable economic growth, requires a growth pace that conserves the environment and its depletable resources. The ultimate goal is to stabilize the population and to use only renewable resources.

NOTE N3.4

The 2004 Nobel Peace Prize

In awarding its 2004 Peace Prize, the Nobel committee recognized the importance of sustainable development in achieving global peace, for the first time ever expanding the word *peace* to involve environmental issues facing the earth and implying that world peace depends on a livable environment. The Nobel Prize winner, Dr. Wangari Maathai, is a Kenyan woman who started an environmental movement by planting 30 million trees across the African continent.

There are two key aspects to economic growth. First, economic growth should be achieved by fully using all the resources available in the economy. This is called the potential (or full-employment) GDP, and GDP should be equal to potential GDP. This is the same as achieving a point on the frontier of the economy's production possibilities curve (PPC) where the available resources are fully utilized (*efficient production*). This aspect of economic growth is similar to the short-term unemployment issues raised during and immediately after the Great Depression.

The second aspect of economic growth is to grow a nation's potential GDP by advancing technology, enhancing worker skills, improving education, and so on. This is equivalent to moving the frontier of the production possibilities curve to the right (and upward).

Although economic growth will expand future consumption possibilities, it may limit current consumption because resources are devoted to capital accumulation to increase the economy's productive capacity. Also, the advancement of technology means that structural unemployment could increase as economic growth progresses, requiring the retraining of workers.

There are two measures specifically developed to estimate the degree to which the economy is achieving its potential GDP. The *Okun gap* or *output gap* is the estimated difference between real GDP and potential GDP. The accumulated Okun gap (created by recessions) since 1973 is approximately $3 trillion. (U.S. GDP in 2003 was $10.8 trillion.)

Another measure of macroeconomic efficiency is the *Lucas wedge,* the accumulated loss of output resulting from the slowdown in productivity (or real GDP per capita). The Lucas wedge that was caused by the oil shocks of the

1970s has been estimated at $48 trillion (or almost *five times* the size of current GDP).

3.5   Price Stability

The economy's *price level* is the average level of prices in the economy. The price level is the basis for measuring changes in the exchange value of money. The price level is a strictly relative value, used only to measure changes in price. It cannot be calculated because it is the average of the unit prices of all of the economy's goods and services, and we would be comparing apples and oranges.

Price-level measurement is important because GDP is a value (monetary) measure, and for accurate year-to-year comparisons, we require adjustments for changes in the price level caused by inflation or deflation. *Inflation* occurs when the price level goes up persistently; the *inflation rate* is the percentage of change in the price level. Inflation reduces the value of money, and unanticipated inflation complicates economic transactions over time. *Deflation* occurs when the price level goes down (i.e., it is negative inflation).

Price stability is desirable because if prices are not dependable, people make decisions based on anticipated inflation (or deflation) rather than on the most efficient ways to make products, invest savings, or maximize consumption. Unanticipated inflation will cause additional problems. Hyperinflation (i.e., an inflation rate that exceeds 50 percent per month) typically causes economic chaos.

There are three major price indexes used to measure estimated inflation:

- Consumer Price Index (CPI)
- Producer Price Index (PPI)
- GDP deflator

The *Consumer Price Index (CPI)* measures the cost of a typical consumer's basket of goods. The basket is meant to measure the average household's purchase cost and price level. The Bureau of Labor Statistics (BLS) of the U.S. Department of Commerce collects thousands of prices each month and compares them to the previous month's prices. The BLS creates a basket of goods and determines the typical quantity in each. Each item is weighted to reflect its relative importance. The formula for the index is

Consumer Price Index = (cost of basket in current year/cost of basket in base year) × 100

The CPI may overstate the actual inflation rate by about one percentage point per year. There are several reasons for the overstatement of actual inflation by the CPI:

- New product bias (disregarding the fact that high-priced new goods are replacing older goods)
- Quality change bias (disregarding the improved quality of new high-priced products)
- Commodity-substitution bias (disregarding changes in spending patterns toward cheaper substitutes)
- Outlet-substitution bias (disregarding people switching to low-cost discount stores)

The *Producer Price Index (PPI),* published monthly by the Bureau of Labor Statistics, is an index of goods used in the wholesale markets and includes raw materials and semifinished and finished products. It is calculated like the consumer price index, although the product "basket" differs.

The PPI is considered an advance inflation indicator, as higher input prices signal inflation caused by increased factor costs.

Another measure of change in price level is the *GDP deflator,* an average of current-year prices as a percentage of base-year prices. The GDP deflator is a weighted average of the price indexes used to deflate GDP. It reflects the broadest range of goods and services (wider than the PPI and CPI) and is widely used as a measure of inflation. The GDP deflator is published by the U.S. Department of Commerce (see Fig. 3-4).

The GDP deflator (base-year method) is defined as

GDP deflator = nominal GDP/real GDP = price level (current year)/price level (base year)

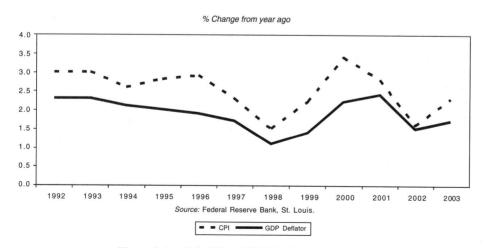

% Change from year ago

Source: Federal Reserve Bank, St. Louis.

Figure 3-4.   U.S. CPI and GDP deflator, 1992–2003.

3.6 Full Employment

Full employment is a key goal in achieving the economy's potential because unemployed workers lose income and can find their future job prospects limited. This could decrease the economy's potential GDP and future growth rate.

Typically, unemployment increases during a recession and decreases during an expansion. However, if labor productivity increases significantly—fewer people produce more GDP—an expansion may not lower unemployment.

The U.S. Census Bureau divides the working-age population (people aged 16 years and over who are not in jail, hospital, or some other institution) into the following categories:

- *Employed.* People working at a full-time or part-time job
- *Unemployed.* People who (1) are without a job but have made efforts to find a job within the past four weeks, (2) are waiting to be called back to work from a layoff, or (3) are waiting to start a new job within 30 days
- *Not in the labor force.* People who are not employed and are not looking for work, i.e., are not unemployed

The *labor force* equals the sum of employed workers plus unemployed workers who are actively looking for work. *Discouraged workers* are unemployed people who have stopped looking for work and are not considered part of the labor force anymore.

The *unemployment rate* equals the number of unemployed/labor force $\times$ 100. The average U.S. unemployment rate from 1963 to 2003 was about 6 percent.

Unemployment is classified into three types:

- *Frictional unemployment.* The result of normal market turnover, such as people entering the labor force and businesses expanding or contracting. Frictionally unemployed workers are searching for good job matches.
- *Structural unemployment.* The result of changes in technology or international competition that require new skills and/or change the location of jobs.
- *Cyclical unemployment.* The unemployment that fluctuates over the course of the business cycle. Unemployment increases during a recession and goes down during an expansion.
- *Seasonal unemployment.* The unemployment that varies by season, such as construction, agriculture, and tourism.

Full employment occurs when there is no cyclical unemployment. The *natural rate of unemployment* equals the sum of frictional and structural unemployment.

During the business cycle, the unemployment rate fluctuates around the natural rate. Potential GDP is real GDP with unemployment equal to the natural rate of unemployment.

3.7   Economic Policy

Government pursues macroeconomic goals by adjusting personal and corporate tax rates and the amount of government spending. This is called *fiscal policy*.

The Federal Reserve (see Chapter 5) controls the nation's *monetary policy*. It pursues macroeconomic goals, in particular price stability, by changing interest rates and by influencing the supply of money.

The pursuit of macroeconomic goals can be challenging. For example, it may require government to stimulate the economy without causing major inflation by keeping budget deficits low. Two specific relationships between macroeconomic variables illustrate these policy challenges:

• Greater output (GDP) usually reduces unemployment. However, the *Phillips Curve* suggests that there may be a negative relationship between inflation and unemployment, suggesting a trade-off between these two macroeconomic goals. For example, as the economy approaches its potential at full-employment GDP, inflation is likely to increase (wage rates are likely to go up in a tight labor market). Conversely, policies attempting to curb inflation may lead to higher unemployment rates.
• *Okun's Law* states that real GDP growth of 2.5 percent *above trend* is required in order to decrease the rate of unemployment by 1 percent. In other words, significant growth in GDP is required to decrease the rate of unemployment.

3.8   Hints

H3.1   Government may supply certain goods and services (e.g., military services) that are not efficiently provided by the private markets; these goods are sometimes called *public goods*. In return, government collects taxes and fees.

H3.2   Employment statistics exclude discouraged workers, who have (temporarily) left the labor market and are no longer looking for work. Officially published unemployment numbers may underestimate actual unemployment, especially when unemployment levels are relatively high (i.e., when the number of discouraged workers is relatively large).

H3.3   The *labor force participation rate* equals labor force/working-age population × 100 (the U.S. rate in 2003 was about 67 percent). The *employment-to-population ratio* is the percentage of working-age people who have a job (the U.S. rate in 2003 was about 63 percent). The labor force participation rate and the employment-to-population ratio have increased over the last decades because more women have entered the labor force.

H3.4   If a person's income has a *cost-of-living adjustment* (COLA), which increases the amount of income received by the rate of inflation, then that person's living standard will not be affected by inflation (e.g., Social Security benefits have a cost of living adjustment).

H3.5   *Demand-pull inflation* occurs when increases in consumer demand outpace the economy's output of extra goods and services. *Cost-push inflation* occurs when increasing input (factor) costs or anticipated final product price increases lead to less supply of products, increasing prices. Inflation is a self-fulfilling prophecy: When consumers expect price increases, they buy more now, creating demand-pull inflation. Suppliers who expect increases in final product prices decrease supply, creating a higher price level.

H3.6   The production sectors of the national economy can be divided into the private and public sectors. The *private sector* includes the economic activity outside government control. This includes the activities of profit-maximizing firms and nonprofit institutions (e.g., private hospitals and private schools). The *public sector* covers economic activity by government agencies for the benefit of the public. This includes local, state, and federal government and public services (e.g., police and fire departments, the military, and public education).

H3.7   *Macroeconomics* studies sectors that go across the whole economy: households, firms, government, and the foreign sector. In contrast, *microeconomics* studies specific industry sectors (e.g., automotive and food processing). Microeconomic demand and supply curves can typically be found by horizontal summation of individual quantities demanded because the quantities are comparable (e.g., automobiles). This is *not* the case for macroeconomic demand, which is the sum of the value of demand across the economy for a specific macroeconomic sector. In macroeconomics, aggregate demand and supply are linked to the price level (the average, aggregate level of prices in the economy, across the board) and not to prices of specific products in an industry sector (e.g., automobiles) as in microeconomics.

The recent applications of the theory of rational expectations are the attempts to link behavior at the individual (microeconomic) level with observed results at the macroeconomic level. This is an important example of the impact of microeconomics on macroeconomics.

There are sometimes subtle differences in definitions and approaches between the two major disciplines of economics; this hint is primarily meant to make you aware of this issue.

Quiz

Choose the one best answer for each question.

Q3.1   Which of the following is an example of monetary policy?
(a) Decreasing the government deficit
(b) Increasing government spending
(c) Increasing the interest rate
(d) Decreasing the tax rate
(e) All of the above

Q3.2   Modern macroeconomics started during
(a) World War II.
(b) the Civil War.
(c) the Great Depression.
(d) World War I.
(e) the 1970s.

Q3.3   Which one is the proper order for the business cycle?
(a) Peak, expansion, recession, trough
(b) Recession, expansion, trough, peak
(c) Expansion, trough, recession, peak
(d) Expansion, peak, trough, recession
(e) None of the above

Q3.4   What is excluded from the GDP?
(a) Illegal market activities
(b) Household services
(c) Underground market activities

(d) The value of intermediate products

(e) All of the above

Q3.5   GDP rose for four quarters in a row and subsequently declined in the next three quarters. How would you describe this situation in terms of the business cycle?

(a) Expansion, peak, recession

(b) Trough, expansion, peak

(c) Expansion, recession, peak

(d) Recession, trough, expansion

(e) Peak, expansion, trough

Q3.6   Which of the following is *not* a macroeconomic goal?

(a) Reduce inflation

(b) Minimize government spending

(c) Increase economic growth

(d) Minimize deflation

(e) Attain full employment

Q3.7   Avoiding high, unpredictable inflation is an important economic goal because with such inflation,

(a) it becomes hard to transact business over time.

(b) savings may lose their value.

(c) more resources are spent on estimating inflation and less on productive activities.

(d) it is difficult to obtain loans at reasonable cost.

(e) all of the above are true.

Q3.8   In the circular flow diagram, which of the following is true in the product market?

(a) Households sell goods and services to businesses.

(b) Households sell resources to businesses.

(c) Businesses sell resources to households.

(d) Businesses sell goods and services to households.

(e) Households buy resources from businesses.

Q3.9   Which of the following is included in the calculation of GDP?

(a) Government purchase of new cars

(b) The purchase of antique furniture

(c) A barber who cuts the hair of his children

(d) An engine produced in a foreign country

(e) A used book purchase

Q3.10 Suppose the extra $10,000 value of a plant's output causes waste in the nearby river at a loss value of $3,000. What is the additional value to GDP?
(a) A decrease of $3,000
(b) An increase of $10,000
(c) An increase of $7,000
(d) A decrease of $7,000
(e) None of the above

Q3.11 Full employment means that:
(a) unemployment is zero.
(b) structural unemployment is zero.
(c) frictional unemployment is zero.
(d) unemployment equals the natural rate of unemployment.
(e) there is only cyclical unemployment.

Q3.12 Okun's Law states that
(a) real GDP growth increases unemployment.
(b) inflation goes up as unemployment increases.
(c) inflation decreases nominal GDP growth.
(d) inflation goes up as unemployment decreases.
(e) real GDP growth above trend is needed for a decrease in unemployment.

Quiz Answers

Q3.1 (c). Changing the interest rate (charged to banks) is one of the tools of the Federal Reserve's monetary policy. The other options are all fiscal policies by government.

Q3.2 (c). Modern macroeconomics started during the Great Depression (1929–1939), when economists realized that the classical theory of price flexibility could not guarantee full employment, as 10 years of high unemployment and stagnation occurred. The leading macroeconomist during that era was John Maynard Keynes (1882–1946).

Q3.3 (e). None of the other options describes the proper order in the business cycle. The order is expansion (GDP goes up), peak (end of expansion), recession (GDP goes down), and trough (end of recession).

Q3.4 (e). Options (a) through (d) are all excluded from GDP. The value of intermediary products is excluded because it is already included in the value of final goods. Also, goods and services provided by people for themselves (e.g., household services) are excluded from the GDP, as are illegal (or underground) activities.

Q3.5 (a). In the business cycle, four quarters of GDP growth indicate an expansion, while three subsequent quarters of decline indicate a recession. The upper turning point where the expansion ends and the recession starts is called the *peak.*

Q3.6 (b). Minimizing government spending is *not* a macroeconomic policy goal (although it may be a *political* goal). Some macroeconomists consider minimizing the government deficit a goal, but this would also require a tax policy to balance the budget. The other options all relate to the macroeconomic goals of price stability, full employment, and economic growth.

Q3.7 (e). Options (a) through (d) are consequences of high, unpredictable inflation rates. Bankers will charge higher interest on loans because the value of money is, unpredictably, decreasing over time. For the same reason, companies have difficulty doing business over time. Savings will be in jeopardy as money loses value (and there's no reliable cost-of-living index to cover uncertainty). Also, people will spend increasing amounts of time (resources) to anticipate future inflation rates. If the rates become very high (e.g., hyperinflation), economic chaos may result.

Q3.8 (d). Please note that the question asks for the activities in the product market. That means businesses selling goods and services to households. Answer (b) (households selling resources) describes the resource (or factor) markets in the circular flow model.

Q3.9 (a). The government purchase of new cars is included in the GDP. The other options are excluded from the GDP: Furniture is not a newly manufactured good, the barber provides a household service, the engine is from abroad and counts as part of another country's GDP, and the used book is not a newly manufactured product.

Q3.10 (b). The loss value of $3,000 to the river is not included in GDP because quality-of-life aspects are excluded from GDP calculation.

Q3.11 (d). Full employment does *not* mean that unemployment equals zero, ruling out (a). Full employment is reached at the so-called natural rate of unemployment, the sum of frictional unemployment and structural unemployment, eliminating answers (b) and (c). Cyclical unemployment is equal to zero at full employment, ruling out (e).

Q3.12 (e). GDP growth usually increases employment, eliminating (a). Inflation may go up as unemployment increases (the case of stagflation, perhaps caused by negative supply shocks), but this is not Okun's Law, eliminating (b). Inflation implies an increase in price levels, which will lead to increased nominal GDP, ruling out answer (c). Answer (d) is a description of the trade-off in the Phillips Curve. Okun's Law states that GDP growth of 2.5 percent above trend leads to a 1 percent decline in the rate of unemployment, so answer (e) is right.

CHAPTER 4

Aggregate Supply and Aggregate Demand

What do we mean by the "market" of the national economy? What are supply and demand?

What does it mean to aggregate supply and demand for all products and services in the economy?

Are aggregate supply and demand curves for the national economy the same kind of curves as those for a single good or service?

What kind of market results do we get when aggregate demand and aggregate supply intersect?

4.1   Introduction

Supply and demand in macroeconomics (aggregate supply and demand) are different from microeconomic supply and demand. Supply and demand in the national economy are *not* formed by the summation of the volumes of all goods and services in the economy because that would be the same as adding cars, Oreos, and toothbrushes.

In order to be meaningful, aggregate supply and aggregate demand are the summations of the value of all goods and services. Therefore, "quantity of (real) GDP" or "quantity of aggregate demand" will refer to the dollar value quantity.

4.2 Aggregate Supply: The Long Run and the Short Run

The *aggregate supply (AS) curve* is the relationship between the quantity of real GDP (at constant prices) supplied and the *price level,* or the average price for goods and services in the economy. In other words, the overall supply in the economy is tied to the general price level.

There is a critical distinction between aggregate supply in the long run and in the short run. The *macroeconomic long run* is the period of time required for all macroeconomic variables—especially the price level—to be completely flexible. This period of time will allow all macroeconomic forces to cancel out and to reach a stable outcome as a result of the full flexibility of price-level changes and resulting quantity changes. This complete price-level flexibility will lead real GDP to reach the potential or full-employment level of GDP. The "long run" is not a specific fixed time frame, but rather refers to any period long enough that all prices will be flexible.

The *long-run aggregate supply (LAS) curve* is the relationship between the price level and real GDP in the long run. Because real GDP equals potential GDP in the long run, LAS is vertical (see Fig. 4-1).

The *macroeconomic short run* is the period of time during which at least some prices are inflexible (i.e., rigid or "sticky"), causing a relatively inflexible or constant price level in the economy. For example, wage rates may be inflexible because of multiyear labor contracts, and firms' fixed capital costs (plants, machines, and equipment) and long-term supply arrangements for raw materials may account for additional factor price inflexibility. In addition, customer delivery contracts and menu costs (the cost of relabeling and updating when prices change) could make final product prices inflexible in the short run.

In the short run, price and quantity adjustments cannot run their course so that real GDP may not be equal to the full-employment level of GDP, resulting in an unemployment rate above (or below) the natural rate of unemployment. Note that as in the definition of "long run," the "short run" is not a fixed, specific time frame, but rather any period short enough that at least some prices will not be fully flexible (and therefore the aggregate price level will not be fully flexible).

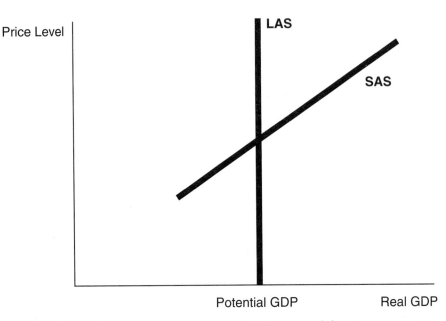

Figure 4-1.   Long-run aggregate supply (LAS) curve and short-run aggregate supply (SAS) curve.

The *short-run aggregate supply (SAS) curve* is the relationship between the quantity of real GDP supplied and the price level in the short run. As illustrated in Fig. 4-1, the SAS curve slopes upward (only the general price level of goods and services produced varies; wage rates and other resource prices are relatively fixed). The aggregate supply curve may become steeper closer to the full-employment level of real GDP because production resources (e.g., qualified labor) will become increasingly scarce.

The LAS curve is determined by potential GDP, and therefore shifts in the LAS curve are similar to shifts in potential GDP (or to shifts in the production possibilities frontier). These shifts could be caused by changes in the full-employment quantity of labor, changes in the quantity of production factors available, or advances in production technology. If the LAS curve shifts, it also causes a shift in the SAS curve because potential GDP has changed.

The SAS curve will shift if the wage rate (or the cost of any other resource) changes. This is the result of the *ceteris paribus* condition that is part of the SAS curve definition: the relationship between the general price level and quantity supplied, provided all other factors are held constant, such as wages, corporate taxes, and costs of raw materials. Because changes in resource costs leave the potential GDP unaffected, this shift in the SAS curve does not cause a shift in the LAS curve.

4.3   Aggregate Demand

The circular flow model (see Chapter 3) demonstrates that the value of output (GDP) creates aggregate income, as when firms pay workers. This creates aggregate demand, as when households use income to consume the goods and services produced by the economy, which has the value of GDP.

The following equalities are therefore the immediate result of the economy's circular flow:

$$GDP = aggregate\ income = aggregate\ demand\ (AD)$$

The total quantity of *aggregate demand* equals the sum of consumption, investment, government purchases, and net exports.

- *Consumption (C)*. Total expenditures by households for goods and services
- *Investment (I)*. Total expenditures by businesses for capital stock (buildings and equipment) and inventory
- *Government expenditures (G)*. Total expenditures by government for goods and services
- *Net exports (X_N)*. Exports *(X)* (the value of the economy's sales of goods and services abroad) minus *imports (M)* (the value of the economy's purchases of foreign goods and services)

In 2003, U.S. GDP was $10.8 trillion, with consumption representing 71 percent, investment 15 percent, government expenditures 19 percent, and net exports −5 percent. Consumption is the main expenditure category, followed by government expenditures, investment, and gross imports.

The *aggregate demand (AD) curve* is the relationship between the quantity of real GDP demanded and the price level. It slopes downward because higher average price levels will decrease consumers' buying power and therefore decrease the quantity demanded. In addition, higher price levels will decrease exports because domestic products are more expensive for the foreign sector (*ceteris paribus*), and lower exports mean lower aggregate demand. A linear aggregate demand curve is illustrated in Fig. 4-2.

The aggregate demand curve may shift as a result of changed expectations (anticipated income, inflation, and so on) or changes in foreign exchange rates. Also, the government may cause a shift by increasing expenditures or lowering taxes (fiscal policy), while the Federal Reserve can cause shifts by making changes in the monetary policy (e.g., the discount rate).

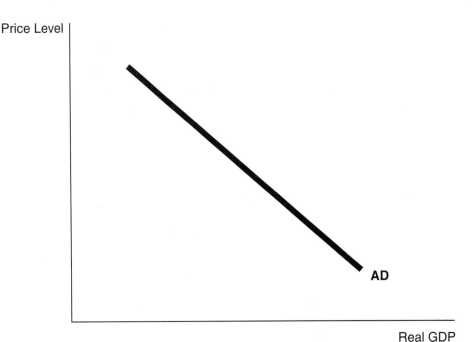

Figure 4-2.   Aggregate demand (AD) curve.

4.4   Macroeconomic Equilibrium

Although the aggregate demand and aggregate supply curves look similar to the microeconomic supply and demand curves (see Chapter 2, "Microeconomics"), the explanation for the slopes of the curves is different. The aggregate demand curve slopes down because consumers use income (and wealth) to increase demand at lower aggregate price levels. The aggregate supply curve's slope may be relatively small (and positive) in the short run because a price-level increase may have a large impact on GDP when producers take advantage of higher profits (higher final product prices combined with relatively inflexible factor costs). As factor costs become increasingly flexible, profitability prospects will decline as GDP approaches potential GDP, and wage rates are likely to rise because of the shortage of labor. In the long run, the curve will be vertical because real GDP equals potential GDP.

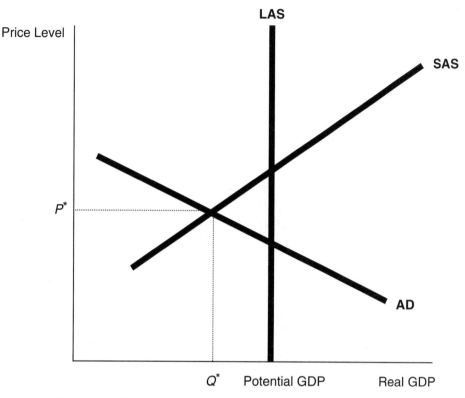

Figure 4-3.   Macroeconomic equilibrium in the short run: recessionary gap.

Long-run macroeconomic equilibrium occurs when aggregate demand and long-run aggregate supply are equal. By definition, in the long run prices will adjust so that real GDP equals potential GDP. Economic growth takes place when the potential GDP increases. Inflation will occur when aggregate demand increases more than long-run aggregate supply.

Short-run macroeconomic equilibrium occurs when aggregate demand and short-run aggregate supply are equal. If the short-run real GDP is below potential GDP, the amount of the difference is called a *recessionary gap* (see Fig. 4-3). An above-full-employment equilibrium occurs when real GDP exceeds potential GDP. The *inflationary gap* is the amount by which real GDP exceeds potential GDP. According to Keynesian theory, instability and business cycles result when aggregate demand and short-run aggregate supply are not growing at the same rate.

4.5 The AS/AD Model

The *AS/AD model* is the macroeconomic supply and demand model that explains how macroeconomic equilibrium is achieved and how shifts of the aggregate supply curves and aggregate demand curves change the macroeconomic equilibrium.

For example, an increase in aggregate demand means that, in the short run, the aggregate demand curve shifts to the right. Consequently, the equilibrium moves along the SAS curve. This means that real GDP increases and the price level rises. The money wage rate rises as a result of the higher prices. Then the SAS curve shifts left, and real GDP decreases while price levels are raised further. In the long run, the SAS curve will shift to the left just enough for real GDP to equal potential GDP. At that point, adjustments cease, and real GDP equals potential GDP. The price level is permanently higher than before the increase in aggregate demand.

As another example, a decrease in short-run aggregate supply means that the SAS curve will shift to the left, and as a consequence real GDP will decrease, and the price level rises. This condition (recession and inflation combined) is known as *stagflation.*

The AS/AD model is helpful in understanding the expected (or predicted) impact of real-world events on the economy.

- *Increase in government expenditures.* Aggregate demand goes up, and the AD curve shifts to the right. This leads to an increase in GDP and an increase in the price level.
- *Decline in household consumption.* Aggregate demand goes down, and the AD curve shifts to the left. This causes GDP, as well as the price level, to go down (similar to the 1930s Depression).
- *Wage rate declines.* Aggregate supply shifts to the right (higher profitability), and GDP goes up while the price level goes down.
- *Oil supply goes down.* Aggregate supply shifts to the left (lower profitability), and GDP goes down while the price level goes up (similar to 1970s stagflation).

The AS/AD model also demonstrates the likely effects of fiscal or monetary policy and can be used to analyze major economic models. For example, neoclassical economists believe that the price mechanism is completely efficient and will ultimately return the economy to the potential GDP. The economy will operate at full-employment levels, and business cycles are mostly responses to changes in technology. Neo-Keynesians believe that the economy typically does not operate at full employment unless fiscal and monetary policy is applied. Changes in aggregate demand and relatively inflexible money wages will cause business cycles to occur. Finally, monetarists believe (like the neoclassicals) that the economy self-regulates efficiently, operating at full-employment level as long as monetary policy is not erratic. They believe that the pace of money growth must be kept steady because changes in the quantity of money are the main source of aggregate demand fluctuations and economic instability.

4.6 The "Bathtub" Theorem

The "bathtub" theorem is a statement about the leakages and injections into the circular flow. The leakages and injections describe the changes in aggregate expenditures. *Leakages* are uses of household income other than consumption of the GDP. They include taxes (sent to government), savings (nonconsumption, by definition), and imports ("lost" GDP as a result of the purchase of output from foreign economies). *Injections* are expenditures by government (including government purchases), business (including investment), or foreign sectors on domestic goods or services (including exports).

The *bathtub theorem* states that an economy grows when injections are greater than leakages, and an economy shrinks if leakages exceed injections.

4.7 The Financing of Flows

National saving equals the saving (i.e., the amount left after consumption) by households and businesses (S) plus government saving $(T-G)$. The amount borrowed by the economy from the foreign sector equals $M-X$.

The economy's *investment (I)* is financed by household saving, government saving, and foreign borrowing:

$$I=S+(T-G)+(M-X)$$

Capital is the amount of plant, equipment, and inventories used to produce goods.

Depreciation (also called *capital consumption*) is the decrease in capital stock as a result of wear and tear and obsolescence.

Gross investment is the total amount of investment.

Net investment is gross investment minus depreciations; it represents the change in the amount of capital stock.

GDP includes gross profits (before depreciation) on the income side and gross investments on the expenditure side.

Government spends taxes by making government purchases. It runs a budget deficit if purchases (G) exceed income from taxes (T), and in this case it effectively borrows the savings of households. Businesses retain profits and capital consumption allowances to finance investment (I). If investment exceeds available funds, then business borrows from households' savings. The offset to household savings would be the borrowing of business and government for I and G.

Exports also inject income into the economy. This is the income created from foreign economies purchasing the domestic economy's products. It can also be the income from this economy that is sent to households outside this economy, called *foreign factor income.*

4.8   Hints

H4.1   The meaning of the term *macroeconomic short run* is defined strictly in the context of macroeconomics, i.e., the inflexibility of the aggregate price level. There is also a *microeconomic short run*, which has a different meaning that is beyond the scope of this book. In macroeconomics, the temporary breakdown of the price adjustment process in the short run is a key feature of Keynesian economic theory (in contrast to classical theory, which assumes full price flexibility).

H4.2   Government spending on goods and services (G) and *government transfer payments* are different. Both involve payments by the government, but transfer payments are not payments for goods and services. As there is no simultaneous (reverse) flow of goods and services, transfer payments are "gifts," and consequently are excluded from aggregate expenditure component G.

H4.3   The AS/AD framework is helpful in explaining economic schools of thought. The classical economists followed Say's law: "Supply determines demand." This means that they believed that aggregate supply (AS) determined GDP. Keynes made the case in the 1930s that aggregate demand (AD) could determine GDP under certain conditions (e.g., price rigidity in the short run).

H4.4   The equality of GDP, aggregate demand, and aggregate income follows from the symmetry of the *circular flow.*

$$\text{Aggregate demand} = \text{GDP} = \text{aggregate income}$$

These equalities will be used frequently to understand the classical and Keynesian models.

Quiz

Choose the one best answer for each question.

Q4.1 The LAS curve is
   (a) horizontal.
   (b) vertical.
   (c) positively sloped.
   (d) negatively sloped.
   (e) positively sloped, except for low GDP, when it's horizontal.

Q4.2 An inflationary gap occurs when
   (a) the AD curve shifts leftward.
   (b) the AD curve shifts rightward.
   (c) GDP is above full-employment GDP.
   (d) GDP equals full-employment GDP.
   (e) GDP is below full-employment GDP.

Q4.3 Which of the following does *not* shift the AD curve?
   (a) An increase in the quantity of money
   (b) A change in the price level
   (c) A change in preferences
   (d) A decrease in taxes
   (e) An increase in consumption expenditure

Q4.4 A technological improvement shifts
   (a) both the SAS and LAS curves to the right.
   (b) the LAS curve to the right, but does not change the SAS curve.
   (c) the SAS curve to the right, but does not change the LAS curve.
   (d) both the SAS and LAS curves to the left.
   (e) neither the SAS nor the LAS curve.

Q4.5 Short-run macroeconomic equilibrium occurs at the level of GDP where the
   (a) AD curve intersects the LAS curve.
   (b) SAS curve intersects the LAS curve.
   (c) economy is at full employment.
   (d) AD curve intersects the SAS curve.
   (e) economy is in an inflationary gap.

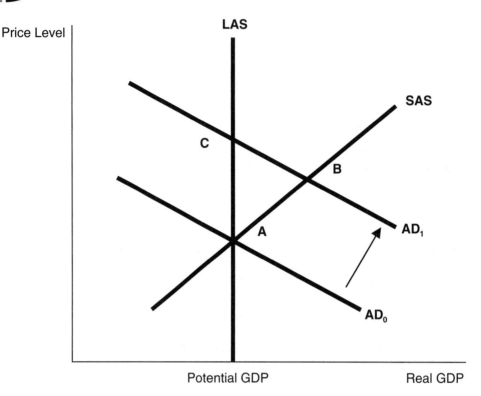

Figure 4-4.　Short-run and long-run equilibrium.

Questions Q4.6, Q4.7, and Q4.8 refer to Fig. 4-4.

Q4.6　Which of the following factors may have shifted the AD curve from AD_0 to AD_1?
(a)　A decrease in net investments
(b)　A decrease in government purchases
(c)　An increase in money wages
(d)　An increase in taxes
(e)　None of the above

Q4.7　Once aggregate demand has shifted to the AD_1 curve, what change has occurred?
(a)　There is a new long-run equilibrium at point B.
(b)　There is a new short-run equilibrium at point B.
(c)　There is a new short-run equilibrium at point C.
(d)　There is a new long-run equilibrium at point A.
(e)　None of the above.

Q4.8   When the economy shown in Fig. 4-4 is moving to the new long-run
        equilibrium, which curve will be shifting?
        (a) The LAS curve shifts to the right.
        (b) The LAS curve shifts to the left.
        (c) The SAS curve shifts to the right.
        (d) The SAS curve shifts to the left.
        (e) None of the above.

Q4.9   An increase in which of the following would cause an increase in the ag-
        gregate supply?
        (a) Labor productivity
        (b) The wage rate
        (c) The price of imports
        (d) Consumer spending
        (e) Interest rates

Q4.10   Based on Fig. 4-5, what is the impact of an increase in the world supply
        of oil on real gross domestic product and the aggregate price level?

	Real GDP	**Price Level**
(a)	Decrease	Increase
(b)	Decrease	Decrease
(c)	Increase	Increase
(d)	Increase	No change
(e)	Increase	Decrease

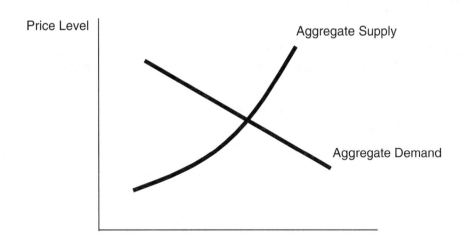

Figure 4-5.   Aggregate supply and aggregate demand.

Q4.11   In the macroeconomic long run,
(a) all prices are flexible.
(b) prices of goods and services are fixed.
(c) wage rates are fixed.
(d) some factor costs are constant.
(e) some wages change, but some don't.

Q4.12   If the labor force decreases, what does the AS/AD model predict will happen?
(a) GDP goes up and the price level increases.
(b) GDP goes up and the price level decreases.
(c) GDP goes up and the price level remains unchanged.
(d) GDP goes down and the price level increases.
(e) GDP goes down and the price level decreases.

Quiz Answers

Q4.1 (b). The long-run aggregate supply curve (LAS) is determined by the full-employment (potential) level of GDP. Therefore, the curve is vertical.

Q4.2 (c). An inflationary gap occurs when a short-run equilibrium exists with GDP above the potential or full-employment GDP (e.g., because of high short-run demand), putting pressure on prices to rise (inflation).

Q4.3 (b). The AD curve depends *ceteris paribus* only on the price level, so a change in any factor *except the price level* will shift the AD curve.

Q4.4 (a). An improvement in technology will increase the quantity supplied, both in the short run and the long run. This shifts both the SAS curve and the LAS curve to the right.

Q4.5 (d). By definition, the short-run equilibrium is the intersection of the AD curve and the SAS curve.

Q4.6 (e). This is a tricky question because none of the first four answers qualifies. For the shift from AD_0 to AD_1 to occur, aggregate demand has to go up for each given price level. Decreases in net investments and government purchases decrease aggregate demand. An increase in money wages (as opposed to real wages) will not have a positive impact on aggregate demand. Neither will an increase in taxes.

Q4.7 (b). As the AD curve has shifted to AD_1, it has created a new short-run equilibrium at the intersection with the SAS curve at point B. Please note that answer (d) is not the correct answer because there is no *new* long-run equilibrium at point A (this is the *old* long-run equilibrium).

Q4.8 (d). The LAS curve is fixed. The SAS curve moves because it is the short-run reaction by suppliers to the higher price levels, adjusting to the potential GDP.

Q4.9 (a). Labor productivity affects the production function directly and therefore the supply of products. The other factors mentioned have an impact on aggregate demand.

Q4.10 (e). The increase in the world supply of oil will shift aggregate supply to the right because it enhances production capabilities at a given price level. This shift to the right will cause the price level to decrease while the real GDP increases.

Q4.11 (a). The macroeconomic long run is the period in which all prices (final products, wage rates, factor costs, and so on) are considered fully flexible.

Q4.12 (d). A decrease in the labor force is a limitation (or restriction) on producers and will cause a leftward shift of the AS curve, leading to a decrease in real GDP as well as a decrease in the price level.

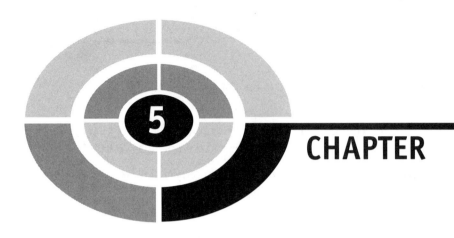

CHAPTER 5

Money and the Federal Reserve System

Money makes the circular flow go around, allowing for the efficient exchange of resources in the economy.
What is money? What are its key functions?
What is the role of banks? What is the role of the Federal Reserve System?
Money has its own economic sector (financial), with a central banking system, the Federal Reserve System, to monitor and control monetary activity.
How much money (and what kind) circulates in the economy? What is the impact of the quantity of money?

5.1 Introduction

The circular flow model (see Chapter 3) shows the importance of money in the national economy. Money is used for all major transactions in the economy, including those in factor markets, product markets, foreign markets, and so on.

Money is any item or commodity that is generally accepted as a means of payment for goods and services or for repayment of debt, and that serves as an asset to its holder. In ancient primitive societies, goods were exchanged for other goods because a widely accepted currency (e.g., gold or silver) was not available. Coins made of valuable metals were the first form of money. Offering the *intrinsic value* of the metal (e.g., the coin's weight in gold), they provided a means of payment that was generally accepted. In modern economies, currency in the form of banknotes and coins has practically no intrinsic value. This kind of currency, established by law as a valid form of financial exchange, is called *fiat money*. In addition, bank deposits are merely entries booked at banks whose value is based on the public's confidence that they are a viable medium of exchange.

Because money in a modern economy is not directly backed by intrinsic value, the financial system works on an entirely fiduciary basis, relying on the public's confidence in the established forms of monetary exchange.

Money has three main functions:

- *Medium of exchange*. It is acceptable in exchange for goods and services. This critical function avoids the inefficiencies of barter exchange.
- *Unit of account*. It is usable for quoting prices.
- *Store of value*. It is durable for exchange at a later date. This requires a stable value so that purchasing power is retained over time (see also Chapter 9, "Price Stability").

5.2   The Supply of Money

Although the general description of money is relatively straightforward, the precise definition of the overall supply of money is complex because of the wide variety of forms of money in modern economies.

The key measures for the U.S. money supply are

- *M1*. The narrowest measure of the money supply. It includes currency in circulation held by the nonbank public, demand deposits, other checkable deposits, and traveler's checks. M1 refers primarily to money used as a medium of exchange.
- *M2*. In addition to M1, this measure includes money held in savings deposits, money market deposit accounts, noninstitutional money market mutual funds, and other short-term money market assets (e.g., "overnight" Eurodollars). M2 refers primarily to money used as a store of value.
- *M3*. In addition to M2, this measure includes the financial assets and instruments of large businesses and financial institutions, e.g., large-denomination

time deposits and term Eurodollars. M3 refers primarily to money used as a unit of account.

- *L*. In addition to M3, this measure includes liquid and near-liquid assets, e.g., short-term Treasury notes, high-grade commercial paper, and bank acceptance notes.

The deposits of the public at banks and other depository institutions are considered money and are therefore included in the M1 money supply. If the public withdraws money from bank deposits to hold money as personal currency ("under the mattress"), this increase in inactive money will affect the banks' ability to extend loans and will influence the supply of money (see the discussion of the Federal Reserve System and fractional banking in this chapter).

Some common forms of public payment may not count as part of the supply of money. Check payments from one person to another are not included in the money supply because checks merely transfer money without being a net addition to the supply of money. Consumer credit cards are not included in the money supply; they are considered instant loans to consumers and therefore are not a net addition to the money supply.

5.3   Banks

A *depository institution* is a firm that takes deposits from the public and uses those deposits to make loans. Examples of depository institutions are commercial banks, thrift institutions (savings and loans, savings banks, credit unions), and money market mutual funds. For simplicity, in the remainder of this book, the term *bank* is used for depository institutions.

Banks provide four basic economic functions:

- They make liquid funds available to consumers and firms.
- They lower the cost of loans because the bank takes the role of single central lender.
- They lower the costs of loan performance monitoring.
- They lower exposure risks by lending to many borrowers.

Although significantly deregulated in the last two decades, banks continue to be subject to two important types of regulation, deposit insurance (e.g., FDIC-insured deposits) and general balance sheet rules (e.g., equity and reserve requirements, deposit and lending rules). After the Depression, commercial banks were barred from investment banking activities. As part of the ongoing banking industry deregulation, these provisions of the *Glass-Steagall Act* were repealed in 2001.

NOTE N5.3A

The Glass-Steagal Act

From 1929 to 1933, 11,000 out of the total of 25,000 U.S. banks failed or were forced to merge with other banks. In early 1933, congressional hearings were held to investigate these unprecedented bank failures. Testimony at the hearings appeared to point to gross misconduct and violation of the public's trust by bankers. In response, Congress passed the Banking Act of 1933, which barred commercial banks from investment banking and vice versa. This provision of the act became known as the Glass-Steagall Act. (The provision was finally repealed in 2001.)

Some economists have argued that the Depression, as opposed to bankers' misconduct, was the immediate reason for the high rate of bank failures. The value of certain assets (e.g., real estate) went down sharply in the first years of the Depression, directly jeopardizing bank loans.

Ironically, the 1933 Banking Act failed to correct the critical weakness in U.S. banking: state-based unit banking with a prohibition on nationwide banking. Few of the 11,000 failed U.S. banks were branch banks, while 90 percent of the failed banks had assets below $2 million. In Canada, a nationwide banking system did not experience major bank failures during the Depression.

NOTE N5.3B

The South Sea Bubble

One of the classic examples of panic occurred in England in the early eighteenth century, the incident known as the "South Sea Bubble." Ironically, the special Bubble Act passed one year after the panic episode did not address the major causes of the panic and ultimately had a negative impact on the country's economic activity.

In 1720, stock speculation reached panic proportions in England during the South Sea Bubble. The South Sea Company was set up in 1711 to manage English trade with South America. In 1719, the company proposed to manage part of England's national debt, the traditional responsibility of the Bank of England. The South Sea Company appeared to offer investors and the government better terms than the Bank of England. Cut-price stock offers made a rapid payback imperative, which required funding by new stock offerings, supported by ever more inflated expectations. The South Sea Company collapsed in 1720 and ruined most of its investors. The Bubble Act of 1721 made the founding of joint-stock companies without royal approval unlawful. This provision slowed down the development of British industry.

Historically, banks have been in the middle of major economic panics. In the nineteenth century, economic systems had developed beyond rural and local boundaries. As a consequence, financial panics affected many sectors of consumption and capital goods industries, causing havoc around the country. The impact was not even limited to domestic economies. Free trade had grown significantly since 1800, and the panics in the nineteenth century revealed the ever stronger connections among major global economies (the United States, England, and France).

Railroad companies defaulting on their bonds triggered the Panic of 1857 in the United States. This caused the assets of banks to be tied up in nonliquid railroad investments, leading to bank closures, as well as sharp increases in U.S. unemployment and a money market panic in Europe. The Panic of 1873, which started with a financial crisis in Vienna in June and in New York City in September, marked the end of the long-term expansion of the world economy that had begun in the late 1840s.

NOTE N5.3C

The Great Crash of 1929

The greatest economic panic may have been the *Great Crash* of the U.S. stock market in 1929, which precipitated the Great Depression.

The first day of panic occurred on October 24, 1929 ("Black Thursday"). Large banks and investment companies stemmed the immediate panic by buying stocks, but on October 29 ("Black Tuesday"), stock prices completely collapsed. Rampant speculation (triggered by low margin requirements for stock purchases), the proliferation of debt-creating holding companies, and large bank loans that could not be liquidated all contributed to the crash.

The *Securities and Exchange Commission (SEC)* was created in the aftermath of the Great Crash to regulate U.S. securities transactions. The financial performance of banks also came under scrutiny, leading to reserve requirements for U.S. banks, monitored by the Federal Reserve System.

5.4   The Federal Reserve System: Organization

Congress created the Federal Reserve System in 1913. The Federal Reserve System consists of 12 Federal Reserve Banks, 25 branches of these banks, the Board of Governors, the Federal Open Market Committee, and the member banks. The

Federal Reserve Banks are owned by the member banks, and their boards are selected by the member banks and the Board of Governors. The *Board of Governors* of the Federal Reserve has seven members serving 14-year terms, staggered so that one's term ends every two years. The members are appointed by the U.S. president and confirmed by the U.S. Senate. The president designates the chairman and the vice chairman of the Board of Governors. The Board of Governors supervises the operations of the Federal Reserve Banks and constitutes the majority of the Federal Open Market Committee. The *Federal Open Market Committee (FOMC)* determines the amounts of government securities and other obligations that Federal Reserve Banks buy or sell. It also manages the Federal Reserve's purchases of foreign currencies. The FOMC is responsible for day-to-day open market operations and meets at least once every three weeks.

Under the *Monetary Control Act of 1980,* all U.S. banks are member banks of the Federal Reserve System.

NOTE N5.4

The Bank of the United States

The history of U.S. banks is directly tied to George Washington's first presidency and his secretary of the Treasury, Alexander Hamilton.

Banking issues played a key role in the development of U.S. political parties, and banking policies figured prominently in several presidential elections, especially in the early years of the nation. The Bank of the United States was chartered by Congress in 1791 amidst an intense debate about the bank's constitutionality (defended by the Federalists, led by the secretary of the Treasury, Alexander Hamilton) and its purported infringements of states' rights (argued by the Democratic-Republicans, led by Thomas Jefferson).

The pro- and anti-central banking debate contributed significantly to the formation of the first American political parties. The controversial bank's 20-year charter was not renewed in 1811. Reconstituted in 1816, it continued to stir debate, with Henry Clay (and the Whigs) in support and Andrew Jackson (and the Democrats) in opposition. The bank issue dominated the 1832 presidential election, in which Jackson defeated Clay. Jackson vetoed the bank renewal act, calling the bank the "prostration of our Government to the advancement of the few at the expense of the many." The Bank Wars were over, and it would be another 80 years before effective regulation of the U.S. private banking industry was instituted by the 1913 creation of the Federal Reserve System.

The Banking Act of 1935 granted the Federal Reserve the power to determine the cash reserves of U.S. commercial banks. Originally designed to prescribe minimum bank balance standards, it was first employed as a policy tool during the 1936–1937 boom to control the supply of money. The cash reserve requirement is more useful as an anti-inflationary measure than as a means to fight a recession because the tool cannot force banks to lend money.

5.5 The Federal Reserve's Central Banking Role

The Federal Reserve System (or the "Fed") is the *central bank* for the United States. A central bank is a "bank for banks" and a public authority that regulates financial firms.

The essential function of the central bank is to be the *lender of last resort* for banks. The lender of last resort is an institution that is at all times willing to lend money to the banks, on its own terms.

The Federal Reserve's lending to banks allows it to have an impact on the rate of interest and the supply of money. It also provides the financial foundation for banks to solve liquidity problems.

As a constitutionally independent federal institution, the Federal Reserve briefs the U.S. Congress on its policies and remains in close contact with the U.S executive branch. However, the Federal Reserve retains ultimate responsibility for its policy.

The Federal Reserve, responsible for the nation's monetary policy, has three major policy tools to manage the supply of money:

- *Required reserve ratio.* The Federal Reserve sets the required reserve ratio, the minimum percentage of their deposits that banks are required to hold as reserves. This establishes the *fractional banking system* that guides money creation by banks. A decrease in the reserve ratio increases lending by banks, and therefore the quantity of money goes up.
- *Discount rate.* The discount rate is the interest rate at which the Fed lends reserves to commercial banks. A decrease in the discount rate means that banks will borrow more from the Fed (because of the lower cost). Consequently, the quantity of money goes up.
- *Open market operations.* Open market operations are the purchase or sale of government securities (U.S. Treasury bills and bonds) by the Fed in the open market. Banks' reserves go up when the Fed buys securities, increasing banks' lending and the quantity of money

Banks create money by making loans. They observe the required reserve ratio, that is, the ratio of reserves to deposits required by regulation. When actual

Figure 5-1. The Federal Reserve's open market policy.

T-account: Baseline Situation

Required Reserve Ratio = 20%

Banks' reserves (Reserve Accounts + Fed Notes) $190, exactly 20% of checkable deposits ($950); no excess reserves.

Money Supply = Checkable Deposits + Customer Fed Notes = $950 + $90 = $1,040

Assets				Liabilities
The Fed				
Treasury Securities	$190	$90	Reserve Accounts of Banks	
		$100	Federal Reserve Notes	
Banks				
Reserve Accounts	$90	$950	Checkable Deposits	
Federal Reserve Notes	$100	$380	Net Worth	
Loans	$1,140			
Bank Customers				
Checkable Deposits	$950	$1,140	Loans	
Federal Reserve Notes	$90			
Treasury Securities	$100			

Continued on next page . . .

Continued . . .

T-ACCOUNT after $20 Treasury securities open market purchase by Federal Reserve (expansionary policy)

Money Multiplier = 1/Required Reserve Ratio = 1/0.2 = 5.0

The $20 Fed purchase of securities translates into 5.0 × $20 = $100 extra checkable deposits.

Money Supply = Checkable Deposits + Customer Fed Notes = $1,050 + $90 = $1,140 (i.e., $100 more than baseline).

Assets	Change		Change		Liabilities
The Fed					
Treasury Securities	+$20	$210	$110	+$20	Reserve Accounts of Banks
			$100		Federal Reserve Notes
Banks					
Reserve Accounts	+$20	$110	$1,050	+$100	Checkable Deposits
Federal Reserve Notes		$100	$380		Net Worth
Loans	+$80	$1,220			
Bank Customers					
Checkable Deposits	+$100	$1,050	$1,220	+$80	Loans
Federal Reserve Notes		$90			
Treasury Securities	−$20	$80			

reserves exceed required reserves, institutions may increase their loans and increase borrowers' deposits; these new deposits create money. The potential change in the total supply of money is equal to the excess reserves multiplied by the *money (or direct deposit) multiplier*. The money (or direct deposit) multiplier equals 1/legal reserve requirement.

The primary tool for the management of banks' reserves is the Federal Reserve's open market policy. Discount rate changes serve mainly as signals, while reserve requirements are rarely changed.

Figure 5-1 shows a so-called T-account. It demonstrates how the Federal Reserve influences the supply of money through open market policies. Assume a legal reserve requirement of 20 percent, so that the money multiplier is $1/0.2 = 5$. By purchasing \$20 in Treasury securities, the Federal Reserve will increase the money supply by $5.0 \times \$20 = \$100$.

The major assets on the Federal Reserve's balance sheet are gold, foreign exchange, U.S. government securities, and loans to banks. Its major liabilities are Federal Reserve notes in circulation (currency) and banks' deposits (reserves).

5.6   Hints

H5.1   In economic terms, *money* is the supply of money, such as M_1 or M_2. It is *not* the same as our informal usage of "money" earned through income (in economic terms, this is "consumer income").

H5.2   The *federal funds rate* is the interest rate at which financial institutions can borrow short-term loans from other financial institutions (e.g., banks borrowing from banks). This rate should not be confused with the discount rate charged to banks by the Federal Reserve. However, changes in the Federal Reserve's discount rate and its open market operations have an impact on the federal funds rate.

H5.3   *Currency* is the notes and coins that are the "current" medium of exchange in a country. Gold and national currencies that act as reserve currency (e.g., the dollar) are referred to as *international currencies* because they are used for settlement of international debts.

H5.4   *Financial innovation,* or the development of new ways of borrowing and lending, is spurred by the economic environment, technology, and regulation. This often complicates the measurement of the economy's money supply, as monitored by the Federal Reserve (see Section 5.2).

H5.5   The Federal Reserve is responsible for enforcing several federal laws to protect consumers in their dealings with state-chartered banks that are members of the Federal Reserve System. These laws include the Truth in

Lending Act, the Community Reinvestment Act, and the Home Mortgage Disclosure Act.

H5.6 The Monetary Control Act of 1980 made all U.S. banks members of the Federal Reserve System and also established uniform reserve requirements for banks and depository institutions, as well as the uniform service charges by the Federal Reserve. To become a member of the Federal Reserve System, a bank has to meet certain capital requirements and be willing to follow the regulations of the Federal Reserve System.

H5.7 The Glass-Owen Bill of 1913 (also called the *Federal Reserve Act*) established the Federal Reserve System and authorized it to control the quantity of money in circulation.

Quiz

Choose the one best answer for each question.

Q5.1   Checking account balances at banks are
    (a) part of M1, M2, and M3.
    (b) part of neither M1 nor M2.
    (c) part of M3 only.
    (d) part of M1 and M2, but not of M3.
    (e) part of M2 only.

Q5.2   Which of the following is considered money?
    (a) A check for $1,000
    (b) A credit card with a $1,000 credit limit
    (c) A deposit of $1,000 cash into a checking account
    (d) A personal I.O.U. for $1,000
    (e) None of the above

Q5.3   The Bank of the United States, chartered in 1791, was strongly supported by
    (a) Thomas Jefferson.
    (b) the Democratic-Republicans.
    (c) Andrew Jackson.
    (d) states' rights supporters.
    (e) Alexander Hamilton.

Q5.4   Who has the day-to-day responsibility for U.S. monetary policy?
    (a) The Board of Governors of the Federal Reserve
    (b) The presidents of the Federal Reserve's regional banks

(c) The member banks of the Federal Reserve
(d) The Federal Open Market Committee of the Federal Reserve
(e) The secretary of the Treasury

Q5.5   If the Federal Reserve lowers the reserve ratio, it _____ the banks' required reserves and _____ the quantity of money.
(a) decreases; increases
(b) decreases; doesn't change
(c) decreases; decreases
(d) increases; increases
(e) increases; decreases

Q5.6   If the legal reserve requirement equals 20 percent, what is the money multiplier?
(a) 3
(b) 4
(c) 5
(d) 1.25
(e) 10

Q5.7   Which of these statements about the federal funds rate are true?
   I. It is influenced by the discount rate.
   II. It is the interest rate that banks charge one another for short-term loans.
   III. It is influenced by open market operations.

(a) I only
(b) II only
(c) I and II
(d) II and III
(e) I, II, and III

Q5.8   A commercial bank holds $100,000 in demand deposit liabilities and $20,000 in reserves. If the required reserve ratio is 10 percent, what is the maximum amount by which the banking system can increase loans?
(a) $25,000
(b) $100,000
(c) $120,000
(d) $150,000
(e) $400,000

Q5.9   The 1935 Banking Act granted the Federal Reserve System the power to
(a) audit U.S. banks.
(b) set cash reserve requirements for U.S. banks.
(c) determine fiscal policy as well as monetary policy.
(d) set the federal funds rate.
(e) make all U.S. banks member banks of the Federal
    Reserve System.

Q5.10   Which action by the Federal Reserve results in an increase in banks' excess reserves?
(a) Increasing the federal funds rate
(b) Increasing the discount rate
(c) Buying bonds on the open market
(d) Selling bonds on the open market
(e) Increasing the reserve requirement

Q5.11   "Lender of last resort" refers to
(a) requesting a new credit card.
(b) the central bank's willingness to lend to banks.
(c) government's financial support of the Federal Reserve.
(d) a bank at the final port of call of a cruise ship.
(e) banks willing to provide loans to customers.

Q5.12   The effective use of fiduciary money depends on
(a) the intrinsic value of money.
(b) the backing of money by gold by the Federal Reserve.
(c) the bank's willingness to exchange currency for silver.
(d) the acceptance of out-of-state checks.
(e) confidence that the money can be exchanged for goods
    and services.

Quiz Answers

Q5.1 (a). Checking account balances held at banks are considered part of M1 (the narrowest form of the money supply) because they represent money used for exchange and transaction purposes. Because checking accounts are part of M1, they automatically are also part of M2 and M3.

Q5.2 (c). A check is a transfer of money, but it is *not* a net addition to the money supply. The credit card line is an instant loan to consumers, but it is not part of the money supply. The I.O.U. may be (informal) "money" between certain parties, but it is not generally acceptable currency and therefore is not a part of the money supply. The cash deposit in the bank is a net addition to the economy's money supply and constitutes money.

Q5.3 (e). Alexander Hamilton, secretary of the Treasury in the cabinet of the nation's first president, George Washington, was a forceful proponent of the (first) Bank of the United States. Jefferson and his party, the Democratic-Republicans, were opposed because they felt that a federal bank would violate the rights of the states [this eliminates answers (a), (b), and (d)]. Andrew Jackson was opposed to the rechartering of the federal bank at a later time, eliminating answer (c).

Q5.4 (d). The responsibility for U.S. monetary policy rests with the Federal Reserve System, with day-to-day operations being managed by the Federal Open Market Committee, chiefly through its daily open market operations. The Federal Reserve briefs Congress regularly on its policies and also stays in close touch with the administration (e.g., the secretary of the Treasury).

Q5.5 (a). If the Federal Reserve lowers the required reserve ratio, it means that banks are allowed to hold less reserves. This permits the banks to increase the amount of loans they make, and therefore increases the supplied quantity of money.

Q5.6 (c). The money (or direct deposit) multiplier = 1/reserve requirement = 1/0.2 = 5.

Q5.7 (e). The federal funds rate is the interest rate on short-term loans between banks and other banks. This rate will be influenced by the Federal Reserve's discount rate and its open market activities.

Q5.8 (b). The single bank's excess reserves are equal to its total reserves minus its required reserves, or $20,000 - (10\% \times \$100,000) = \$10,000$. We find the loan availability in the total banking system by applying the money (or direct deposit) multiplier (= 1/reserve requirement = 1/10 percent = 10) to the $10,000 excess reserves to get $100,000.

Q5.9 (b). The 1935 Banking Act provided the Federal Reserve with the power to determine cash requirements for banks. Originally intended to provide basic guidelines for banking practices, it quickly became a tool to manage the supply of money, especially to limit inflation. It was the Monetary Act of 1980 that made all U.S. banks member banks of the Federal Reserve System.

Q5.10 (c). The buying of bonds by the Federal Reserve increases funds for the sellers, i.e., the banks, and therefore increases their excess reserves. All other answers are actions that will decrease excess reserves.

Q5.11 (b). The central bank ("bank of banks") is the lender of last resort for banks, protecting their liquidity.

Q5.12 (e). Fiduciary (Latin for "trust") money means that people have confidence that the money being used can be exchanged for valuable goods and services. Often, government has legally decreed what the currency is. Please note that the intrinsic value of the money [answer (a)] is not critical in a fiduciary system. People do *not* require that the money itself have value (coins in silver or gold).

CHAPTER 6

The Money Market

Money facilitates the flow of resources in the circular model of the macroeconomy. Not enough money will slow down the economy, and too much money can cause inflation because of higher price levels.

Either way, monitoring the supply and demand for money is vital for the Federal Reserve's monetary policy, which aims to stabilize price levels and to support economic growth.

The rate of interest is the price mechanism that achieves equilibrium in the money market.

6.1   The Demand for Money

The *rate of interest* is the price paid in the money market for the use of money (or loans). The rate is a percentage of the amount borrowed.

If a person holds $1,000 in currency, the opportunity cost of holding the money is the interest that could be earned on the $1,000 in an interest-bearing account. The opportunity cost of holding money goes up if the interest rate increases, which may lead to decreased consumption and increased saving. Conversely, if the interest rate

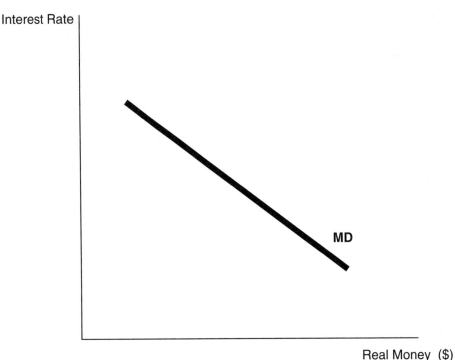

Figure 6-1.   The negatively sloped money demand curve MD.

is low, it is relatively cheap to borrow money and the quantity of money demanded goes up (see Fig. 6-1). Therefore, the demand for currency has a negative relationship with the interest rate.

Sources of the *demand for money* are

- *Transaction demand.* Money demanded for day-to-day payments through balances held by households and firms (instead of stocks, bonds, or other assets). This kind of demand varies with GDP; it does not depend on the rate of interest.
- *Precautionary demand.* Money demanded as a result of unanticipated payments. This kind of demand varies with GDP.
- *Speculative demand.* Money demanded because of expectations about interest rates in the future. This means that people will decide to expand their money balances and hold off on bond purchases if they expect interest rates to rise. This kind of demand has a negative relationship with the interest rate.

The total demand curve for money MD has a negative relationship with the rate of interest (see Fig. 6-1).

Changes in other factors (held constant along the curve, *ceteris paribus*) will lead to shifts in the demand curve for money. Increases in the economy's price level will increase the demand for money (note that the demand for money is tied to the interest rate, not the price level). If real GDP increases, the demand for money increases because of the higher demand for products. Also, when banks develop new money products that allow for easier, low-cost withdrawal, the demand for money will decrease, such as banks offering savings accounts with shorter (or less stringent) time deposit requirements and lower penalties for withdrawal.

6.2   The Supply of Money

The Federal Reserve (see Chapter 5, "Money and the Federal Reserve System") is responsible for determining the supply of money. Its Federal Open Market Committee uses daily open market operations to influence the creation of money by banks and to guide the availability of money in the economy. The Federal Reserve also has an impact on the creation of money by banks through reserve requirements and the discount rate, that is, the interest rate at which banks can borrow from the Federal Reserve as the lender of last resort. Changes in the supply of

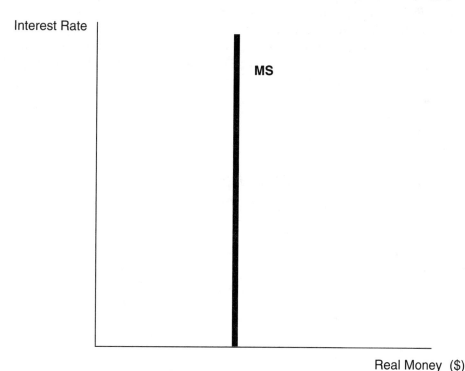

Figure 6-2.   The vertical money supply curve MS.

money will affect the interest rate and therefore the cost of borrowing money. This will have an impact on consumption and investment levels in the economy.

For simplicity, we assume that the *supply of money* is a constant, indicated by the vertical line MS in Fig. 6-2.

6.3   The Money Market and the Equilibrium Rate of Interest

The rate of interest functions as the price in the money market (compare this to the price level in the AS/AD model). Money has a time value, and its use is bought and sold in the *money market* in return for the payment of interest (see also note N6.3). The financial institutions that deal in government securities and loans, gold, and foreign exchange make up the money market. The money market is not a specific physical location but consists of transactions made electronically or by phone. Equilibrium in the money market occurs when the MD and MS curves intersect at the *equilibrium interest rate*, as shown in Fig 6-3.

If the Federal Reserve were to decide to increase the quantity of money from MS to MS′, the supply of money curve would shift to the right, resulting in a decrease in the equilibrium interest rate. The lower cost of borrowing could spur higher consumption and investment.

NOTE N6.3

Keynesian Interest Rate Theory

According to Keynesian theory, the rate of interest is determined as a price in two markets:

- *Investment funds.* The rate of interest balances the demand for funds (required for investment) and the supply of funds (from savings). If investors can earn a 10 percent return on a capital investment project (e.g., building a factory), they will be willing to pay a rate of interest of up to 10 percent. Households delay consumption by saving (and are rewarded by earning interest) depending on their *time preference* and the rate of interest. Savings percentages can differ significantly from one nation to another. The U.S. savings rate in 2004 was about 0.2 percent, while the savings rate in China was roughly 40 percent.

The equilibrium interest rate goes down from r^* to r'^* as the money supply curve shifts to the right from MS to MS' (e.g., when the Fed increases the quantity of money).

> MS = money supply
> MD = money demand

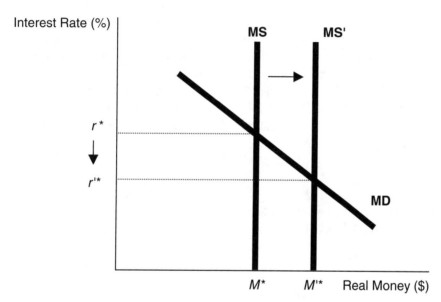

Figure 6-3. Money market equilibrium.

- *Liquid assets.* Households and businesses may have reasons to hold assets in liquid form (i.e., readily available money). Because borrowers require cash in the long term (that doesn't need to be repaid to the lender immediately), they are willing to compensate lenders for giving up liquidity. Keynes introduced the influence of the *liquidity preference* on the interest rate. The classical economists, who considered investment funds as the critical market for the interest rate, disregarded the topic of liquidity preference.

Although intermediaries can achieve equality between the rates of interest in the two markets, the potential lack of balance between the investment and money markets was essential to Keynesians, who claimed that it caused unemployment in the short run.

6.4 The Impact of Money

In the macroeconomic short run, some prices (e.g., wage rates affected by labor contracts) will be inflexible. This causes economic fluctuations, with real GDP either below potential GDP (recessionary gap) or above potential GDP (inflationary gap).

The Federal Reserve's monetary policy has an immediate, short-run impact on the economy. In particular, higher interest rates will decrease investment because it becomes more expensive to borrow money, and will also decrease consumption because consumers will tend to save more as interest rate returns increase. In addition, as higher U.S. interest rates increase the demand for dollars on the foreign exchange markets (because of the higher returns on U.S. deposits), the higher dollar will decrease exports by making them increasingly expensive. This means that real GDP growth and the inflation rate slow when the Federal Reserve raises the interest rate. The reverse occurs when the interest rate is lowered.

AD = aggregate demand
SAS = short-run aggregate supply
LAS = long-run aggregate supply

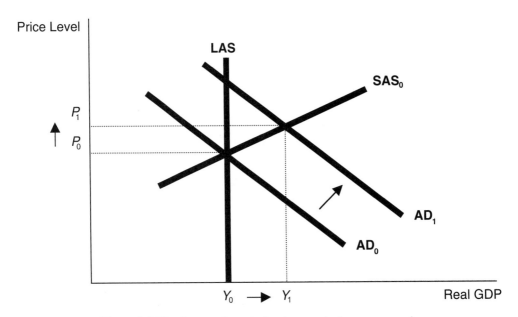

Figure 6-4. The short-run impact of an increase in the money supply.

AD = aggregate demand
SAS = short-run aggregate supply
LAS = long-run aggregate supply

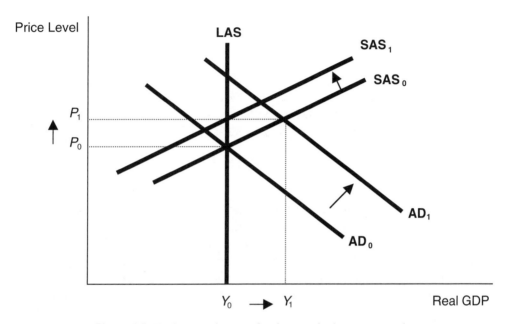

Figure 6-5. The long-run impact of an increase in the money supply.

Monetary policy can be applied in the short run, when the economy faces an inflationary gap (real GDP exceeds potential GDP). The Federal Reserve may then pursue a policy to avoid inflation by decreasing the quantity of money and raising the interest rate. The higher interest rate decreases investment, consumption, and net exports, as discussed in the previous paragraph. This decrease in aggregate demand will decrease real GDP and lower the price level. In the macroeconomic long run, prices are assumed to be fully flexible, and this will move real GDP toward potential GDP.

If the economy is at its long-run equilibrium and the Federal Reserve increases the money supply, it will increase aggregate demand, causing a shift of the AD curve from AD_0 to AD_1 (see Fig. 6-4). Consequently, the price level goes up, as well as the real GDP. This means that an inflationary gap exists, with the actual unemployment rate being below the natural rate. The tightness in the labor market will lead to a rise in the money wage rate. Because of higher labor costs, the short-run aggregate supply curve SAS will shift to the left (from SAS_0 to SAS_1; see Fig. 6-5), returning real GDP to the level of potential GDP.

6.5   The Quantity Theory of Money

The *quantity theory of money* holds that changes in the money supply MS directly influence the economy's price level, but nothing else. This theory follows from the *equation of exchange*:

$$M \times V = P \times Y$$

where M = quantity of money
V = velocity of money (i.e., the average number of times a unit of money is used during a year to purchase GDP's goods and services)
P = price level
Y = real GDP

The equation of exchange essentially states that the economy's nominal GDP or expenditures ($P \times Y$) equal the money actually used in the economy ($M \times V$). According to the quantity theory of money, velocity V is not affected by the quantity of money M and is considered constant: $V = V_{constant}$. Also, potential real GDP (i.e., long-run equilibrium) is not affected by M and is considered constant: $Y = Y_{constant}$. It now follows directly from the equation of exchange ($M \times V_{constant} = P \times Y_{constant}$) that changes in M are equal to the changes in P, in the long run. This view of the equation of exchange expresses the (neo)classical *neutrality of money*, that is, money affects only nominal values but not real values. In other words, the money supply leaves real output unaffected.

Historical evidence suggests that the money growth rate and the inflation rate are positively related in the long run. However, the year-to-year relationship is weaker.

6.6   Hints

H6.1   The equation of exchange does not hold in the short run, as the economy does not immediately adjust because of price inflexibility. Although the relationship between M and P may not be causal, as suggested by quantity money theorists, it appears that there is a correlation between M and P in the long term. Therefore, growth in M can be used as a statistical estimate for the rate of inflation, that is, the Federal Reserve can be effective in stabilizing prices. It's less clear what the Federal Reserve's impact on short-term real GDP and real interest rates is.

H6.2   The Federal Reserve's primary goal since 1979 (when the United States was plagued by high rates of inflation) has been to stabilize prices. The Federal

Reserve's purpose (from "Purpose and Functions," Washington D.C., Federal Reserve Board of Governors) is "to promote effectively the goals of maximum employment, stable prices, and moderate long-term interest rates."

H6.3   The Federal Reserve has a choice between setting money supply targets (which will affect short-term interest rates) or setting goals for short-term interest rates. It cannot set targets for money and interest simultaneously because of the interaction between the two factors.

H6.4   The *prime rate* is the interest rate that commercial banks charge their best customers for short-term loans. This rate is important because it is a reference rate for many types of commercial and consumer loans. See Fig. 6-6.

H6.5   Irving Fisher (1867–1947) designed the exchange equation $MV = PY$ (the equation is also called the *Fisher equation*). This equation became the foundation for the quantity theory of money and plays a prominent role in monetarist models. Fisher, a mathematician by training, was professor of political economy at Yale University. He also developed the theory of index numbers.

Quiz

Choose the one best answer for each question.

Q6.1   Transaction demand for money increases when
(a) GDP goes down.
(b) GDP goes up.
(c) interest rates fall.
(d) interest rates rise.
(e) unanticipated payments are expected to increase.

Q6.2   If the interest rate is expected to change in the future, what type of money demand will be affected?
(a) Speculative
(b) Transaction
(c) Precautionary
(d) Day-to-day payments
(e) There will not be any effect on money demand

Q6.3   Which of the following factors does *not* shift the money demand curve?
(a) Real GDP
(b) Nominal GDP

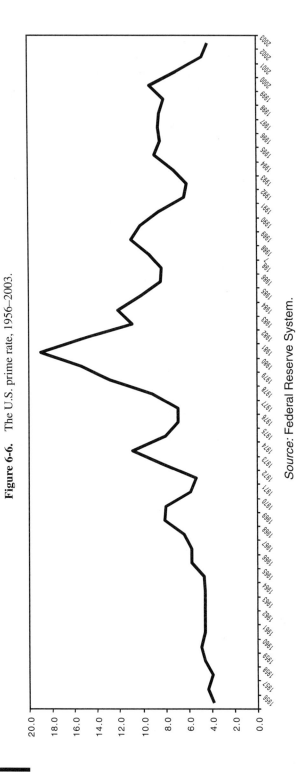

Figure 6-6. The U.S. prime rate, 1956–2003.

Source: Federal Reserve System.

(c) Rate of interest

(d) Price level

(e) Financial innovation

Q6.4   The Federal Reserve's anti-inflation policy will _____ the quantity of
money and _____ the interest rate.

(a) not change; not change

(b) increase; lower

(c) increase; raise

(d) decrease; lower

(e) decrease; raise

Q6.5   In the long run, an increase in the quantity of money

(a) shifts the AD curve rightward.

(b) shifts the AD curve leftward.

(c) shifts the SAS curve rightward.

(d) shifts the SAS curve leftward.

(e) does none of the above.

Q6.6   If nominal GDP equals $10 trillion and the quantity of money is $5 trillion, what is the velocity of money in the economy?

(a) ½

(b) 50

(c) 4

(d) 2

(e) None of the above

Q6.7   Historically, higher growth in the money supply is associated with

(a) higher growth of real GDP.

(b) higher inflation rates.

(c) lower inflation rates.

(d) lower discount rates.

(e) none of the above.

Q6.8   Which of the following most likely increases the velocity of money?

(a) Declining interest rates

(b) Declining personal income

(c) Increased unemployment

(d) Declining price levels

(e) Higher frequency of paychecks

Q6.9   Interest rates and the money supply are most likely to change in which
way when the Federal Reserve sells bonds?

Interest Rates	Money Supply
(a) Increase	Decrease
(b) Increase	Increase
(c) Decrease	Increase
(d) Decrease	Decrease
(e) No change	Decrease

Q6.10 The neutrality of money refers to the situation in which
   (a) increases in interest rates are matched by increases in bond prices.
   (b) increases in the money supply leave real output unaffected.
   (c) increases in interest rates are matched by decreases in bond prices.
   (d) decreases in the money supply cause short-term interest rates to go up.
   (e) money has neither a nominal nor a real impact on the economy.

Q6.11 If real GDP equals potential GDP and the velocity of money is constant, what happens if the supply of money increases?
   (a) Unemployment goes up.
   (b) The price level goes down.
   (c) The price level goes up.
   (d) Real GDP goes down.
   (e) Real GDP goes up.

Q6.12 Higher interest rates will _____ firms' capital investments and _____ household consumption.
   (a) increase; increase
   (b) decrease; increase
   (c) decrease; not change
   (d) decrease; decrease
   (e) not change; decrease

Quiz Answers

Q6.1 (b). The transaction demand for money goes up when the day-to-day payment needs of households and firms increase. This kind of money demand depends on GDP growth. If GDP goes up, transaction demand increases. Transaction demand does not depend on the rate of interest. Money demand resulting from unanticipated expenses is called *precautionary demand,* not transaction demand.

Q6.2 (a). If interest rates are expected to change in the future, this will trigger speculative demand (e.g., maintaining money balances to delay the purchase of bonds), as opposed to transaction or precautionary demand. "Day-to-day payments" refers to transaction demand.

Q6.3 (c). Changes in nominal GDP, real GDP, and the price level will affect the demand for money and shift the curve. Also, financial innovation will shift the curve. Changes in the rate of interest will *not* shift the curve itself but will lead to a move along the curve.

Q6.4 (e). The Federal Reserve will decrease aggregate demand by raising the interest rate (investments go down) and decreasing the money supply, curtailing the money available for spending on goods and services.

Q6.5 (d). In the long run, the labor market causes wages to go up; therefore the SAS curve moves to the left.

Q6.6 (d). The equation of exchange is $MV = PY$, where $PY = $ nominal GDP. If $PY = \$10$ trillion and $M = \$5$ trillion, then $V = 2$.

Q6.7 (b). The statistical record appears to back up the quantity theory in the long run: the higher M, the higher P.

Q6.8 (e). Spending is likely to accelerate because of the shorter time frame, causing an increase in velocity. Please note that a decrease in price level [answer (d)] leads to a decline in V, provided M remains the same and real GDP is unchanged.

Q6.9 (a). When the Federal Reserve sells bonds, it reduces the money supply through the banks, increasing the interest rate.

Q6.10 (b). The neutrality of money indicates that money affects only nominal price and output levels, not real levels. Please note that answer (e) is *not* correct; money has an impact on nominal values.

Q6.11 (c). From the equation of exchange, $M \times V = P \times Y$, it follows that if Y is constant and V is constant, the increase in M will lead to an increase in the price level P. This is similar to the quantity theory of money.

Q6.12 (d). The higher interest rates will increase the cost of borrowing money for capital investments, causing investments to decrease. Households' return on savings increases with higher interest rates, and they will use a larger portion of their disposable income for savings instead of consumption, thereby decreasing consumption.

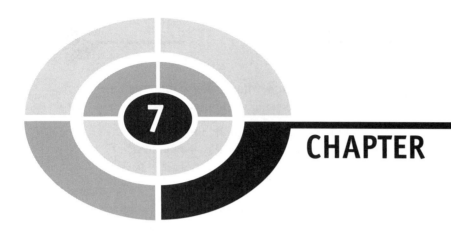

CHAPTER 7

Global Economics

Why do countries trade? What kind of trade is likely to develop?
What is the impact of restrictions on trade? How critical is free trade for global economic growth?
What is the role of international finance? Of exchange rates? What drives the value of the dollar and other major currencies?

7.1 Introduction

Historically, nations managed economies from the domestic point of view. The emergence of extensive free trade in the nineteenth century heralded the beginning of the "global" economy and its interdependencies. As early as the 1850s, financial crises and panics in one country could have major repercussions in other countries. In the 1930s, the Great Depression plunged the United States and most of the Western world, including Great Britain and Germany, into a prolonged economic stagnation. This led countries to impose trade restrictions in order to protect their domestic economies, and the resulting decline in international trade made the stagnation worse.

In order to address the increased need for global coordination, the 1944 conference at Bretton Woods led to a global currency system and to the establishment of the International Monetary Fund (IMF). In addition, the postwar General Agreement on Tariffs and Trade (GATT) was a multination commitment to removing barriers to trade.

Since World War II, global economic connections have become ever stronger, evidenced by growing import and export ties and by the emergence of major free-trade groups such as the European Union, NAFTA, Mercosur, and ASEAN. In addition, the World Trade Organization (WTO) is dedicated to worldwide progress in free trade. For example, worldwide textile quotas were lifted in 2005 by global WTO agreement. These kinds of multinational decisions characterize the modern global economy.

Comparative advantage is the factor that drives international trade. A country has a comparative advantage in the production of a good if the country can produce it at

The slope of the production possibilities frontier at point A represents the opportunity cost (or trade-off) of making one product instead of another.

At point A, the opportunity cost of producing one extra automobile is 100 bushels. This is equivalent to the slope (= Δ bushels of grain/Δ cars) of the PPC at point A.

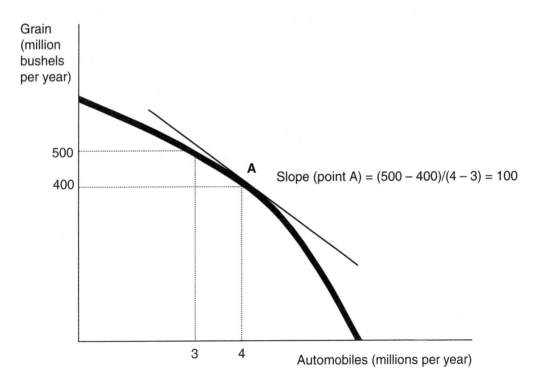

Figure 7-1.   The slope of the production possibilities curve is the opportunity cost.

a lower opportunity cost than any other country (see also H7.1). The slope of the country's production possibilities curve (PPC) is the opportunity cost (see Fig. 7-1).

A nation gains from trade by specializing in the production of goods for which it has a comparative advantage and trading those goods for other goods. With international trade, a nation receives a higher relative price for the goods it exports and pays a lower relative price for the goods it imports. Therefore, by efficiently pooling the productive resources of various countries, international trade allows nations to consume outside their PPCs. The added consumption is equivalent to the gains from trade.

7.2 Barriers to Trade

Governments may decide to restrict trade to protect domestic industries. The main methods used to restrict trade are *tariffs*, or taxes on imported goods, and *nontariff barriers*, or any actions other than tariffs that restrict international trade (e.g., quotas). See Fig. 7-2 for the illustration of the effect of a tariff.

A tariff decreases the supply of the imported good. The new supply curve with the tariff lies above the old supply curve by the amount of the tariff (the length of the arrow). The price rises from P_0 to P_1, and the quantity decreases from Q_0 to Q_1. The government's tariff revenue is indicated in Fig. 7-2.

The tariff reduces the gains from trade. The decrease in imports to the domestic economy means that foreigners can buy less from the domestic economy. Therefore, the value of domestic exports decreases by an amount equal to the drop in the value of domestic imports.

Nontariff barriers include quotas and voluntary export restraints. *Quotas* are quantitative restrictions on the maximum amount of a good that can be produced, and *voluntary export restraints* are agreements between governments in which the exporting nation agrees to limit the volume of its exports. For example, the worldwide lifting of textile quotas (by WTO agreement) caused major concerns on the part of U.S. textile manufacturers, who feared an avalanche of low-cost Chinese imports into the United States. After the potential threat of import tariffs emerged, the Chinese government agreed to a so-called voluntary quota, establishing self-imposed restrictions on textile exports to the United States. This was a way to gradually move from a quota-directed to a free-trade-based system for textiles.

Like tariffs, nontariff barriers raise the prices of imported goods and decrease the quantities imported. Unlike the situation with a tariff, however, the government gets no revenue from a nontariff barrier. For quotas, the revenue from the higher price goes to importers, and in the case of voluntary export restraints it goes to foreign exporters.

Although many reasons are given for protection, most of the suggested protective measures raise the cost of doing business substantially and are fundamentally

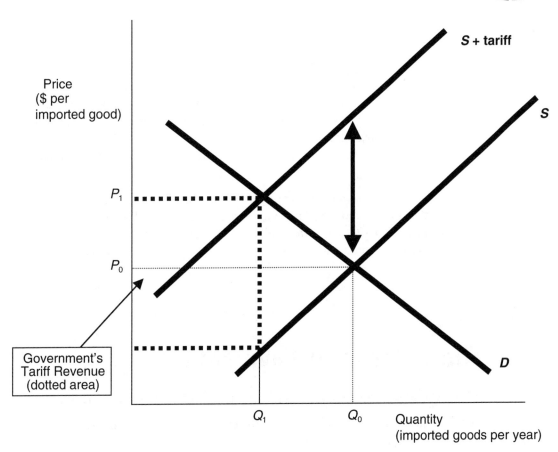

Figure 7-2.   The effect of a tariff.

flawed. A selection of those protective arguments follows (with comments on the corresponding flaws).

- "We need to protect industries that are critical to our national defense." Most industries are vital for defense. It's best to subsidize selected industries.
- "We need to protect this young industry so that it can 'grow up' and compete successfully in global markets." Firms can finance their own start-ups; if needed, direct subsidies are most efficient.
- "We need to protect this industry from foreign competitors who sell goods below cost." Only monopolies can persistently sell below cost, and regulation is the most efficient way to control this.
- "We need to protect U.S. jobs; imports cost U.S. jobs." Free trade may cost jobs in importing countries, but it creates jobs in exporting countries. Tariffs will only raise the cost of products.

- "We need tariffs to compete with cheap foreign labor." U.S. labor is more productive than cheap foreign labor. U.S. firms can compete successfully in industries where they have the comparative advantage because of high (relative) productivity.

Barriers to trade occur if nations rely on revenue from tariffs as a source of income. In addition, tariffs occur when certain industries, under siege, lobby politicians for trade restrictions.

Several international organizations and agreements seek to stimulate global free trade, among them

The *General Agreement on Tariffs and Trade (GATT)*, an international agreement designed to reduce tariffs and increase international trade.

The *World Trade Organization (WTO)*, to which the United States belongs, which requires that nations more closely obey GATT rules. China is one of the countries that recently joined the WTO.

7.3   The Balance of Payments

The balance of payments accounts keep track of international transactions:

- *Current account.* This account records exports, imports, net interest, and net transfers. The current account balance equals exports minus imports, net interest, and net transfers.
- *Capital account.* This account records foreign investment in the United States and U.S. investments abroad.
- *Official settlements account.* This account shows changes in U.S. official reserves, the government holdings of foreign currency.

The total balances of these three accounts must sum to zero.

A nation that is borrowing more from abroad than it is lending is a net borrower; if the reverse is true, the nation is a net lender. A debtor nation owes more to foreigners than foreigners owe to it; the reverse means that it is a creditor nation.

National income accounting provides a framework for analyzing the current account. From the two equations $GDP = C + I + G + X - M$ and $GDP = C + S + T$, it follows that

$$X - M = (T - G) + (S - I)$$

This means that net exports $(X-M)$ equal the government surplus or deficit $(T-G)$, plus the private-sector surplus or deficit $(S-I)$. In 2003, the U.S. government sector had a $548 billion deficit and the private sector a surplus of $42 billion, so net exports had a net deficit of $506 billion.

The consequence of high U.S. government debt is the need to borrow money, mostly abroad, because savings rates in the United States are very low. This creates a foreign financial dependency for the United States that affects the supply and demand for U.S. dollars and the level of U.S. interest rates. This dependency also necessitates active policy to support the level of the U.S. dollar—that is, pursuing a "strong" U.S. dollar.

7.4   Foreign Exchange Rates

The *foreign exchange market* is the market in which the currencies of different nations are traded. The three main functions of the foreign exchange market are to transfer purchasing power, provide credit, and minimize the exchange risk. The price at which one currency can be exchanged for another is called the *foreign exchange rate*.

The foreign exchange market is conducted by phone, wire service, and other such means and is not tied to a specific location. While the market is dominated by banks, transactions are conducted by foreign exchange dealers and brokers, individuals, and companies for transaction and investment purposes. Arbitrage trading takes place as a result of global exchange rate and interest rate variations. New York and London are the centers for speculation in foreign exchange futures.

Currency appreciation occurs when one currency rises in value in relation to another currency. *Currency depreciation* occurs when one currency drops in value relative to another currency.

The demand for U.S. dollars is negatively related to the U.S. exchange rate. If the exchange rate falls, the quantity of exports increases, and so the quantity of dollars demanded increases.

A shift in the demand curve for U.S. dollars is caused by the U.S. interest rate differential (the U.S. interest rate minus the foreign interest rate). A rise in the U.S. interest rate differential increases the demand for U.S. dollar assets and shifts the demand curve for U.S. dollars to the right. In addition, a rise in the future exchange rate increases the current demand for U.S. dollars and shifts the demand curve for U.S. dollars rightward.

People supply dollars when they buy other currencies to pay for U.S. imports or to buy foreign assets. As illustrated in Fig. 7-3, the supply of U.S. dollars is

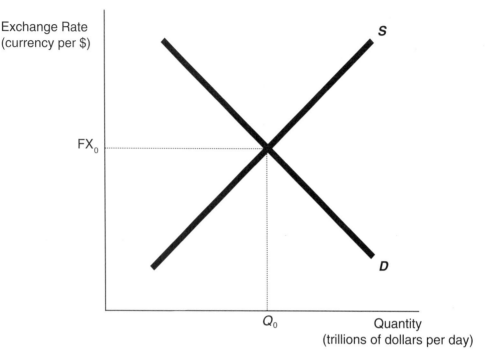

Figure 7-3. A foreign exchange market: the U.S. dollar exchange rate (FX$_0$) results from the worldwide supply of (S) and demand for (D) dollars.

positively related to the exchange rate. If the exchange rate rises, the quantity of U.S. imports increases, which increases the quantity of U.S. dollars supplied.

As with the demand curve, two factors can change the supply of U.S. dollars and shift the supply curve for U.S. dollars. An increase in the interest rate differential decreases the demand for foreign assets and thereby decreases the supply of U.S. dollars. A rise in the expected future exchange rate decreases the current supply of U.S. dollars as people hold dollars to sell later at the higher rate.

Figure 7-3 illustrates how demand and supply determine the equilibrium exchange rate FX$_0$. Changes in the demand and supply (shifts in the demand and supply curves) change the exchange rate.

Two basic fundamentals help drive the foreign exchange markets:

- Exchange rates adjust so that the currencies of different nations can buy the same amount of goods and services (*purchasing power parity*).
- Exchange rates adjust so that the return from investing in assets in different nations is the same (*interest rate parity*).

NOTE N7.4

History of Foreign Exchange Rates

Prior to 1914, exchange rates were fixed in terms of gold, trade was mostly in physical goods, and capital flows were limited. Current account deficits would be paid first in foreign currency; after that, imports would be paid for by shipping gold, reducing the money supply in the shipping country. There was full convertibility into gold.

The *gold standard* was suspended during World War I. After the war was over, countries experienced rapid inflation because the gold standard was reintroduced at prewar rates. The gold standard had mostly been abandoned by the early 1930s. The experimentation with floating rates during the Depression (when international trade fell by almost 50 percent) led to a further loss of confidence in the international system of payments.

In June 1944, the *Bretton Woods* conference established the monetary structure for the postwar world. As a result, the IMF and the World Bank were founded to promote international monetary cooperation, and international currencies were fixed to the U.S. dollar. The American government agreed to buy gold on demand at $35 an ounce, leaving the dollar the only currency on a gold standard and becoming the de facto reserve currency for the world,

The Bretton Woods system broke down in the 1970s when American deficits caused an excess supply of dollars, putting pressure on U.S. gold reserves. The convertibility of the dollar was suspended in August of 1971 and the major global currencies were allowed to float, a situation that persists today.

In December 1971 the IMF Group of Ten established the *Smithsonian Agreement*, which provided for fixed rates with some kind of flexibility. Most major currencies have remained floating ever since. In 1999, most of the EU countries fixed their rates of exchange irrevocably and joined the European currency, the *euro*. Official interest rates in the 12 euro countries are now set by the *European Central Bank* (ECB) in Frankfurt, Germany. The governors of the national central banks are among the members of the ECB's rate-setting governing council.

7.5   Global Interdependence

U.S. fiscal and monetary policy affects international financial flows, especially given the U.S. budget and trade imbalances. In turn, this effect on international financial markets will influence the U.S. economy. For example, significant trade

and budget deficits lead to the need to borrow money from abroad. To stimulate the flow of foreign funds into the United States, the value of the dollar should be relatively stable (i.e., there should be no runaway inflation that lowers the value of money). In addition, U.S. interest rates should be attractive to foreign investors (i.e., relatively high).

Along with the Federal Reserve, central banks across the world (the European Central Bank and the Central Banks of China and Japan) can support (and protect) the U.S. dollar by buying dollars in foreign exchange markets. The Federal Reserve can also maintain relatively high interest rates to increase the attractiveness of investing in U.S. dollars, which improves the dollar's foreign exchange rate.

NOTE N7.5A

China's Monetary Policy

In early 2004, China's central bank, the People's Bank of China, imposed tighter controls on bank loans and instituted policies to avoid excessive growth. Consequently, the Chinese stock market lost significant value. The new policy also led to a decrease in worldwide commodity prices on the expectation of lower demand from China.

In late 2004, the central bank in China increased interest rates for the first time in a decade. This time, the stock market hardly lost money, as the move by the bank had been widely anticipated and had been taken into account in the valuation of stocks. The interest rate increase was meant to slow down economic growth and limit inflation in the Chinese economy.

Asian economies, in particular those of China's top five trading partners (Japan, South Korea, Malaysia, the Philippines, and Taiwan), and the Australian economy have become increasingly reliant on trade with China to achieve growth. Further moves by China's government and central bank to slow down growth, specifically the decrease in the growth of Chinese imports, will have a significant impact on the growth of those countries.

NOTE N7.5B

The European Union

In 1957, the Treaty of Rome formally established the customs union of France, West Germany, Italy, Belgium, the Netherlands, and Luxemburg. These countries became known as the European Economic Community (EEC). After merging with the European Coal and Steel Community and Euratom in 1967, the new organization adopted the name of European Community (EC).

In 1973, the United Kingdom, Denmark, and Ireland became members of the European Community. In 1981, Greece joined the EC, followed by Portugal and Spain (1986) and Austria, Finland, and Sweden (1995). The name of the organization was changed to *European Union (EU)* in 1993.

In 2004, the EU was enlarged from 15 to 25 countries by the addition of Poland, Hungary, the Czech Republic, Slovakia, Slovenia, Latvia, Estonia, Lithuania, Cyprus, and Malta. Also in 2004, the EU voted to formally start membership negotiations with Croatia and Turkey.

By 1968, the European Community had eliminated all internal import duties, established a common external tariff, and adopted the Common Agricultural Policy (CAP).

Because the EC was not a complete single market (e.g., there were country variations in qualifying requirements for the professions and differences in technical standards), the 1986 Single European Act called for the eventual abolition of all restrictions on free trade within the EC. The Schengen Treaty involved decisions on wide-ranging areas aimed at achieving consistency and openness among EC members:

- Abolition of exchange controls
- Recognition of professional and academic qualifications
- Abolition of restrictions on internal transport
- Liberalization of the markets in air services, public procurement, life insurance, and banking
- Abolition of frontier controls

The Treaties of Maastricht (1992), Amsterdam (1997), and Nice (2000) are de facto amendments to the original 1957 Treaty of Rome. They formally confirmed the new free-trade arrangements and established qualified majority decision making within the EU.

The executive management of the EU is vested in the European Commission, while issues of policy are presented to the Council of Ministers by the commission. Decisions by the EU's current membership (25 countries) require either unanimity (each country has veto power) or a majority of 75 percent of the total votes (votes are partially weighted by the size of the country). A unanimous vote is required for decisions relating to taxation and social security. The European Parliament has significant legislative authority but currently lacks true power. The European Court of Justice has the ultimate power to review and interpret treaty arrangements, acting similarly to the U.S. Supreme Court.

7.6   Hints

H7.1   There are two quick formulas to determine who has the comparative advantage (e.g., for Product X) between two countries with linear PPCs, using either input or output quantities (see also H1.3).

Input Method
1. Divide the inputs required for 1 unit of Product X by the inputs required for 1 unit of Product Y.
2. The country with the lowest ratio (or opportunity cost of producing Product X) has a comparative advantage for Product X.
3. The other country will have a comparative advantage for Product Y.

Output Method
1. Divide the output for Product Y by the output for Product X.
2. The country with the lowest ratio (or opportunity cost of producing Product X) has a comparative advantage for Product X.
3. The other country will have a comparative advantage for Product Y.

H7.2   Conflicts between internal and external policies can develop when a country has a *balance of payments deficit* during a recession. Correcting the deficit requires a rise in the country's price of imports, a decrease in the price of exports, and a rise in interest rates. Currency depreciation has an inflationary effect and may require contractionary monetary policy, which is inconsistent with a recessionary situation.

Quiz

Choose the one best answer for each question.

Q7.1   Which of the following statements is true? In 2003,
    (a) trade in services accounted for about 50 percent of total U.S. exports.
    (b) agricultural products accounted for over 50 percent of total U.S. exports.
    (c) the U.S. government left the World Trade Organization (WTO).

    (d) the value of U.S. imports was greater than the value of
        U.S. exports.

    (e) U.S. exports exceeded U.S. imports in value.

Q7.2   Which of the following is considered a U.S. service export?
    (a) A French tourist spends a night in a U.S. hotel.
    (b) A Mexican person buys dinner while traveling in
        Mexico.
    (c) In the Netherlands, a Dutch citizen buys a computer
        made in the United States.
    (d) A U.S. citizen buys a theater ticket in London.
    (e) In Canada, a U.S. citizen buys clothing imported from
        China.

Q7.3   The maximum gains from trade occur when
    (a) there is no international trade.
    (b) nations use tariffs rather than quotas.
    (c) nations use voluntary trade restrictions.
    (d) nations trade with other nations and produce according
        to their comparative advantage.
    (e) each nation uses quotas to protect its highest-cost
        industries.

Q7.4   Who benefits from a tariff on a good?
    (a) Domestic consumers
    (b) Domestic producers
    (c) Nobody
    (d) Foreign consumers
    (e) Foreign producers

Q7.5   Which of the following is a valid reason for protecting an industry?
    (a) The industry is in its early stages and needs assistance
        to compete internationally.
    (b) The industry is unable to compete with low-wage for-
        eign countries.
    (c) The industry is necessary to diversify the nation's pro-
        duction.
    (d) Protection keeps richer nations from exploiting the
        workers of poorer nations.
    (e) None of the above reasons is a valid reason for pro-
        tection.

Q7.6   Which of the following describes the likely impact of China's contractionary monetary policy?
(a) It leads to increased prices for commodities on world markets.
(b) It increases the value of the Chinese stock market.
(c) It is likely to limit the economic growth of China's major trading partners.
(d) It increases commercial loans by Chinese banks.
(e) It increases domestic consumption in China.

Q7.7   Stability of the U.S. dollar exchange rate is a worthwhile goal of monetary policy because
(a) it limits the impact of foreign exchange fluctuations on corporate earnings by U.S. global companies.
(b) it benefits international trade in goods and services.
(c) it limits speculation and future instability.
(d) it limits consumers' risks in foreign transactions.
(e) all of the above apply.

Q7.8   The modern global economy is characterized by
(a) supra-national organizations (e.g., the WTO) pursuing global free trade.
(b) domestic economic goals of countries.
(c) protectionist trade pacts between nations.
(d) decreasing monetary policy coordination.
(e) increased quotas and tariffs.

Q7.9   If demand for U.S. dollars decreases, the international value of the dollar _____ and U.S. exports _____.
(a) doesn't change; increase
(b) increases; decrease
(c) increases; increase
(d) decreases; increase
(e) decreases; decrease

Q7.10 Foreign exchange rates are determined by parity of which two factors?
(a) Export prices and inflation
(b) Purchasing power and interest rates
(c) Budget deficit and trade deficit
(d) Imports and exports
(e) Trade deficit and inflation

Q7.11 The nation's current account balance is
   (a) gross investments minus depreciation.
   (b) net foreign transfers.
   (c) saving minus investment.
   (d) consumption minus saving.
   (e) exports minus imports, net foreign interest, and net foreign transfers.

Q7.12 The overall balance of the current account, the capital account, and the official settlements account is
   (a) the trade deficit.
   (b) the value of exports.
   (c) the capital flow balance.
   (d) zero.
   (e) the value of net interest.

Quiz Answers

Q7.1 (d). The value of U.S. imports has exceeded the value of U.S. exports in recent years.

Q7.2 (a). A foreign person is purchasing a U.S. service (a night in a hotel).

Q7.3 (d). Maximum gains from trade occur if nations trade according to production specialization consistent with comparative advantage.

Q7.4 (b). Domestic producers of the good will gain from the tariff because the price of the product will increase.

Q7.5 (e). All of the reasons for protection provided in answers (a) through (d) are faulty.

Q7.6 (c). Contractionary monetary policy is meant to limit aggregate demand and reduce inflation. This will limit the growth prospects of countries relying on major exports to China.

Q7.7 (e). The pursuit of stable exchange rates generally reduces risky rate fluctuations for U.S. and international consumers and U.S. and international producers alike, and removes a major source of speculation from the exchange markets.

Q7.8 (a). Increasingly, supra-national organizations (e.g., the WTO) are playing a major role in determining the global economic environment.

Q7.9 (d). If the demand for U.S. dollars goes down, the international value of the dollar decreases. This makes exports relatively cheap and leads to an increase in exports.

Q7.10 (b). The factors are purchasing power parity (exchange rates adjust to the point where one currency buys the same amount of goods and services as another currency) and interest rate parity (exchange rates adjust to the point where the return from investing in assets in different nations is identical).

Q7.11 (e). The current account balance equals exports minus imports, net foreign interest, and net foreign transfers.

Q7.12 (d). The total of the three accounts should balance out; therefore, the overall balance is zero.

PART THREE

The Goals of Macroeconomics

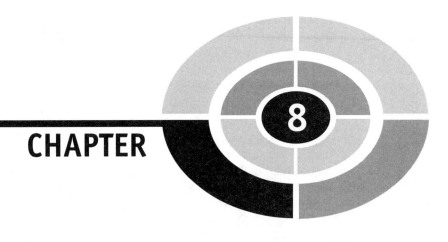

CHAPTER 8

Economic Growth

Why is economic growth a major macroeconomic goal?
What is required to achieve economic growth? What is the role of labor productivity, human capital, and education? Capital productivity? Advances in technology?
What are the major economic theories about the growth of potential (or full-employment) GDP?

8.1   Introduction

Economic growth is the increase in a country's national income, or the growth of GDP. GDP growth is essential for improvement of the *standard of living*, as measured by GDP per capita. In addition, economic growth is a general sign that a country's economic activity is successful.

Economic growth and potential (full-employment) GDP are directly related because effective economic growth requires the efficient use of the economy's resources. In addition, as Okun's Law illustrates, significant economic growth is required to decrease the actual rate of unemployment and achieve full employment.

Optimal growth theory analyzes the level of economic growth required to maximize GDP per capita. The *golden rule of capital accumulation* suggests that the optimal growth path is the one that maximizes consumption per worker over time. The key to finding this maximum is finding a level of capital per worker such that the marginal productivity of capital (equals profitability in a perfectly competitive economy) equals the growth rate of the population.

Theories of economic growth focus on increases in labor productivity resulting from improved education and skills, intensive usage of capital, and the progress in production technology. Increasingly, the importance of sustainable growth, which takes into account the earth's population and its environment, is emphasized in modern economic growth theory. However, growth in GDP is not identical to growth in general human welfare. The broader costs of GDP growth (e.g., pollution, noise, and destruction of the countryside) are not included in the GDP.

The growth percentage of U.S. GDP, reported on a quarterly basis, is probably the most closely watched economic statistic. An example of a typical quarterly GDP growth report by the U.S. Department of Commerce is: "The nation's economy expanded at a 3.7 percent annual rate in the most recent quarter, exceeding the 3.3 percent rate from the quarter before, when consumer expenditures were diminished due to the high price of oil. Continued growth is still threatened by escalating energy prices, modest income growth, and increasingly large budget and trade deficits."

NOTE N8.1

Economic Development

Economic development studies national differences in economic growth and GDP per capita. It tries to answer the question of why developing nations consistently remain behind advanced countries.

After World War II, the main focus of development was investment in infrastructure and industrial and agricultural projects. Those efforts proved largely ineffective without first addressing the basic conditions for growth (e.g., health and education). More recently, the development of institutions to create free markets has been a major objective. As Fig. 8-1 illustrates, Ethiopia's per capita GDP, one of the lowest in the world, lags far behind the per capita GDP in major Western countries.

Figure 8-1.   GDP per capita, by nation.

GDP per Capita, Current U.S. Dollars, 2003

World	5,500
OECD[1]	29,310
European Monetary Union (EMU)	22,850
Latin America and Caribbean	3,260
East Asia and Pacific	1,080
Heavily Indebted Poor Countries (HIPC)	350
Selected Nations	
United States	37,610
Japan	34,510
United Kingdom	28,350
Germany	25,250
France	24,770
Canada	23,930
Australia	21,650
Italy	21,560
Spain	16,990
Greece	13,720
Republic of Korea	12,020
Slovenia	11,830
Czech Republic	6,740
Costa Rica	4,280
Latvia	4,070
Lebanon	4,040
Argentina	3,650
Botswana	3,430
Brazil	2,710
Russian Federation	2,610
Iran	2,000
Algeria	1,890
Jordan	1,850
Bosnia-Herzegowina	1,540
Egypt	1,390
China	1,100
Ukraine	970
Honduras	970
Indonesia	810
India	530
Vietnam	480

Continued on next page . . .

Continued . . .

Pakistan	470
Bangladesh	400
Nigeria	320
Eritrea	190
Luxembourg (highest GDP/capita)	43,940
Ethiopia (lowest GDP/capita)	90

[1]Organization of Economic Cooperation and Development (includes all major Western economies)

Source: World Bank, *World Development Indicators.*

8.2   The Foundation for Economic Growth

The foundation for successful economic growth requires that the economy have the proper institutions (e.g., markets and monetary exchange) and legal environment (e.g., property laws), enhanced by a public policy that provides incentives for economic activities such as saving, investment, and technological innovation.

Requirements for the effective exchange of goods and services in a free-market economy are

- *Markets* that enable buyers and sellers to carry out transactions and that signal information (e.g., through prices) to assist people in adjusting the quantities supplied and demanded. Sometimes markets do not provide all the signals needed to make informed, rational decisions. See note N8.2 for examples of market failures.
- *Property rights* that are clearly assigned (and/or free trade in property rights). For example, we would not want to buy a house or a car if it is unclear whether the potential seller holds title to the asset.
- *Monetary exchange* that is built on the market's trust and confidence in payment procedures. This is critical to final exchange transactions, especially when markets are relatively new (e.g., PayPal as the means of payment on eBay).

The economy's productive capability is determined by the availability of natural resources, human resources, capital goods, and technology and by public policy (including social and economic regulations). This is analogous to the production possibilities curve (PPC) presented in earlier chapters. For example, if the availability of certain natural resources (e.g., oil) in the economy declines, this will immediately affect the economy's growth prospects.

Public policy can play a critical role in achieving growth by providing incentives for saving, capital investment, and the accumulation of capital (plants, equipment, and so on.). Also, incentives can be given for investment in human capital (the skills

and talents of people acquired through education) and for advances in technology (e.g., robotics in manufacturing that improve labor productivity).

Major government policies to increase growth include research and development, targeting high-technology industries, and improving the quality of public education.

Advances in production technology may lead to increased structural unemployment as unskilled workers are laid off. It is imperative that retraining of those workers takes place to avoid persistently high rates of unemployment. The natural rate of unemployment, which includes the rate of structural unemployment, may rise as a result of significant technology progress.

NOTE N8.2

Market Failure

Market failure is said to occur when free trade and self-interested behavior do not result in a mutually beneficial result for buyers and sellers.

The existence of "failing markets" acts as a constraint on economic growth, and some form of government intervention through regulation will be required when market failures happen. There are several types of failure:

- The parties in a transaction don't have the same information (e.g., the sale of a lemon car).
- Property rights do not exist (e.g., clean air) or property rights are unclear (e.g., ambiguous legal title to an asset).
- Transaction costs are very high. Transaction costs are the costs of participating in the process of buying and selling. For example, effort is required to change prices (e.g., relabeling, brochures, marketing documents), also called menu pricing costs.
- Some goods and services, e.g., the military, are public and cannot be produced very well by private efforts.
- There are (near) monopoly industries, which are prone to inefficiencies and require regulation.

8.3   Labor Productivity

Labor is a factor of production that includes the number of people involved in the production of goods and services as well as people's physical and intellectual skills. The productivity of labor is a key driver of wage rates and economic growth.

Labor productivity equals real GDP divided by aggregate labor hours, that is, real GDP per hour of labor. The productivity of labor is an immediate indicator of the economy's per capita income potential, and labor productivity is therefore directly linked to the standard of living.

Growth in labor productivity includes the growth in capital per hour of labor and advances in technology. *Capital per hour of labor* measures the intensity of capital usage (plants, equipment, machinery, and so on.) per fixed hour of labor input. *Technology* is the knowledge of the methods of producing goods and services. It encompasses both scientific knowledge and applied knowledge of production, such as practical know-how. Modern technology includes both physical techniques and methods of organization. New investments will include updated technology, and therefore advances in technology are critical to achieving economic growth.

The *labor productivity curve* (see Fig. 8-2) is the relationship between capital per hour of labor and labor productivity, assuming that technology remains the same (*ceteris paribus*). The curve is an illustration of the *law of diminishing returns;* that is, as extra units of labor are employed, the output per unit produced by those extra units of labor will go down. This result is caused by the increasing difficulty of finding the required labor skills as production continues to increase.

Increases in labor productivity are due to either increased use of capital per hour of labor or advances in technology. There is simple rule of thumb that estimates how much of the labor productivity growth is due to increased use of capital per hour of labor. The *one-third rule* states that a 1 percent increase in capital per hour of labor leads to a 1/3 percent increase in labor productivity.

Growth in labor productivity resulting from technology can now be estimated: It is that part of the growth in labor productivity that cannot be attributed to growth in capital. For example, if labor productivity growth equals 8 percent and the increase in capital per hour of labor is 9 percent , then the one-third rule implies that $1/3 \times 9$ percent $= 3$ percent of the labor productivity growth is due to increased capital per hour of labor. Therefore, 5 percent (8 percent − 3 percent) of the labor productivity growth is due to technology advances.

The objective of *growth accounting* is to estimate the contributions of the sources of growth (e.g., technology) to total GDP growth:

- Changes in the inputs of the factors of production (e.g., labor, capital)
- Changes in the quality of labor
- Total factor productivity (e.g., contributions of technology)

An empirical analysis of the U.S. economy from 1929 to 1969 provided the following growth accounting results (based on specific factor/GDP share assumptions).* The average annual growth rate of GDP of 3.33 percent was estimated to be composed of

Accounting for United States Economic Growth, 1929–1969, Denison, 1974.

The productivity curve shows how real GDP per hour of labor (labor productivity) changes as a result of the replacement of labor by capital, going from point A to point B on the curve (= increased capital per hour of labor while technology is held constant).

A shift from LP_0 to LP_1 indicates an advance in technology (e.g., robotics).

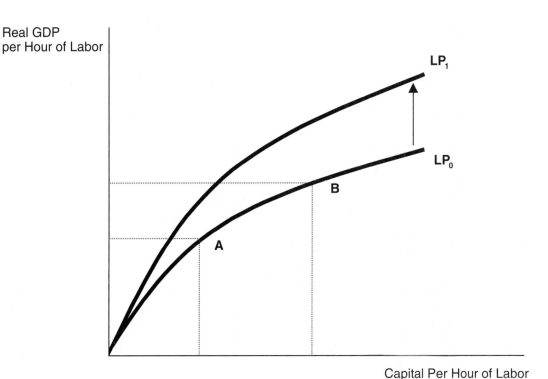

Figure 8-2.   The labor productivity (LP) curve.

- 1.31 percent due to growth of labor input
- 0.50 percent due to capital growth rate
- 1.52 percent due to technology progress

The "*new economy*" refers to economic activity created by information technology (IT), which includes computer hardware and software, computer services, telecommunications, and other IT-related products and services. These activities, as distinct from the "old economy" (e.g., food, cars, and plastics), are still only a relatively small part of the total economy. Some economists expect that the new economy will move economic growth to new levels through gains in productivity and global trade.

The Internet emerged as a powerful digital technology in the first half of the 1990s. U.S. productivity indeed increased in the 1990s, but the large majority of this increase was directly due to the IT sector itself and not to productivity enhancements in other sectors. So far, there is no clear evidence of the positive global impact of IT on productivity.

8.4   Technology and Economic Growth

Models of economic growth differ in their assumptions about the role of technology. The new growth theory directly links economic growth and advances in technology by focusing on the decisions of profit-maximizing firms and the high (expected) profits from new technology discoveries. In this view, innovation becomes a main source of economic growth, shifting the labor productivity curve upward. Capital growth occurs, and income and consumption rise, leading to more innovation. This will move the labor productivity curve upward even further. The economic growth will continue as long as technological innovation takes place. This new growth model is important because its explanation of the role of technology within the economic model is distinctly different from that of the classical and neoclassical growth models that have dominated thinking about economic growth.

The classical growth model considered technology a factor that could not be explained by the economic model itself. Therefore, technology is an exogenous variable, that is, one that is outside the classical economic model. The classical growth thinking tied any increases in GDP per capita (i.e., wages above the minimum subsistence level) to a rise in population. The extra population (or increased labor supply) would lower wage rates again, back to the original minimum wage rate. Therefore, changes in GDP per capita would always be temporary. Empirical studies have shown that population growth is usually independent of economic growth, contradicting a key assumption of classical growth theory.

The neoclassical growth model linked higher GDP per capita to technology progress that increases saving and investment, and thus capital growth. This would allow capital per hour of labor to grow (and therefore labor productivity). As in classical thinking, technological development is a factor outside of the neoclassical model. The neoclassical growth model predicts that nations will ultimately converge to identical GDP per capita incomes. The numbers in Fig. 8-1 indicate that we are not yet at that point.

8.5   Global Economics and Economic Growth

In determining domestic economic growth objectives, the U.S. government's fiscal and monetary policies need to take *global economics* into account.

In theory, free international trade is a major contributor to a nation's economic growth. Comparative advantage indicates the goods and services that would lead to mutually beneficial international trade. The U.S. government historically has been a staunch supporter of international free trade, and the United States is a member of the *World Trade Organization (WTO)*, whose stated objective is the worldwide removal of trade barriers.

In practice, when certain domestic industries are under siege from effective foreign low-cost producers, industry lobbies may pressure members of Congress to pursue trade restrictions. For example, U.S. textile industry representatives asked for protective tariffs to limit the impact of Chinese imports resulting from the full removal of quotas in 2005. Ultimately, no formal tariffs were imposed, and China agreed to voluntary trade restrictions in the form of a self-imposed U.S. export quota.

Another example of the conflict between international free trade and domestic interests is U.S. imports of Canadian lumber. In order to protect the U.S. lumber industry, the Byrd Amendment provides that the income from tariffs on Canadian lumber imports is redistributed to U.S. lumber companies. The WTO declared this policy illegal because it creates a double penalty for Canadian lumber companies. Consequently, the United States was fined by the WTO for this practice. These examples illustrate the increasing interdependence of domestic and international trade policies and the impact of international organizations (e.g., the WTO) on the conduct of U.S. economic policies.

Other major interdependent aspects of domestic policy and global economics are the U.S. trade and budget deficits and the resulting need for international borrowing by the United States. Also, the choice of U.S. interest rates and foreign exchange rate policies for the dollar are critical in international trade and global economics. Aspects of these complex relationships are discussed in later chapters.

8.6 Hints

H8.1 Changes in labor productivity are usually measured by an index of labor hours divided into an index of output. For example, if the 2004 production index stands at 132 (2,000=100) and the index of labor hours worked stands at 110, then the labor productivity index is 120 (i.e., 132/110). This is known as the *partial productivity index* because it includes changes in other factors as well (land and capital).

H8.2 The measurement of *total labor productivity* is complex and practically difficult. The main reasons are that

- Factor inputs will vary over time.
- Industries with high capital intensity (e.g., manufacturing) will have different results from sectors with high labor intensity (e.g., services).
- Variations in the quality (e.g., education and training) of labor inputs will occur.

Quiz

Choose the one best answer for each question.

Q8.1   Economic growth is required to
(a) reduce unemployment.
(b) increase the standard of living.
(c) increase the national income.
(d) demonstrate a nation's economic success.
(e) do all of the above.

Q8.2   In a country without laws specifying clear property rights, markets will be _____ and economic growth will be _____.
(a) efficient; severely limited
(b) efficient; fully supported
(c) efficient; constant
(d) inefficient; severely limited
(e) inefficient; fully supported

Q8.3   If capital per hour of labor increases by 12 percent and real GDP per hour of labor increases by 10 percent, what is the estimated labor productivity growth resulting from technology?
(a) 6 percent
(b) 8 percent
(c) 10 percent
(d) 12 percent
(e) 22 percent

Q8.4   Which of the following are considered to be part of technology?
(a) Practical production know-how
(b) Methods of production organization
(c) Applied science knowledge
(d) Theoretical science knowledge
(e) All of the above

Q8.5 Which of the following is considered to be part of the new economy?
(a) The car industry
(b) The steel industry
(c) The computer hardware industry
(d) The chemical processing industry
(e) The food processing industry

Q8.6 An assumption of classical growth theory is that
(a) saving is critical in determining economic growth.
(b) population growth increases when real GDP per person increases.
(c) capital plays the major role in economic growth.
(d) human capital is the ultimate cause of economic growth.
(e) technology advances are the key driver of economic growth.

Q8.7 Markets, property rights, and monetary exchange
(a) guarantee economic growth.
(b) are irrelevant to economic growth.
(c) are required for economic growth, but do not guarantee that it will take place.
(d) are fully established in all economies across the world.
(e) are fully established in developing nations.

Q8.8 Which theory predicts that nations will eventually converge to the same level of real GDP per person?
(a) Classical
(b) Keynesian
(c) Neo-Keynesian
(d) Neoclassical
(e) New theory of economic growth

Q8.9 The labor productivity curve is the relationship between
(a) real GDP and labor input.
(b) labor input and wage rate.
(c) real GDP per hour of labor and capital per hour of labor.
(d) capital per hour of labor and labor input.
(e) labor productivity and wage rate.

Q8.10 Which theory of economic growth concludes that growth can continue indefinitely?
I. Classical
II. Neoclassical
III. New theory

(a) I only

(b) II only

(c) III only

(d) I and III

(e) II and III

Q8.11   Continuing economic growth requires

(a) investment in education.

(b) advances in technology.

(c) saving.

(d) investment in new capital.

(e) all of the above.

Q8.12   The market for lemon cars fails to work because

(a) property rights are unclear.

(b) transaction costs are high for sellers.

(c) buyer and seller don't have the same information.

(d) lemon cars are public goods.

(e) the market for lemon cars is a monopoly.

Quiz Answers

Q8.1 (e). Economic growth is arguably the most important economic statistic. Okun's Law suggests that it takes economic growth above its trend to decrease unemployment. Economic growth (or growth in real GDP) is equivalent to growth in national income, so an increase in one is an increase in the other. The (economic) standard of living is equal to real GDP per capita, and without growth in GDP there can be no increase in the standard of living (for populations that do not decrease). Finally, economic growth is considered testimony to the economic success of a nation.

Q8.2 (d). In markets where property rights are not clear, it will be difficult to establish a price. (What are buyers paying for? Part of a house?) Therefore, markets will operate inefficiently, and there will be severe constraints on economic growth. This question shows the importance of public policy (law and regulations) in achieving economic growth.

Q8.3 (a). Apply the one-third rule: A 1 percent change in capital per hour of labor causes 1/3 percent change in real GDP per hour of labor. The 12 percent change in capital per hour of labor causes $1/3 \times 12$ percent $= 4$ percent change in real GDP per hour of labor. The total change in real GDP per hour of labor is

10 percent, so the estimated impact of technology is 10 percent $-$ 4 percent $=$ 6 percent.

Q8.4 (e). The definition of technology is wide and encompasses basic scientific knowledge, applied science, organizational methods, and practical physical know-how.

Q8.5 (c). The new economy consists of all information technology–related industries, as opposed to the "classical" or old economy (food, cars, steel, chemicals, and so on.). Therefore, the computer hardware industry is part of the new economy.

Q8.6 (b). This assumption is critical in classical growth theory; it leads to subsistence wages for people.

Q8.7 (c). These institutions (markets, property rights, and monetary exchange) are necessary but not sufficient for growth. For ongoing growth, the economy requires incentives for saving, investment in capital (including human capital), and advances in technology.

Q8.8 (d). The neoclassical growth theory predicts that all nations will converge to the same level of per capita income.

Q8.9 (c). The labor productivity curve is the relationship between real GDP per hour of labor (labor productivity) on the y axis, and capital per hour of labor (the relative use of capital vs. labor) on the x axis. The curve is an example of the law of diminishing returns.

Q8.10 (c). Only in the new theory of growth can growth continue as the natural course of the economy. Technology is an integral part of this growth theory, as opposed to the classical and neoclassical theories of growth, which consider technology to be outside of the model.

Q8.11 (e). Continuing growth requires saving and investment in capital, as well as human capital investment (education) and technology advances.

Q8.12 (c). In the market for lemon cars, the (potential) seller has information that the (potential) buyer hasn't; this difference in access to information leads to market failure. The market requires regulation to protect potential buyers.

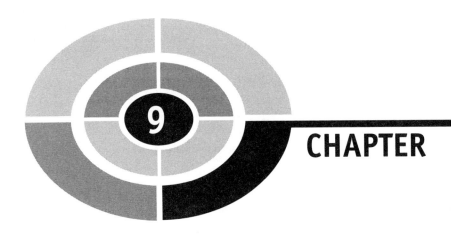

CHAPTER 9

Price Stability

Maintaining price stability is a major goal of macroeconomic policy that is primarily the responsibility of the Federal Reserve System.
What are the risks of price instability? What exactly is inflation? How does it happen? What are its major negative effects?
What is the relationship between unemployment and inflation?
How does inflation affect other economic goals in the short term? In the long term?

9.1 Introduction

The *stability of prices* is critical to economic growth because people make decisions based on expected future prices. If those expected prices become unstable, this causes uncertainty that will have a negative impact on all economic activity.

Inflation, the persistent increase of prices across the whole economy, causes consumers to accelerate demand and producers to delay supply because both groups expect prices to increase. This increases prices as a result of both higher demand and lower supply. Therefore, inflation is self-fulfilling and prone to accelerate unless effective anti-inflationary policies are implemented. Inflation is the most common type of price instability in the economy. However, persistent price decreases (deflation) do happen and also have a major destabilizing influence. A recent example is the economy of Japan from 2001 to 2004.

9.2   The Price Level

Inflation is a sustained increase in the general level of prices in the economy. The scope of price increases during inflation is significant because inflation is neither a persistent price increase for just one single product nor a one-time increase in the average price level. Inflation is an ongoing price increase, across the board, with a significant impact on the economy.

The importance of sustained price increases is that they influence people's expectations about future prices. In addition, inflation has a self-fulfilling nature: Once certain prices change and people are uncertain whether the inflation will stop, there can be a "domino" effect, leading to a continuous string of increases.

Nations sometimes decide on a specific inflation target (e.g., the United Kingdom's target is 2.5 percent) in order to provide a clear trigger for monetary policy by the (independent) central bank. As soon as inflation moves beyond the target, the central bank will intervene with anti-inflationary policies.

Modest inflation (e.g., below 2 percent) is unlikely to have a destabilizing impact on price expectations and behavior. At this level, inflation typically will not jeopardize the perceived value of money. High rates of inflation (e.g., the double-digit inflation after the 1970s oil crisis) will change economic behavior and also affect foreign trade. Economic chaos follows if inflation reaches the unprecedented levels described in the following note.

NOTE N9.2

Germany's Hyperinflation in 1923

In the wake of World War I, Germany experienced an escalating rate of inflation rooted in the debts that Germany incurred in financing its war effort. The *hyperinflation* of 1923 was triggered by the French-Belgian occupation of the Ruhr Valley, Germany's industrial center. The occupation was meant to force Germany to provide compensation for losses suffered by other countries in the war. In response, the German government urged the closing of factories. This immediate loss of major productive activity, combined with the government's continued support of the 1923 Ruhr strike, caused runaway inflation. Idling workers were paid in a currency that was inflating so rapidly that printers stopped putting numbers on new bills. Restaurant prices went up while customers were eating, and workers were paid twice a day. The highest inflation rate was reached on November 15, 1923. That day, it took 4.2 trillion (4,200,000,000,000) German marks to buy one U.S. dollar. The political and economic collapse of Germany was barely avoided after the government ended its resistance to the Ruhr occupation, sponsored currency reform, and rescheduled the war reparation payments.

9.3   Major Types of Inflation

Although there is no agreement on the precise causes of inflation, there are usually three major explanations: demand-pull inflation caused by excess aggregate demand, cost-push inflation caused by high costs, and inflation caused by excess money supply. Ultimately, the causes are related and point to an economy that is reaching beyond its capacity to produce output. Consequently, some form of austerity program is required to bring price changes back to modest levels.

Demand-pull inflation is caused by persistent excess aggregate demand over aggregate supply in the economy. This condition can persist if there is a larger money supply that accommodates the rise in prices or the financing of a government budget gap.

In Fig. 9-1, the shift in aggregate demand (from AD_0 to AD_1) moves the price level from P_0 to P_1. If there is no further increase in aggregate demand, the long-run price level will stabilize at P_2, a one-time change in the price level.

For demand-pull inflation to materialize, the right shift of the AD curve needs to continue. Increases in the quantity of money (money supply inflation) resulting in persistent right shifts of the demand curve are required for demand-pull inflation.

Cost-push inflation is caused by a rise in the costs of production of goods and services. Typically, money wage rates and the cost of raw materials are the main sources of cost-push inflation. A rise in costs will decrease short-run aggregate supply, raising the price level and decreasing GDP.

Deflation is a sustained reduction in the general level of prices. Often, although not necessarily, this is accompanied by declines in output and employment (e.g., the Great Depression). Deflation is different from *disinflation,* which is a reduction in the rate of inflation. Although deflation has been uncommon over the last 50 years, it recently emerged in Japan. One of the difficulties in addressing deflation is that monetary policy may not be effective because of the extremely low interest rates.

NOTE N9.3A

Japan's Deflation of 2001–2004

In the hope of spurring demand and reversing price declines, the Japanese central bank held the rate of interest at practically zero from 2001 to 2004. The long

AD = aggregate demand
LAS = long-run aggregate supply
SAS = short-run aggregate supply

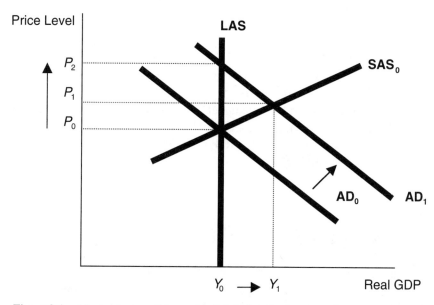

Figure 9-1.   The beginning of demand-pull inflation: the increase of aggregate demand from AD_0 to AD_1 lifts price levels from P_0 to P_1 to P_2.

period of deflation led to a decrease in Japan's extremely high prices of food, clothes, and real estate and moved prices closer to those of other countries. However, corporate profits lagged under deflation, which depressed investment demand. Consumer demand remained low as households delayed purchases because they anticipated lower prices. Also, incomes did not increase, which led to a tightening of spending. Interestingly, a bit of inflation would help greatly in this case.

The combination of a rising price level (inflation) and lower GDP (stagnation) is called *stagflation*. If, in response to the short-run decline of GDP, the Fed increases the quantity of money, aggregate demand increases, leading to further price rises. The rise in price level causes another cost hike, and cost-push inflation results. Cost-push pressures will not lead to sustained inflation unless they are accompanied by sufficient monetary expansion.

NOTE N9.3B

1970s Oil Crisis

In 1973, the oil-producing nations quadrupled the price of crude oil. This led to annual inflation rates of up to 25 percent, triggering extremely high interest rates in the developed world. Stagflation, or a drop in GDP together with high inflation, resulted. In reaction, nations improved production efficiency to become less dependent on foreign oil, and consumers started driving more fuel-efficient automobiles. Since 1970, the U.S. *oil consumption per unit of real GDP* has declined by 50 percent as a result of high-tech manufacturing and fuel-efficient machinery and vehicles. This relative decline has eased the U.S. dependence on oil. However, because of the sustained growth of U.S. GDP, the absolute U.S. demand for this nonrenewable resource is still high.

9.4   The Impact of Inflation

People can prepare for anticipated inflation by indexing incomes, benefits, loans, and so on. A cost-of-living index can offer theoretical protection against this type of inflation. In general economic terms, rational agents can take anticipated inflation fully into account in their actions and decisions and protect themselves.

Although anticipated inflation does not affect real GDP, it still represents a cost to the economy because people will spend more rapidly and will devote extra time to deciding how to do this best. If the rate of inflation becomes high, people will spend more time, effort, and money on this, and methods of payment will be adapted to fast-changing money values. Also, anticipated inflation reduces saving because the after-tax return from saving decreases. This ultimately decreases investment and the economy's capital stock, and so long-run GDP growth declines.

Unanticipated inflation is likely to have a negative impact across the whole economy. Lower than expected inflation decreases firms' profits and therefore increases the rate of cyclical unemployment. Higher than expected inflation leads to frictional unemployment when people leave jobs for higher expected wages.

Unanticipated inflation leads to a redistribution of income between borrowers and lenders. When inflation is higher than expected, borrowers will gain and lenders will lose. Both borrowers and lenders are dissatisfied when they are faced with unanticipated inflation: Higher than expected inflation means that borrowers would like to have borrowed more and lenders would like to have loaned less.

9.5   The Phillips Curve

The *Phillips Curve* is the relationship between the inflation rate and unemployment. The importance of the curve is that it illustrates the challenge of achieving low unemployment and low inflation simultaneously. A certain level of unemployment implies a particular rate of wage increase. Any further decline in unemployment will raise wages because of the tightening of the labor market, and will cause more inflation. Policy officials face a trade-off between unemployment and inflation targets—for example, 5 percent unemployment and 2 percent inflation or 3 percent unemployment and 7 percent inflation.

The *short-run Phillips Curve* assumes that the expected inflation rate and the natural employment rate are constant. The curve is negatively sloped: The higher the rate of unemployment, the lower the rate of inflation (and vice versa). See Fig. 9-2.

The short-run Phillips Curve is related to the short-run aggregate supply (SAS) curve. A surprise increase in aggregate demand moves the economy along the SAS

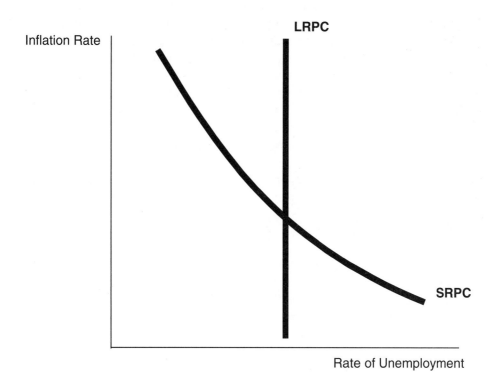

Figure 9-2.   Phillips Curve: short-run (SRPC) and long-run curves (LRPC).

curve, leading to a higher price level (inflation up) and an increase in GDP (unemployment down).

The Phillips Curve shifts as a result of changed expectations about inflation. If more inflation is expected, workers and firms build those expectations into their wages and prices, and this results in inflation. If prices are expected to rise less in the future, the Philips Curve shifts to the left.

The *long-run Phillips Curve* is the relationship between inflation and the unemployment rate when the inflation rate equals the expected inflation rate. The long-run Phillips curve is shown in Fig. 9-2. The curve is vertical at the economy's natural unemployment rate.

NOTE N9.5

Alban William Housego (A. W. H.) Phillips (1914–1975)

In 1958, A. W. H. Phillips, a New Zealander, published "The Relation between Unemployment and the Rate of Change of Money Wage Rates in the United Kingdom, 1861–1957." This article presents the evidence for a significant relationship between the percentage change in wage rates and the rate of unemployment: the lower the unemployment, the higher the rate of change of wages. This became later known as the Phillips Curve. The important implication of the curve is that the macroeconomic goals of low unemployment and low inflation may not be consistent.

In practice, the relation between unemployment and inflation has been too unstable to make definite judgments about the Phillips Curve.

9.6   Global Economics and Price Stability

A relatively high rate of domestic inflation could decrease foreign investment because of the prospect of lower economic growth. This could lead to a decline in the international value of the dollar and cause instability in the foreign currency markets, affecting international trade and international capital flows. Because *domestic price instability* may cause international price instability, the Federal Reserve has one extra reason to pursue domestic price stability. Also, currency depreciation will have an *inflationary impact* (e.g., importing inflation through the higher-rated foreign products) and will affect domestic price stability.

9.7 Hints

H9.1 The inflation rate equals $(P_1 - P_0)/P_0 \times 100$, where P_1 is the current (yearly or quarterly) price level and P_0 is the price level a year ago.

H9.2 When oil prices went up in the 1970s, countries that did not have sufficient oil suffered a decline in their standard of living. However, these countries did not accept the lower standard of living and tried to compensate by an "easy" money policy. This inevitably led to high inflation because there was no productive capability (aggregate supply) to adjust to increased aggregate demand.

Quiz

Choose the one best answer for each question.

Q9.1 Which of the following is considered a rate of inflation of 10 percent?
(a) An ongoing increase of 10 percent per year in the price of a gallon of milk
(b) A one-time 10 percent increase in the prices of all goods
(c) An ongoing increase of 10 percent per year in the prices of all goods
(d) A one-time 10 percent rise in the price of a gallon of milk
(e) A one-time increase of 10 percent in the Consumer Price Index

Q9.2 In demand-pull inflation, the aggregate demand curve shifts to the _____, and the short-term aggregate supply curve shifts to the _____.
(a) left; left
(b) left; right
(c) right; left
(d) right; right
(e) none of the above

Q9.3 Stagflation occurs when
(a) the price level rises while output goes down.
(b) the price level rises for three consecutive quarters.
(c) the price level goes down and output decreases.
(d) the price level doesn't change and output goes up.
(e) the price level doesn't change and output goes down.

Q9.4   Which of the following statements describes cost-push inflation?
(a) A one-time increase in the wage rate
(b) A rise in the price of factor costs that persists because
of increases in the quantity of money
(c) An increase in aggregate demand that causes costs to
go up
(d) An increase in the supply of money that causes higher
factor costs
(e) A decrease in aggregate supply, followed by tight
money policy

Q9.5   Higher anticipated inflation
(a) decreases the economy's price level.
(b) decreases unemployment.
(c) increases economic growth.
(d) decreases economic growth.
(e) has no impact on unemployment or economic growth.

Q9.6   The short-run Phillips Curve shows the relationship between the rate of
inflation and the rate of unemployment when
(a) the natural rate of unemployment changes as unemployment changes.
(b) actual inflation exceeds expected inflation.
(c) expected inflation exceeds actual inflation.
(d) expected inflation equals actual inflation.
(e) expected inflation does not change.

Q9.7   If the inflation rate turns out to be higher than anticipated, then
(a) lenders will lose and borrowers will gain.
(b) lenders will gain and borrowers will lose.
(c) there will be no impact on lenders, but borrowers will
gain.
(d) there will be no impact on borrowers, but lenders will
gain.
(e) there will be no impact on lenders, but borrowers will
lose.

Q9.8   The short-run Phillips Curve crosses the long-run Phillips Curve at the
(a) natural interest rate.
(b) nominal interest rate.
(c) actual inflation rate.
(d) expected inflation rate.
(e) equilibrium price level.

Q9.9   Monetary policy is least effective in dealing with problems of
(a) deflation.
(b) unemployment.
(c) inflation.
(d) hyperinflation.
(e) stagflation.

Q9.10   In a deflationary economy, aggregate demand is low because
(a) consumer incomes are depressed.
(b) corporate profits are down.
(c) consumer demand is low because of expected future
     price decreases.
(d) investment prospects are negative.
(e) all of the above are true.

Q9.11   Nations establish inflation targets because they want
(a) to reach the target value of inflation.
(b) to beat other nations' targets.
(c) to set high target values for inflation.
(d) central banks to act automatically if inflation reaches
     the target.
(e) central banks to decide policy on a discretionary basis
     if inflation reaches the target.

Q9.12   Disinflation is
(a) a reduced rate of inflation.
(b) deflation.
(c) negative inflation.
(d) a zero rate of inflation.
(e) a rate of inflation between normal inflation and hyper-
     inflation.

Quiz Answers

Q9.1 (c). Inflation is a persistent increase in the economy's general price level,
not a one-time increase in the price level or a persistent price increase for a specific good or service. The one-time increase of 10 percent in the Consumer Price
Index is not yet inflation, but if it were to repeat itself, it could be considered a
first step toward inflation.

Q9.2 (c). In demand-pull inflation, the aggregate demand increases, which raises the price level. Therefore, money wages go up, leading to a decrease in the short-term aggregate supply (i.e., the curve shifts to the left).

Q9.3 (a). Stagflation occurs when GDP declines (*stag*nation), while there are rising price levels at the same time (in*flation*).

Q9.4 (b). Cost-push inflation starts off as a rise in factor prices, but it requires expansionary monetary policy to persist as cost-push inflation.

Q9.5 (d). High anticipated inflation decreases GDP growth. First, the after-tax return from saving goes down when anticipated inflation is high, decreasing saving and therefore decreasing investments in capital stock. Second, high anticipated inflation diverts resources because people spend more time avoiding the losses from inflation.

Q9.6 (e). The short-run Phillips Curve is the relationship between the unemployment rate and the inflation rate, holding constant the expected inflation rate and natural unemployment rate.

Q9.7 (a). Borrowers will need to pay back less than expected because the value of currency is lower than originally anticipated. Unfortunately for the lender, the borrower's gain is the lender's loss.

Q9.8 (d). The short-run Phillips Curve holds the expected inflation rate constant, moving along the curve.

Q9.9 (e). Stagflation is the simultaneous decline of real GDP and inflation. To stimulate GDP, an expansionary monetary policy is called for, but to combat inflation, a contractionary policy is required. It's not clear what the best policy is.

Q9.10 (e). In a deflationary economy, persistent price decreases will move consumer income and corporate profits downward and affect expectations, leading to low current consumption and investments, further decreasing aggregate demand.

Q9.11 (d). Inflation targets are set to trigger an automatic response by the central bank: If inflation reaches the target, the central bank automatically starts anti-inflationary policies. This is in line with modern bank policy, which requires credibility and transparency. There is no discretion involved by the central bank, so (e) is not correct.

Q9.12 (a). Disinflation is a reduced rate of inflation, a desired result of anti-inflationary policies.

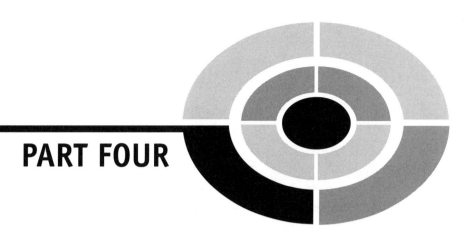

PART FOUR

Macroeconomic Models

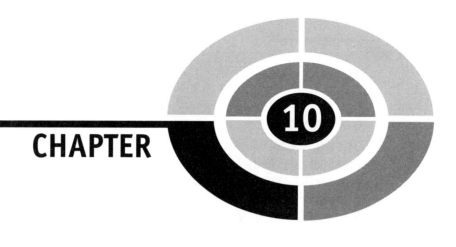

CHAPTER 10

The Classical Model

Classical economists believe in the self-correcting mechanism of markets.
The founder of classical economics, Adam Smith (1723–1790), proposed that an
"invisible hand" guides the economy to equilibrium. Imbalances in the system
(e.g., unemployment) will be temporary, and the price mechanism ensures full-
employment equilibrium in the long run.
What does the classical model mean in macroeconomics? What kind of eco-
nomic policies support this model?

10.1   The Classical Equilibrium

The *classical model* assumes free competition in markets: A large number of buyers
and sellers participate in the markets for products and factors of production, and no
market participant will dominate the market (e.g., monopoly); all prices are flexible,
and adjustment to changing demand and supply takes place immediately. Because
aggregate expenditure equals output, the markets will adjust to full-employment levels, as if guided by an "invisible" or "hidden" hand. This leads to two major classical
economic conclusions:

- The price level is fully flexible; real GDP is determined independent from the price level ("money is neutral").
- The economy will operate at a full- (or natural) employment level.

The first conclusion is described as the classic dichotomy of real and nominal variables (also known as the *neutrality of money*). *Real variables* in the economy (e.g., real GDP, unemployment, and consumption) are the effective indicators of economic performance. *Nominal variables* (e.g., nominal GDP, price level, and inflation rate) are indicators of dollar values and the cost of living in the economy.

The *classical dichotomy* states that at full employment, the forces that determine real variables are independent of the forces that determine nominal variables. The flexibility of prices and wages implies that markets will automatically correct to achieve full employment. For example, if products are not selling and employees are laid off, the market self-corrects to full employment because firms will lower prices to sell off inventory and because workers will accept lower wages and firms will rehire them at those wages. Price and wage levels may change values, but these will be nominal changes. The nominal changes will offset each other, and purchasing power will remain the same.

According to the classical view of macroeconomic equilibrium, there is no need to analyze factors influencing nominal variables, but only those that have an impact on real variables.

The classical economists were not very interested in macroeconomics, especially the business cycle. There was simply no need for government to interfere because price flexibility would resolve any temporary imbalance. This classical view of economics had a powerful influence on U.S. administrations in the nineteenth and early twentieth centuries, including the administration of President Herbert Hoover (1929–1933), who faced the beginning of the Great Depression.

NOTE N10.1A

Adam Smith

Adam Smith (1723–1790), a Scottish philosopher, published *An Inquiry into the Nature and Causes of the Wealth of Nations*, the first comprehensive system of political economy, in 1776. Smith was interested in the factors leading to increased wealth in a community, and he recognized the contribution of the manufacturing industry separately from the traditional agricultural sector. He believed that the economic system was harmonious, requiring a minimum of government interference (also known as

laissez-faire, laissez-passer). Although individuals were motivated by self-interest, they acted for the good of the whole, guided by a "hidden hand" (or *"invisible hand"*) made possible by the free play of competition, the essential ingredient of the efficient economy. In Smith's own words: "It is not from the benevolence of the butcher that we expect our dinner, but from his regard to his own interest."

NOTE N10.1B

Jean-Baptiste Say

Jean-Baptiste Say (1767–1832), a French economist, is best known for *Say's Law,* a law of markets that states that supply creates its own demand. In the long run, the law appears to be true. Ultimately, the overall supply will create income, which is either used for consumption or saved. The savings will be used to lend money to other consumers so that the complete value of supply will ultimately be consumed. However, the short-term version of Say's Law (i.e., there is no overproduction in the short run) proved false, as Keynes would demonstrate in the 1930s (see Chapter 11, "The Keynesian Model").

10.2   The Factor Market for Labor

In the classical model, GDP is produced using the factor resources of labor and capital. The relationship between GDP and labor is critical because it shows the classical interaction between economic growth and unemployment.

The *production function* is the relationship between real GDP and the quantity of labor employed (*ceteris paribus*). A production function is illustrated in Fig.10-1. When employment increases, it means that labor (as a factor of production) increases, causing a move from point A to point B in the graph, leading to a higher real GDP outcome.

The demand for labor and the supply of labor depend on the *real wage rate,* the quantity of goods and services an hour of labor earns. The *demand for labor* is the relationship between the real wage rate and the quantity of labor that firms demand, where the quantity of labor demanded is the number of labor hours hired by all firms in the economy. As the real wage rate increases, the quantity of labor demanded decreases. The *marginal product of labor* is the additional real GDP produced by an additional hour of labor. The *law of diminishing returns* states that as

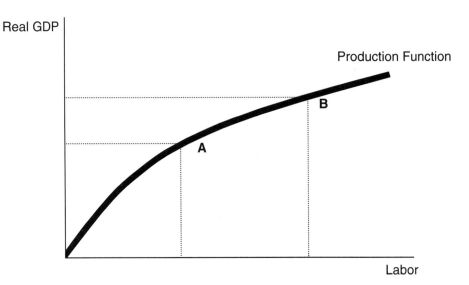

Figure 10-1.   The production function depicts the relationship between labor input and GDP output.

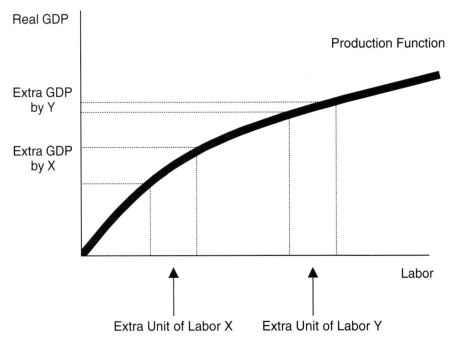

Figure 10-2.   Law of diminishing returns: extra units of labor yield increasingly smaller additions to GDP.

the quantity of labor increases, *ceteris paribus*, the marginal product of labor goes down (see Fig. 10-2).

Because the marginal product of labor goes down as employment increases, firms will hire additional workers only if the real wage rate falls. Therefore, the labor demand curve LD (see Fig. 10-3) slopes downward. The demand for labor increases, and the LD curve shifts to the right when the marginal product of labor increases.

The *quantity of labor supplied* is the number of labor hours that all the households plan to work. The *supply of labor* is the relationship between the quantity of labor supplied and the real wage rate (provided all other influences remain the same).

The labor supply curve LS slopes upward, as illustrated in Fig. 10-4, because higher real wage rates increase the amount of goods and services that can be purchased for an hour's work.

The *equilibrium employment*, determined in the labor market (see Fig. 10-5), and the production function determine potential GDP, as demonstrated in Fig. 10-6.

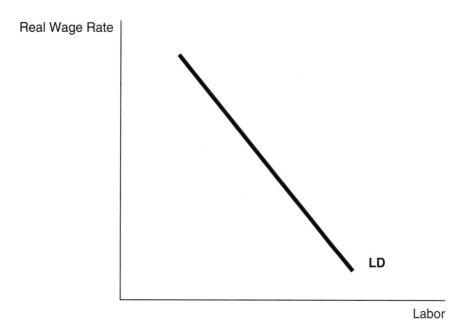

Figure 10-3.   Labor demand curve LD: The demand for labor decreases as the real wage rate goes up.

Real Wage Rate

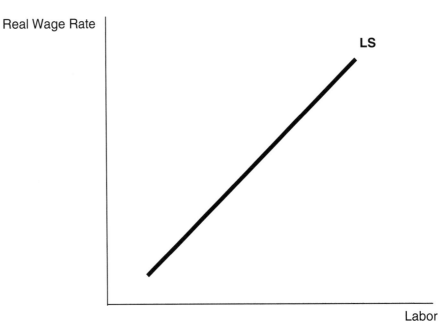

Labor

Figure 10-4.   The labor supply curve LS: the supply of labor increases as the real wage rate goes up.

Real Wage Rate

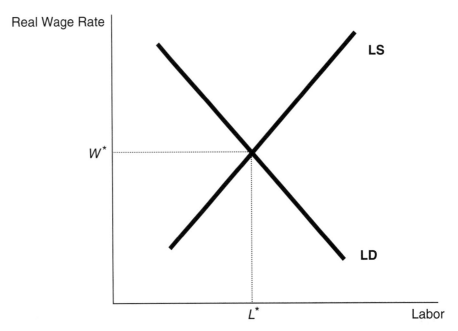

Figure 10-5.   The labor market reaches equilibrium when the labor demand curve LD and the labor supply curve LS intersect, resulting in labor quantity L^* and real wage rate W^*.

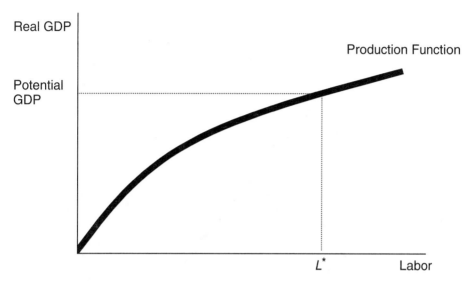

Figure 10-6.   Potential GDP resulting from equilibrium labor quantity L^*.

10.3   The Factor Market for Capital

The *capital stock* is the total quantity of plants, equipment, buildings, and inventories. *Gross investment* is the total purchase of new capital. *Depreciation* is the wearing out and scrapping of capital. The change in the capital stock, *net investments,* is equal to gross investments minus depreciation.

The return on capital is the *real interest rate* (the nominal interest rate minus the inflation rate). Investment depends on the difference between the *expected profit rate* and the real interest rate.

Investment demand (ID) is the relationship between the real interest rate and the amount of investment, *ceteris paribus*. A decrease in the interest rate leads to increased investment demand. A change in expected profits will shift the ID curve. The investment demand curve is shown in Fig. 10-7.

Saving depends on the real interest rate (the higher the rate, the more saving). Factors that cause a positive shift in saving supplied are increases in disposable income and wealth and decreases in expected future income. *Saving supply* (SS) is the (positive) relationship between the real interest rate and the quantity of saving. The saving supply curve is shown in Fig. 10-7.

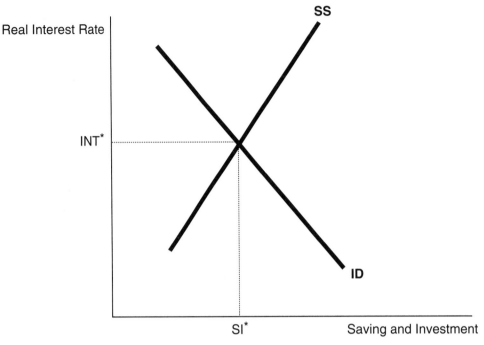

Figure 10-7. The capital market: the real interest rate is determined by investment demand and saving supply. Equilibrium is achieved at SI* and INT* when the saving supply curve SS and the investment demand curve ID intersect.

10.4 Labor Productivity

Labor productivity is defined as real GDP per hour of work and signifies the average output per fixed labor input (hour). Labor productivity increases when physical capital (plants and equipment) and human capital (skills and training obtained from education) increase. Labor productivity also increases when advances in technology take place. An increase in labor productivity shifts the production function upward (see Fig. 10-8) and increases the economy's potential GDP.

Over the last 20 years, the rising population of the United States has increased the supply of labor. In addition, capital stock (plants, equipment, and so on) has increased and technology has advanced, increasing both the demand for labor and the productivity of labor. U.S. potential GDP increased because the equilibrium employment level has increased, and also because the production function has shifted upward. This has provided for generally robust GDP growth in the United States in the last 20 years (see Fig. 10-9).

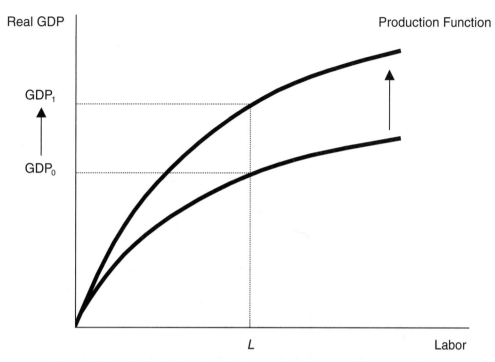

Figure 10-8.   Production function: the impact of an increase in labor productivity.

10.5   Hints

H10.1   An increase in population increases the supply of labor, and therefore the equilibrium employment increases. The production function does not shift. The economy moves along its unchanged production function to a higher GDP level.

H10.2   An increase in labor productivity shifts the production function upward. It also increases the demand for labor, so employment increases. Potential GDP goes up as employment rises, and also because the production function shifts upward.

H10.3   The *money wage rate* is the number of dollars an hour of labor earns. The *real wage rate* is the quantity of goods and services an hour of labor earns.

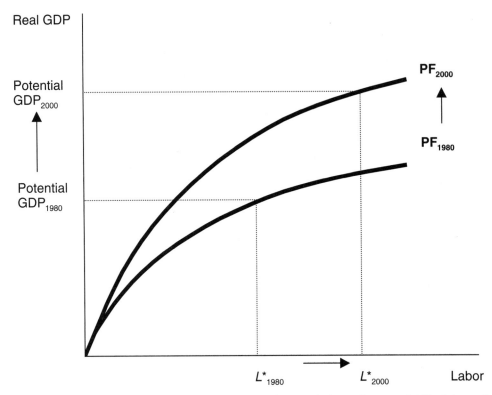

Figure 10-9. Growth in U.S. potential GDP, 1980–2000. The increase is due to the upward shift of the production function (improved labor productivity and technology) and the increase in the equilibrium employment L^*.

Quiz

Choose the one best answer for each question.

Q10.1 According to the classical economists, competition is _____ and prices are _____.

(a) free; inflexible

(b) limited; inflexible

(c) free; flexible

(d) free; constant

(e) limited; flexible

Q10.2   *Laissez-faire, laissez-passer* means that
    (a) government policy is critical to achieving potential GDP.
    (b) a fixed, low wage rate is required for full employment.
    (c) government should not interfere with the economy.
    (d) monetary policy is important to avoid inflation.
    (e) free markets must be regulated to achieve beneficial
        results for participants.

Q10.3   If the demand for labor goes up, the equilibrium quantity of employment
    _____ and potential GDP _____.
    (a) decreases; doesn't change
    (b) decreases; decreases
    (c) increases; doesn't change
    (d) increases; increases
    (e) doesn't change; increases

Q10.4   The change in capital stock is equal to
    (a) gross investments.
    (b) net investments minus depreciation.
    (c) depreciation.
    (d) net investments.
    (e) change in quantity of plants.

Q10.5   An increase in the real interest rate
    (a) shifts the investment demand curve to the right.
    (b) shifts the investment demand to the left.
    (c) increases the quantity of investment, but doesn't shift
        the investment demand curve.
    (d) decreases the quantity of investment, but doesn't shift
        the investment demand curve.
    (e) doesn't change the quantity of investment.

Q10.6   The production function is the relationship between
    (a) real GDP and the quantity of labor.
    (b) real GDP and capital stock.
    (c) capital per hour of labor and labor productivity.
    (d) real GDP and labor productivity.
    (e) capital stock and the quantity of labor.

Q10.7   Of the following, which ones are real variables?
    I. Price level
    II. Rate of inflation
    III. Employment

(a) I only
(b) II only
(c) III only
(d) I and II
(e) II and III

Q10.8   If corporate taxes go up, what is the likely impact on net investments?
(a) Don't change
(b) Decrease
(c) Increase
(d) Depends on the kind of taxation
(e) Depends on the amount of depreciation

Q10.9   An increase in population causes
(a) the labor demand curve to shift leftward.
(b) the labor demand curve to shift rightward.
(c) the labor supply curve to shift leftward.
(d) the labor supply curve to shift rightward.
(e) no change in the supply or the demand curve.

Q10.10   If the nominal interest rate is 15 percent and the inflation rate is 5 percent, the real interest rate is
(a) 5 percent.
(b) 10 percent.
(c) 15 percent.
(d) 20 percent.
(e) 35 percent.

Q10.11   U.S. potential GDP has increased in the last 20 years because equilibrium employment _____ and the production function _____.
(a) decreased; shifted upward
(b) increased; shifted downward
(c) decreased; shifted downward
(d) increased; shifted upward
(e) didn't change; shifted upward

Q10.12   An increase in population leads to _____ shift of the production function, and an increase in labor productivity leads to a(n) _____ shift of the production function
(a) an upward; upward
(b) a downward; upward

(c) no; downward

(d) no; upward

(e) a downward; downward

Quiz Answers

Q10.1 (c). The classical economists assumed free markets with many buyers and sellers (e.g., no monopolies); they also assumed that all prices (product, wage rate, and so on) were fully flexible.

Q10.2 (c). *Laissez-faire, laissez-passer* is the classical economists' view that through the hidden (or invisible) hand, free markets will achieve a result that's beneficial to all. Government should not interfere with this process.

Q10.3 (d). The shift in the demand curve increases equilibrium employment and moves potential GDP to a higher level *along* the production function.

Q10.4 (d). The change in capital stock (plant, equipment, and so on) is equal to net investment, or gross investment minus depreciation. This is a value or dollar total (not a quantity total).

Q10.5 (d). The investment demand (ID) curve is the relationship between the real interest rate and the quantity of investment, *ceteris paribus*. This means that we are isolating the relationship between this specific rate and this specific quantity, while assuming that everything else (e.g., profit expectations and technology) is constant. Therefore, the curve doesn't shift, and we can expect a decrease in investment demand when the real interest rate increases, as we move along the downward-sloping investment demand curve.

Q10.6 (a). The production function is the relationship between real GDP (on the *y* axis) and the quantity of labor (on the *x* axis), that is, the equilibrium outcome of the labor market.

Q10.7 (c). Employment is a real variable; inflation rate and price level are dollar-value (nominal) variables.

Q10.8 (b). Corporate taxes will decrease the rate of return on investments and will probably lead to fewer investments.

Q10.9 (d). The increase in population causes an increase in the supply of labor (for the same wage rate), and the labor supply curve shifts rightward.

Q10.10 (b). The answer is 10 percent. The real interest rate equals the nominal interest rate of 15 percent minus the 5 percent inflation rate.

Q10.11 (d). The supply of and demand for labor have increased, leading to higher equilibrium employment. Advances in technology increased labor productivity and shifted the production function upward.

Q10.12 (d). The change in population will lead to a movement along the production function but will not shift the curve. An increase in labor productivity will move the production function upward.

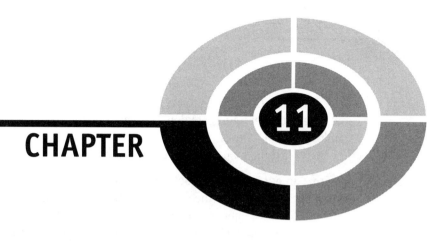
The Keynesian Model

How do we reduce unemployment if the classical model doesn't work and prices do not adjust (rigid or "sticky" prices)?
In the 1930s, John Maynard Keynes, a British economist, proposed that increasing the economy's aggregate demand was the solution to this problem.
According to Keynes, stimulating consumption, investment, and government expenditure would ultimately lead to GDP at full-employment level.

11.1   Introduction

In the 1930s, the United Kingdom faced the effects of extreme deflation in a stagnant economy. Consistent with classical beliefs in the benefits of flexible prices, classical theory held that in a downturn, wage rates and the rate of interest would fall and eventually would lead to improved profitability prospects and new investments, improving employment. U.K. policy makers recommended that labor unions accept a wage cut in order to improve the profitability of producers.

John Maynard Keynes proposed a different, innovative solution.

He observed that a stagnant equilibrium below full employment was possible because of a unique combination of factors: Very low interest rates removed the incentive to save (low savings supply), while negative business prospects kept firms from investing (low investment demand). Under these conditions, Keynes noted that stimulation of aggregate demand was critical to move the economy to the full-employment GDP level.

There are three major assumptions in the Keynesian model:

- Firms do not change product prices in the (very) short run because of such things as menu costs (the costs of relabeling, redesigning contracts, and so on), and factor costs may also be rigid because of long-term contracts (e.g., wages and factor input purchases). This means that the aggregate price level is fixed and that firms will sell the amount that is demanded, implying that GDP is determined by aggregate expenditures. The horizontal or *"flat" aggregate supply curve* at relatively low GDP and fixed price level is called the Keynesian segment of the supply curve.
- *Aggregate expenditures*—the sum of consumption expenditures, investment, government purchases, and exports minus imports—equals national income. Therefore, there is a direct relationship between aggregate demand and aggregate income.
- GDP and aggregate expenditures have a special two-way influence: An increase in real GDP increases aggregate expenditures, and an increase in aggregate expenditures increases real GDP. For example, if consumption, as a part of aggregate expenditures, goes up, it will increase income, but consumption will go up even further because of the (positive) propensity to consume at higher income levels (consumption function).

NOTE N11.1

The Great Depression

The Great Depression (1929–1939) was the longest and most severe economic downturn ever experienced by the Western world. Because the United States was the major creditor and financier of post-World War I Europe, the downturn in the U.S. economy caused the collapse of the economies of Britain and Germany. To protect their respective economies, nations used tariffs and quotas, which reduced international trade and caused further economic decline.

The U.S. economic decline from 1929 to 1933 was unparalleled:

- Stock values dropped to 20 percent of their earlier value.
- Some 11,000 of the 25,000 banks collapsed.
- Unemployment increased from 3.5 percent to 30 percent of the labor force (16 million unemployed).

- The value of international trade declined by 50 percent.
- GDP declined from \$103.8 billion in 1929 to \$55.8 billion in 1933.

The economic, agricultural, and relief policies of the New Deal administration under President Franklin Delano Roosevelt mitigated the effects of the Depression and restored a sense of confidence to the American people. Before the Great Depression, governments relied on abstract market forces for economic correction. After the Great Depression, government assumed a principal role in ensuring economic stability. It is generally agreed that the complete business recovery in the United States after the Great Depression was not achieved until government began to spend heavily for defense in the early 1940s.

11.2   The Consumption Function

The two-way influence between GDP and aggregate expenditure is possible because not only does the increase in aggregate expenditure lift GDP, but the additional GDP will lift aggregate expenditure even more because of the *consumption function*, or the propensity to consume more when income increases. The consumption function is the driver of the multiplier process that lifts GDP and aggregate expenditures incrementally. In the Keynesian model, the multiplier process is fully effective in raising GDP because the aggregate supply curve is horizontal. Changes in aggregate demand translate into changes in GDP and are not muted by an upward-sloping aggregate supply curve.

The consumption function is the relationship between consumption expenditure and disposable income (see Fig. 11-1). The slope of the consumption function is the *marginal propensity to consume (MPC)*, or, the change in consumption expenditure resulting from a change in disposable income:

$$\text{Marginal propensity to consume (MPC)} = \Delta C / \Delta YD$$

where ΔC = change in consumption (Δ stands for change)
  ΔYD = change in disposable income
   YD = disposable income = total income − taxes = $Y - T$

The amount of consumption when disposable income is zero is called *autonomous*. This is equal to the intercept (y axis), or C_{AUT} in Fig. 11-1. Above this amount, consumption is called *induced consumption*.

The consumption function will shift as a result of changes in the real interest rate, wealth, or expected future income. Because a change in real GDP changes disposable income, it will change consumption expenditure.

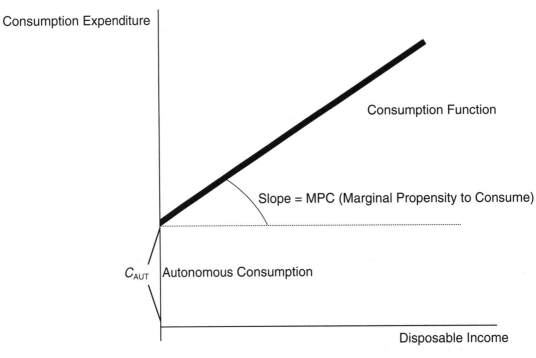

Figure 11-1.   The consumption function.

The saving function is the relationship between saving and disposable income. The *marginal propensity to save (MPS)* is the change in savings that results from a change in disposable income, or

Marginal propensity to save $(MPS) = \Delta S / \Delta YD$

where ΔS = change in saving (Δ stands for change)
ΔYD = change in disposable income

Households' disposable income is either used to consume or to save, so the consumption expenditure plus saving equals disposable income, which implies (see Hint H11.5 for details):

Marginal propensity to consume + marginal propensity to save = 1

Please note that:

• *Disposable income* is the after-tax income earned from supplying labor for the production of goods and services. Consumer loans (e.g., credit cards) are financial transactions and are not part of disposable income.

- If domestic savings S are insufficient (the 2004 U.S. savings rate was about 0.2 percent) to finance investment I, foreign financing becomes critical.

11.3   The Multiplier Process

The two-way relationship between real GDP and aggregate expenditures is caused by the *multiplier process*. In this section, we show an example of this process.

The *spending (or expenditure) multiplier* is the amount by which a change in autonomous expenditure (e.g., government expenditure to stimulate demand) is multiplied to determine the change in the equilibrium values of expenditures and GDP. The multiplier is larger than 1 because a change in autonomous expenditure also changes the induced expenditures.

In a simple economy (one without taxes or imports),

$$\text{Spending multiplier} = 1/\text{MPS} = 1/(1 - \text{MPC})$$

For example, a $1 million increase in the total amount of investment in an economy will set off a chain reaction of increases in expenditures.

Initially, $1 million is added as income. If 80 percent of that additional income is spent, a total of $800,000 will be added to incomes. This means that total income has now been raised by $1 million (the initial expenditure) plus $800,000, or $1.8 million. In turn, the extra income of $800,000 causes 80 percent of $800,000 to be expended and added to incomes, and so on. The process continues, and, ultimately, the initial investment times the factor $1/(1 - 80\%)$ is added to income, or $5 \times \$1$ million $= \$5$ million.

An important assumption of the multiplier process is that either the supply of money or the velocity of money will increase to allow the extra spending to occur.

11.4   The Keynesian Equilibrium

The Keynesian macroeconomic equilibrium is different from the standard demand and supply equilibrium, or the intersection of the aggregate demand curve and the aggregate supply curve. The Keynesian equilibrium occurs when

$$\text{Real GDP} = \text{aggregate expenditures (AE)} = C + I + G + (X - M)$$

Note: The *45-degree line* is a reference line through the origin that has a 45-degree angle relative to the x axis; it contains all the points with identical values on the x axis and the y axis (i.e., $y = x$).

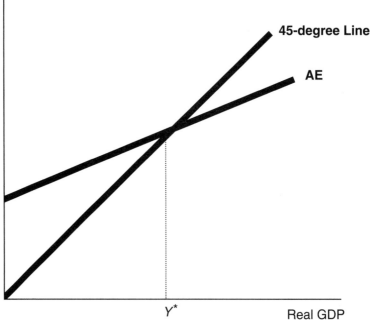

Figure 11-2.   Aggregate expenditure.

In order to show the Keynesian equilibrium graphically, the 45-degree line is used to indicate all points with real GDP = AE. The intersection of this 45-degree line and the AE function $C + I + G + (X - M)$ is the Keynesian macroeconomic equilibrium. If real GDP exceeds the equilibrium level, it means that unplanned inventories will accumulate. If real GDP is below the equilibrium level, inventories will be drawn down in an unplanned manner.

The relationship between aggregate expenditure and real GDP is demonstrated in Fig. 11-2.

NOTE N11.4

John Maynard Keynes (1883–1946)

During World War I, Keynes held a post at the U.K. Treasury, and he participated in the negotiations for the Versailles Peace Treaty of 1919 that ended World War I. He resigned his post because he felt that German war reparation payments had been set too high. In 1936, he published his major work, *The General Theory of*

Employment, Interest, and Money. In World War II he again served in the U.K. Treasury and was responsible for the negotiations with the United States on the Lend-Lease Act. Keynes was a leading participant in the 1944 Bretton Woods conference that established the post-World War II international economic organization, including the International Monetary Fund (IMF).

11.5   The Keynesian Model and the AS/AD Model

Changes in the price level will change disposable income, which will change aggregate expenditures and therefore affect the Keynesian equilibrium. Changes in the price level demonstrate the relationship between aggregate demand and price (or the AD curve). An increase in the price level lowers disposable income, shifting the aggregate expenditure curve downward (see Fig. 11-3).

The downward shift from AE_0 to AE_1 leads to a decline from Y_0 to Y_1 in equilibrium GDP. The two points are points on the aggregate demand curve (the relationship between GDP and the price level) (see Fig. 11-4).

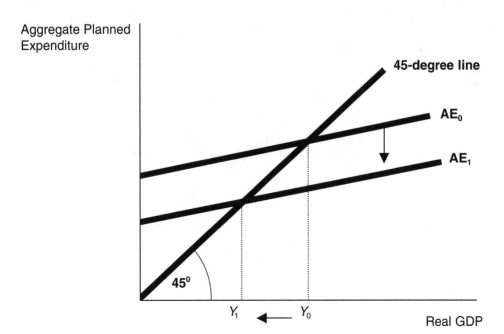

Figure 11-3.   Increase in the price level and the AE curve.

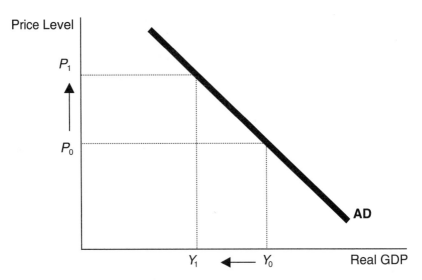

Figure 11-4. Increase in the price level and the AD curve.

The change in real GDP is smaller than the shift of the AD curve
SAS = short-run aggregate supply curve

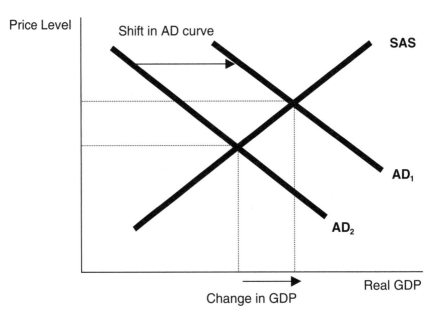

Figure 11-5. A shift in aggregate demand AD.

Figure 11-6. Comparison of the AS/AD model and the Keynesian model.

AD = aggregate demand
AE = aggregate expenditures
AS = aggregate supply

	AS/AD Model	**Keynesian Model**
Price flexibility?	Yes	No; fixed short-run price level
Vertical axis?	Price level	Aggregate expenditures (AE)
Aggregate demand?	AD curve	AE curve
AS shifts?	Yes	No
Multiplier effect?	Muted; AS curve not horizontal	Full; AS curve horizontal

The increase in the price level from P_0 to P_1 leads to a decrease in the equilibrium quantity demanded from Y_0 to Y_1. This is a movement along the AD curve because the AD curve is the relationship between price and quantity, *ceteris paribus*.

The aggregate demand curve will shift when autonomous expenditure changes for any reason other than a change in the price level. The size of the shift is equal to the spending multiplier multiplied by the change in autonomous expenditure. The results are shown in Fig. 11-5.

In the long run, real GDP returns to potential real GDP and does not change as a result of a change in aggregate expenditures; that is, in the long run, the multiplier is zero.

Key differences between the *AS/AD model* and the *Keynesian model* are provided in Fig. 11-6.

11.6   U.S. Unemployment Rate, 1990–2004

The *U.S. unemployment rate* (published monthly by the Department of Labor) is a closely followed statistic. It signals the general growth (or stagnation) of the economy and provides insight into the "willingness to hire" of U.S. businesses (another key statistic is private jobs created). One complication of the unemployment rate measure is that the labor force may shrink if people face long-term unemployment

Full-time workers; monthly.

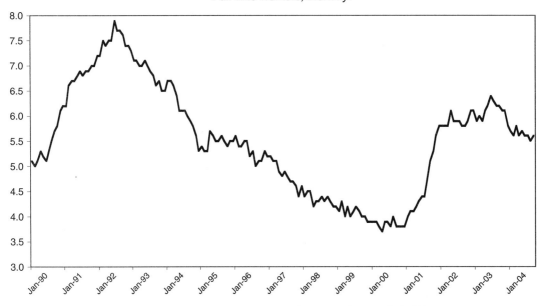

Figure 11-7. Unemployment rate (% of the labor force), 1990–2004.
Source: U.S. Department of Labor.

("discouraged workers"), so a lower percentage is not always the result of more hiring.

Figure 11-7 illustrates the cyclical nature of the unemployment rate. After consistent declines from 1992 to 2000, the rate jumped in 2001 and stayed between 5.5 and 6.0 percent during the 2002–2004 period. During the 1992–2000 period, the unemployment rate reached a low of 3.5 percent, probably close to the natural rate of unemployment.

11.7 Hints

H11.1 The concept of the multiplier is critical in Keynes's model. The initial *autonomous* increase in aggregate expenditures causes national income to go up; this *induces* additional spending (e.g., because of the propensity to consume), increasing income further, and so on. In this model, the equality of savings and investment (equilibrium) is achieved by adjustments in national income (through the multiplier), unlike in the classical model, which balances savings and investment strictly through the interest rate.

H11.2 Multiplier formulas:

MPC (marginal propensity to consume) = change in consumption
divided by change in income

MPS (marginal propensity to save) = change in saving divided
by change in income

Investment multiplier = $1/(1 - \text{MPC}) = 1/\text{MPS}$

The investment multiplier multiplied by the change in investment (e.g., new factories and new equipment) equals the change in GDP.

Government spending multiplier = $1/(1 - \text{MPC}) = 1/\text{MPS}$

The government spending multiplier multiplied by the change in government spending (e.g., new roads and new bridges) equals the change in GDP.

Tax multiplier = $-\text{MPC}/(1 - \text{MPC}) = -\text{MPC}/\text{MPS}$

The tax multiplier multiplied by the change in taxes (e.g., lump-sum taxes) equals the change in GDP.

The investment multiplier is always equal to the value of the government spending multiplier. The investment and government spending multipliers are always positive. The tax multiplier is always negative.

H11.3 Keynes identified that aggregate expenditures $[C + I + G + (X - M)]$ equals national income. The observation of this fundamental equality ultimately developed into the *National Income Accounts*, a tabulation of national income and expenditures that shows the transactions between economic sectors. This special form of "bookkeeping" that tracks the activities in the national economy is now a common practice.

H11.4 The *short-run aggregate supply (SAS) curve* can be thought of as having three separate ranges (see Fig. 11-8):

- *The Keynesian range*. At relatively low GDP, the SAS curve will be horizontal because of fixed price levels. Changes in aggregate demand will have a full multiplier impact on GDP.
- *Intermediate range*. At moderate levels of GDP, below potential GDP, the SAS curve will be upward-sloping. Changes in aggregate demand will have a partial multiplier effect on GDP.
- *Classical range*. In this range, GDP equals potential GDP, and the SAS curve is vertical. Changes in aggregate demand will cause

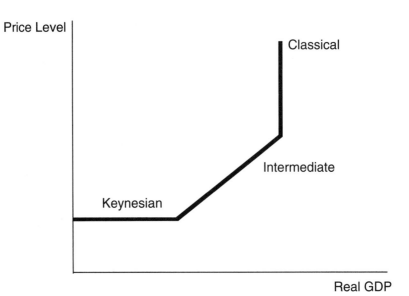

Figure 11-8. The three ranges of the aggregate supply curve AS.

changes only in the price level. Therefore, increases in aggregate demand will only lead to inflationary conditions.

H11.5 Because households' *disposable income* is used either to consume or to save, the consumption expenditure plus saving equals disposable income, or

$$C + S = \text{YD}$$

which means, for changes Δ,

$$\Delta C + \Delta S = \Delta \text{YD} \quad \text{or} \quad \Delta C/\Delta \text{YD} + \Delta S/\Delta \text{YD} = 1 \quad \text{or} \quad \text{MPC} + \text{MPS} = 1$$

H11.6 Equilibrium is defined by $\text{GDP} = Y = \text{aggregate demand} = C + I$ (in a simple economy, without government and foreign sectors). In this special case, there is an easy alternative way to state the equilibrium requirement:

$$Y = C + I$$

$$Y - C = I$$

$$S = I$$

Saving = investment

Saving is a leakage from the circular flow, while investment spending is an injection that balances the leakage from saving.

Quiz

Choose the one best answer for each question.

Q11.1   The Keynesian aggregate supply curve is
  (a) downward-sloping, because product prices are fixed.
  (b) vertical, because the rate of employment is fixed.
  (c) upward-sloping, because factor prices are fixed.
  (d) horizontal, because the price level is fixed.
  (e) vertical for low GDP and upward-sloping for high GDP.

Q11.2   The U.S. savings rate is very low; what does this mean for the value of the spending multiplier?
  (a) Very small; positive value
  (b) Very small; negative value
  (c) Very large; positive value
  (d) Very large; negative value
  (e) Zero

Q11.3   During the 1930s Depression, there was price _____ with _____ interest rates.
  (a) deflation; low
  (b) deflation; high
  (c) inflation; low
  (d) inflation; high
  (e) stability; high

Q11.4   If investment increases by $400, leading to an equilibrium expenditure of $1,000, then
  (a) the multiplier is 1.5.
  (b) the AS curve is vertical.
  (c) the multiplier is 0.5.
  (d) the multiplier is 2.5.
  (e) the AE curve is horizontal.

Q11.5   Income taxes _____ the value of the multiplier.
  (a) triple
  (b) increase

(c) do not change

(d) sometimes increase, sometimes decrease

(e) decrease

Q11.6   The aggregate expenditure (AE) curve is the relationship between
(a) consumption and disposable income.
(b) the total of $C+I+G+(X-M)$ and disposable income.
(c) national income and investment.
(d) household expenditures and the price level.
(e) aggregate expenditures and the price level.

Q11.7   If investment decreases, what causes the strongest negative impact on GDP?
(a) A steeper short-run AS curve
(b) A flatter short-run AS curve
(c) A higher value of the marginal propensity to consume
(d) Lower income taxes
(e) A lower value of the marginal propensity to save

Q11.8   During the Great Depression, countries used _____ and international trade _____.
(a) more tariffs; increased
(b) less tariffs; decreased
(c) more tariffs; decreased
(d) less tariffs; increased
(e) no tariffs; increased

Q11.9   A change in _____ does not change autonomous expenditure.
(a) price level
(b) interest rate
(c) real GDP
(d) the short-run supply curve
(e) the long-run supply curve

Q11.10   Included in aggregate expenditure are
(a) consumption expenditures, saving, and government purchases.
(b) investments, saving, and net exports.
(c) investment, government purchases, disposable income, and imports.

  (d) consumption expenditures, investment, government purchases, and net exports.
  (e) government purchases, disposable income, and net exports.

Q11.11 Which of the following statements about the U.S. monthly unemployment rate from 1995 to 2000 is true?
  (a) It was below 6 percent at all times.
  (b) It was above 8 percent for several months.
  (c) It was above 6 percent at all times.
  (d) It reached a high of 12 percent.
  (e) It reached a low of 6 percent.

Q11.12 What is the value of the long-run multiplier?
  (a) A large negative value
  (b) 1
  (c) 0
  (d) Infinite
  (e) 10

Quiz Answers

Q11.1 (d). The Keynesian aggregate supply curve is horizontal because the short-run price level is fixed. Therefore, firms will sell whatever is demanded; that is, aggregate demand determines GDP. This situation occurs when GDP is relatively low and significant excess capacity exists.

Q11.2 (c). Assume a small marginal savings rate, such as a 1 percent MPS, which means that the spending multiplier (1/MPS) equals $1/(0.01) = 100$. Please note that the spending multiplier is never zero or negative.

Q11.3 (a). The Depression in the 1930s caused massive unemployment, lack of demand, excess productive capacity, and low prices (deflation), combined with low interest rates. The low interest rates were not sufficient to move new investment because of negative prospects and the existing overcapacity.

Q11.4 (d). The multiplier = equilibrium expenditure/initial amount = $1,000/$400 = 2.5$.

Q11.5 (e). Income tax reduces disposable income and therefore decreases the induced consumption expenditure change.

Q11.6 (b). The AE curve is the relationship between planned aggregate expenditures $C+I+G+(X-M)$ and disposable income.

Q11.7 (b). The flatter the SAS curve, the stronger the impact of a change in aggregate demand—in this case, the stronger the negative impact on GDP of a decrease in aggregate demand (investment decrease). In Keynes's theory, the SAS curve is horizontal and changes in aggregate demand have a maximum (multiplier) impact on GDP.

Q11.8 (c). During the Great Depression, countries tried to protect their domestic economies by increasing tariffs. This decreased international trade (by 50 percent) and accelerated the decline in countries' GDP, further deepening the economies' depression.

Q11.9 (c). By definition, autonomous expenditure is independent from real GDP.

Q11.10 (d). Aggregate expenditure, by definition, is the sum of consumption expenditure, investment, government purchases, and net exports. It does *not* include saving or disposable income (or only imports).

Q11.11 (a). During 1995 to 2000 (with 2000 included), the rate of unemployment never exceeded 6.0 percent. The rate declined from just over 5.5 percent in 1995 to almost 3.5 percent in 2000, with the latter number being very close to the natural rate of unemployment.

Q11.12 (c). In the long run, real GDP equals potential real GDP. At that point, real GDP does not change as a result of a change in aggregate expenditures. This means that in the long run, the multiplier is zero.

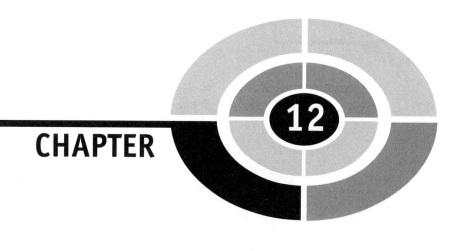

CHAPTER 12

The Business Cycle

What is the business cycle? Why do business cycles occur?
What causes the fluctuations in GDP? Should we attempt to dampen cycles? If
so, what is the best way to do it?
What are the main economic theories of the business cycle? What policy tools
are available?

12.1   Introduction

The up-and-down pattern of GDP growth over time, consisting of recessions and expansions, is called the *business cycle*. Although the length and the intensity of cycles may vary, the cycles themselves appear to be a permanent feature of economic activity. The business cycle is probably tied to the expectations of consumers and producers and to the lag between investment decisions and capital accumulation. However, there are other plausible reasons for GDP fluctuations. A variety of models emphasize specific explanations for the business cycle, prescribe different policies, and offer different points of view on whether it is feasible (and desirable) to stabilize the cycles. For example, a monetarist would claim that any policy designed

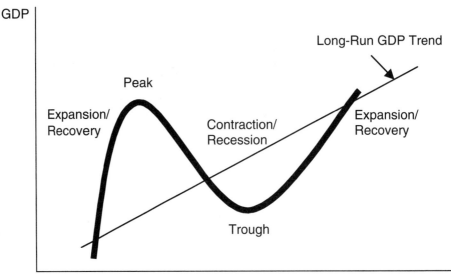

Figure 12-1.   The business cycle: fluctuations of GDP.

to dampen cycles will only further destabilize the business cycle, while a Keynesian would argue that stimulating aggregate demand is critical to avoid a long-term recession. Others highlight the impact of external events (oil shortages, population increases, wars, and so on) or stress the influence of specific economic decisions (capital accumulation, net investments, and so on). In this chapter, we provide a comprehensive summary of business cycle models.

The *business cycle* is the fluctuating pattern of GDP growth over time, consisting of expansions (recovery) and contractions (recessions); see Fig. 12-1.

There is no agreement about the reasons for the sometimes erratic fluctuations in GDP. Major influences are the volatile mix of consumer and producer expectations, as well as fixed investment and inventory cycles. External shocks (e.g., the 1974 oil embargo) and the timing of government policies also contribute to the development of business cycles.

Although the severe swings of economic activity during the Depression and World War II have not been repeated in the last 50 years, it is unclear to what extent economic policy is capable of significantly dampening the business cycle.

After World War II, the U.S. economy experienced sporadic contractions (average length about one year), while enjoying significant periods of expansion (average length about four years). More recently, the U.S. economy experienced a one-year recession in 2001 after a unique 10-year expansion during the 1990s. On average,

GDP rises to a new high after each recession. The average gain in an expansion is 22 percent (the average decline in a recession is −6 percent).

12.2   Consumer and Producer Expectations

Consumer expectations play an important role in the business cycle; for example, an increase in positive expectations will contribute to aggregate demand because consumption is likely to be up.

NOTE N12.2

Consumer Confidence

Consumer confidence is households' perception of economic progress. It has an impact on spending (and saving) plans in the short run. Index results from surveys are published in the United States by the Conference Board and by the University of Michigan; they primarily report on whether consumers are feeling more or less optimistic about the economy.

The *accelerator model* states that net capital investment depends on changes in GDP. For example, if aggregate demand increases and the economy is at capacity (potential GDP), the required increase in GDP has to be achieved by additional investment:

$$\text{Net investment} = \text{accelerator} \times \text{change in GDP}$$

The accelerator model demonstrates the importance of net investment in durable capital goods (e.g., plant and equipment) as a driver of business cycles. Typically, when investments go down, contractions occur, and when investments go up, expansion takes place.

Producer (and distributor) expectations and investment are captured by a series of results, including

- Investment intentions (plans for capital spending)
- Inventories (inventories or stocks held by producers and distributors)
- Fixed investment

Stock buildup could be the first sign of a decrease in aggregate demand and signal a downturn in the economy; conversely, a decrease in inventories may be a sign of increased aggregate demand.

12.3 Classical Models

Members of the *Classical School* (e.g., Smith and Ricardo) were aware of economic fluctuations, but they did not develop a theory of the business cycle. Classical economists considered all fluctuations to be strictly temporary, and therefore business cycles were not a major focus of interest for them.

Members of the *Neoclassical School* (late nineteenth and early twentieth centuries) were the first to develop a model of the business cycle. Like the Classical School, the neoclassical economists assumed that pure competition takes place in markets. This means that a multitude of buyers and sellers interact, without any special influence of monopoly and other factors distorting competition. These neoclassical markets will balance buyers and sellers at the market equilibrium, and government is not supposed to intervene. The *neoclassical model* of the business cycle therefore states that cycles are merely temporary deviations from the potential (full-employment) GDP and that the price mechanism will ultimately restore the economy to full-employment levels. Keynes's views in the 1930s cast significant doubt on the neoclassical approach of hands-off government.

The *monetarist theory* of the business cycle regards the quantity of money as the main source of economic fluctuations. The impulse for fluctuations will be the changes in the growth rate of the quantity of money. A lower growth rate of the quantity of money will decrease aggregate demand. Ultimately, money wages respond to the change in price level and the short-run aggregate supply (SAS) curve shifts until the economy achieves its potential GDP. This view is similar to the classical argument (see Fig. 12-2).

The *new classical theory* of the business cycle, developed after World War II, is based on the rational expectations of individual firms and consumers. The *rational expectations model* emphasizes that people's expectations, based on the available information and their understanding of the economy, directly determine current economic behavior. Individuals and businesses use information efficiently by analyzing and forecasting prices, interest rates, and money supply, and they decide on the basis of those forecasts. Widely expected policy moves (anticipated policy actions) will have no impact because they have already been taken into account in people's decisions. Only unanticipated (surprise) moves will have an impact on changing people's behavior. This result is due to the *policy ineffectiveness theorem*, which says that if prices and wages are flexible and if people hold rational expectations, then any government policy to stimulate demand will have no impact on GDP (or employment) unless the *policy is unanticipated*. Government should provide a stable environment by strictly adhering to long-term moderate policies (including balanced budgets), as well as predictable growth in the money supply.

Aggregate demand moves to the left (AD_0 to AD_1), lowering the price level and GDP.

SAS = short-run aggregate supply

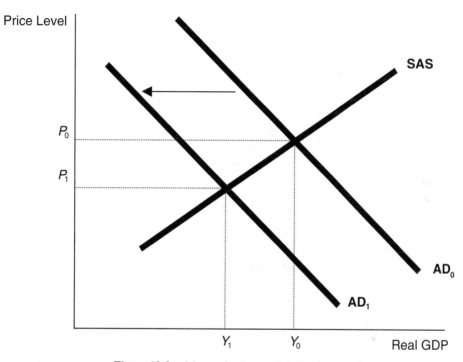

Figure 12-2.   Monetarist theory of the business cycle.

New classical theory expects that saving and investment tend to balance when the interest rate changes and that anticipated changes in aggregate demand will have no impact on real wages and GDP. People (under rational expectations) will take anticipated changes into account when they make their decisions, and therefore policies to achieve change will not be effective. The real impulse in the new classical theory is unanticipated changes in aggregate demand.

12.4   Keynesian Models

The *Keynesian model* of the business cycle emphasizes price rigidity and economic expectations as a source of GDP fluctuations. According to Keynes, short-run price rigidity prevents neoclassical price dynamics from restoring the economy to the

A change in aggregate demand (AD_0 to AD_1) has a large impact on GDP because the short-run aggregate supply (SAS) curve is horizontal (as a result of fixed prices).

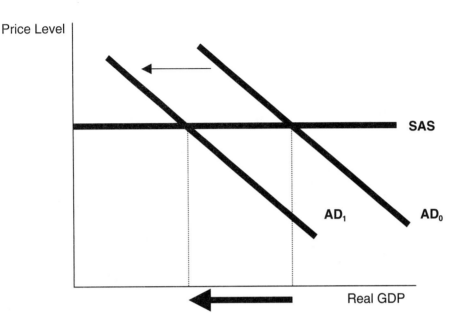

Figure 12-3. Keynesian theory of the business cycle.

full-employment level. This could be caused by wage rates that do not go down even if aggregate demand falls, such as those in labor union contracts. Therefore, the economy can stagnate in a recession.

The Keynesian impulse for fluctuations is a change in firms' expectations about sales and profits, which will affect investment decisions. The change in investment increases aggregate demand. In the short run, this change in aggregate demand has a large impact (i.e., the full multiplier effect) on GDP because the supply curve SAS is horizontal as a result of fixed prices (see Fig. 12-3).

The *New Keynesian* model is based on the theory of rational expectations (like the new classical model) and emphasizes unanticipated shifts in the aggregate demand (AD) curve that move the economy along the short-term aggregate supply (SAS) curve as real wage rates change. The New Keynesians emphasize the business practices and institutions that may cause short-run price inflexibility (e.g., long-term contracts and transaction costs), which is not consistent with the price flexibility required in the policy ineffectiveness theorem. Therefore, unlike in the new classical model, *anticipated* change does play a role in New Keynesian models. For example, New Keynesians believe that an anticipated increase in aggregate demand—after prices have been fixed—will still have a positive impact on real wages and real GDP.

12.5   The Impact of Technology

Some models of the business cycle focus on technology rather than on aggregate demand as the main force for the cycle. The Real Business Cycle model is an example.

The *Real Business Cycle model* regards progress in technology as the main impulse for the business cycle. Changes in productivity resulting from innovation will affect investment demand and labor demand and cause changes in the business cycle. For example, during a recession, both investment and labor demand decline. As investment demand goes down, it lowers the real interest rate. Because of the replacement of labor by capital (because the lower interest rate makes capital relatively cheaper), demand for labor continues to decline (see Fig. 12-4). The long-run aggregate supply (LAS) curve shifts to the left, decreasing employment. The aggregate demand (AD) curve also shifts to the left as a result of the decrease in investment, and GDP goes down, while the price level falls.

A strong feature of the Real Business Cycle model is that it captures both business cycle and economic growth (i.e., potential GDP). In addition, it appears to be consistent with microeconomic data on labor supply, labor demand, and investment demand.

Aggregate demand (AD) shifts to the left (AD_0 to AD_1), while long-run aggregate supply (LAS) also shifts to the left (LAS_0 to LAS_1). This decreases GDP and the price level.

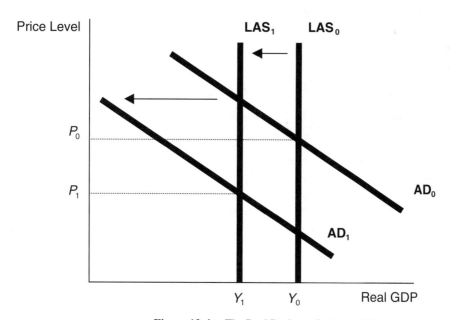

Figure 12-4.   The Real Business Cycle model.

The arguments against the Real Business Cycle model are that money wages are probably not fully flexible in the short run and that the substitution effect (i.e., replacing labor with capital) is not strong enough to account for major changes in employment.

NOTE N12.5

Real Business Cycle Theory and the 2004 Nobel Prize in Economics

The 2004 Nobel Prize for Economics was awarded to Edward Prescott from the United States and Finn Kydland from Norway. Prescott and Kydland's Real Business Cycle model attributes changes in business cycles to changes in technology or other supply shocks (e.g., oil price increases). They found that technological progress could account for 70 percent of the swings of American business cycles after World War II, with stagnating technological innovation causing contractions and surges in innovation causing expansions.

The influence of the Real Business Cycle model has been significant, leading to the incorporation of technology, productivity, and external shocks in explaining recessions. However, it is unclear whether the Great Depression could be explained by changes in technology.

12.6   The Great Depression and Institutional Reform

In its first four years, the Great Depression significantly diminished U.S. GDP while the unemployment rate grew from 3.5 percent to 30 percent. The initial source of the Great Depression was uncertainty and pessimism, which reduced investment and consumption expenditures. The continuing decline in aggregate demand turned the initial recession into the Great Depression:

- Aggregate demand continued to decrease because of growing uncertainty and pessimism.
- Bank failures and the collapse in the quantity of money caused aggregate demand to decrease.

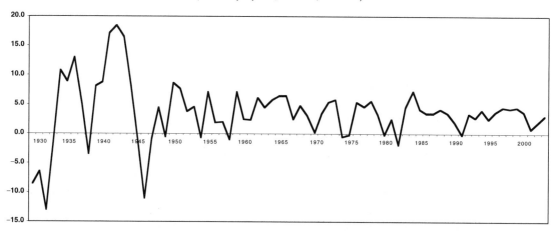

(Seasonally adjusted, chained 2,000 dollars)

Figure 12-5.   U.S. GDP, 1930–2003, % change vs. year ago.
Source: U.S. Department of Commerce, Bureau of Economic Analysis.

Most economists do not consider it likely that a decline similar to the Great Depression will occur again because of the modern safeguards built into the financial system:

- Bank deposit insurance is provided by the Federal Deposit Insurance Corporation (FDIC).
- The Federal Reserve has an active role as the central banking authority.
- There has been extensive regulation of the financial markets [e.g., the Securities and Exchange Commission (SEC)].

Generally, the Great Depression led to regulatory reform of the financial markets and financial institutions, as well as improved fiscal and monetary policies to ensure economic stability. These steps appear to have been very successful. Since World War II, the number (and duration) of recessions has been limited, while periods of expansion have been numerous (see Fig. 12-5).

12.7   Hints

H12.1   Large-scale computer models have improved the forecasting of business cycles. However, current forecasting of GDP fluctuations still remains imprecise.

H12.2 *Cyclical unemployment* is caused by a lack of demand for labor (usually during a recession). Because the input volume varies most in capital goods industries (e.g., the automotive industry), workers in those industries are most at risk of becoming cyclically unemployed.

H12.3 New Keynesians emphasize rational institutions (e.g., labor unions) and transaction costs as factors leading to price rigidity. An example of producers' transaction costs is menu costs. *Menu costs* are the practical costs incurred by producers when they change prices (e.g., relabeling products and re-entering prices into systems). These transaction costs may be the explanation for discontinuous "jumps" in prices, rather than smooth, tiny increments. It also helps to explain that money may not be neutral (a Keynesian argument, opposed to the classical view).

H12.4 The *misery index* is a quick indicator of consumer confidence. There are two main varieties:

- The rate of (consumer) inflation plus the rate of unemployment
- The rate of (consumer) inflation plus the rate of interest

Inflation is estimated by the Consumer Price Index (CPI).

The higher the misery index, the higher consumers' misery is supposed to be. (*Note*: The index works only for positive rates of inflation.)

H12.5 Several types of indicators can be used to anticipate and verify the movement of the business cycle. Leading indicators move 6 to 12 months ahead of GDP, coincident indicators move with it, and lagging indicators are about 6 months behind the cycle.

- *Leading indicators*. interest rates begin to increase about 18 months ahead of output peaks. Business confidence, share prices, housing starts, and companies' cash flow surplus peak about 8 to 16 months ahead of GDP. Consumer credit, car sales, and manufacturing orders peak about 6 months ahead, while retail sales peak 2 to 3 months in advance.
- *Coincident indicators*. GDP is the main reference point during the cycle.
- *Lagging indicators*. Capacity utilization peaks about 1 month after output. Job vacancies peak about 3 months later, growth in average earnings after 4 months, and growth in unit labor costs after 5 months. Productivity, unemployment, and inflation turn up 6 months after the peak of GDP. Investment, order backlogs, and stocks peak around 12 months after output.

Quiz

Choose the one best answer for each question.

Q12.1   An average expansion lasts _____ as an average recession.
  (a) four times as long
  (b) about as long
  (c) half as long
  (d) twice as long
  (e) eight times as long

Q12.2   Which of the following statements is true?
  (a) Since World War II, business cycle swings have become less severe.
  (b) Producer intentions do not have an influence on the business cycle.
  (c) If interest rates go up, the misery index goes down.
  (d) The causes of business cycles are precisely known.
  (e) The longest post-World War II GDP expansion was six years.

Q12.3   According to the theory of rational expectations, government's *anticipated* policy will
  (a) fool some of the people all of the time.
  (b) fool all of the people some of the time.
  (c) fool some of the people some of the time.
  (d) fool all of the people all of the time.
  (e) never fool anybody.

Q12.4   Which of the following is a true statement about the neoclassical business cycle theory?
  (a) Monopolies are the driving force causing cycles.
  (b) Economic policy is critical in dampening cycles.
  (c) Deviations from potential GDP are not temporary.
  (d) Product advertising contributes to GDP expansion.
  (e) Government should never interfere in markets.

Q12.5   What major factor drives expansions in the Real Business Cycle model?
  (a) Unexpected declines in aggregate demand
  (b) Advances in technology
  (c) Anti-inflationary monetary policy

(d) Less government spending

(e) Increased corporate taxation

Q12.6   What is the key impulse in the monetarist model of the business cycle?

(a) Innovation

(b) Changes in aggregate demand

(c) Changes in the quantity of money

(d) Unanticipated changes in economic policy

(e) Anticipated changes in economic policy

Q12.7   Regulatory economic reforms resulting from the Great Depression were

(a) nonexistent.

(b) limited to new banking regulations.

(c) insignificant.

(d) significant, but ineffective.

(e) significant and effective.

Q12.8   During an average expansion, real GDP climbs by about _____.

(a) 22 percent

(b) 5 percent

(c) 11 percent

(d) 55 percent

(e) 1 percent

Q12.9   The Federal Deposit Insurance Corporation (FDIC)

(a) insures banks against bad loans.

(b) insures bank deposits.

(c) lends reserves to banks.

(d) manages banks' reserve requirements.

(e) sets bank discount rates.

Q12.10   In the 1990s, the U.S. economy experienced

(a) the longest expansion in U.S. history.

(b) one of the most severe recessions in U.S. history.

(c) several complete business cycles.

(d) one complete business cycle.

(e) the highest peak in GDP yearly growth in U.S. history.

Q12.11   Which of the following statements is true about the New Keynesians' beliefs?

(a) Prices are flexible in the short run.

(b) The growth in the quantity of money is the main impulse for business cycles.

(c) New technology is the main impulse for business cycles.

(d) Prices are rigid in the short run because of transaction costs.

(e) Consumers do not behave according to rational expectations.

Q12.12   Which of the following is typically caused by a recession?
(a) An increase in structural unemployment
(b) An increase in frictional unemployment
(c) An increase in cyclical unemployment
(d) A decrease in discouraged workers
(e) A decrease in the natural rate of employment

Quiz Answers

Q12.1 (a). Since World War II, the average expansion has lasted four years, while the average recession has lasted one year.

Q12.2 (a). The swings in GDP growth have become less severe since World War II. Please note that the longest GDP expansion was 10 years, during the 1990s.

Q12.3 (e). People with rational expectations will take government's anticipated policies into account, and therefore policy will not have an impact. Only surprise policies will lead to a change of behavior.

Q12.4 (e). The neoclassical economists want a hands-off approach by government because perfect markets (price mechanism; many buyers, many sellers; no monopolies, no advertising influence) will correct any deviations from full-employment GDP.

Q12.5 (b). The key impulse leading to business cycles in the Real Business Cycle model is technological innovation.

Q12.6 (c). Changes in the growth rate of the quantity of money will move aggregate demand and affect GDP. Ultimately, GDP will return to potential GDP (similar to the neoclassical argument).

Q12.7 (e). Significant regulatory changes include banking regulations (e.g., reserve requirements, FDIC insurance) and stock market regulations (the creation of the SEC). Those changes have been effective: The post-World War II GDP growth has been largely positive and very stable relative to the 1930s.

In addition, fiscal and monetary policies have been improved to provide economic stability.

Q12.8 (a). The average gain in an expansion is 22 percent. (The average decline in a recession is −6 percent.) On average, GDP rises to a new high after each recession.

Q12.9 (b). By insuring deposits, the FDIC prevents bank failures. It removes bank customers' concerns about the safety of their deposits, a primary cause for "runs" on banks.

Q12.10 (a). Starting in the early 1990s, the economy expanded until the 2001 recession, a period of about 10 years, the longest expansion in U.S. history.

Q12.11 (d). The New Keynesians adhere to the rational expectations theory, but they believe that institutional transaction costs (e.g., labor contracts) and other transaction costs (e.g., menu costs) cause temporary price rigidity and therefore lead to imbalances between supply and demand, causing business cycles.

Q12.12 (c). A recession leads to temporary layoffs (e.g., in the auto industry) until GDP goes up again and rehiring takes place. This is called *cyclical unemployment*. *Structural unemployment* is caused by new technology, and *frictional unemployment* is caused by worker transitions from one job to another. The natural rate of unemployment (frictional + structural) is typically not affected by recessions. In a recession, the number of discouraged workers typically increases.

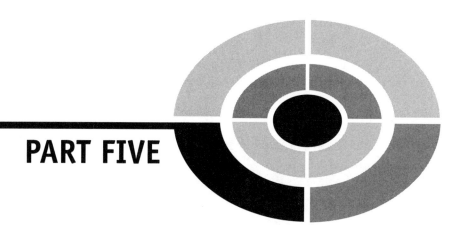

Macroeconomic Policy

CHAPTER 13

Fiscal Policy

What is the best way for government to manage its budget (taxes-expenditures)?
Should the budget remain balanced at all times?
How effective are increases in government spending? Do they stimulate economic activity? How effective are changes in taxation?
Are budget deficits appropriate tools for enhancing aggregate demand and increasing GDP growth?
What does government's fiscal imbalance mean for future generations?

13.1   Introduction

The government can influence the disposable income of households and the net income of firms by changing the rate of personal and business taxation (T), thereby changing the economy's outcome. The choice of the volume of government spending (G), a part of the economy's aggregate demand, will also have an impact on the economy's results.

Fiscal policy is the use of the federal budget [i.e., taxation (T) minus spending (G)], to achieve macroeconomic goals. The goal of an expansionary fiscal policy is to stimulate aggregate demand; it involves increased government spending and decreased taxation. In contrast, contractionary fiscal policy ("tightening" fiscal policy) includes higher taxes and less government spending. This policy may be followed to reduce inflation.

The government's balanced budget objective refers to the aim of keeping spending in line with taxation ($T = G$). If the government spends more than its income, it incurs a budget deficit. This has an impact on the money market and interest rates because the government will be forced to borrow money. The U.S. Congress has pursued laws to require balanced federal budgets, but the constitutionality of those measures is unclear.

Federal budget management continues to present challenges in the relations between the executive and legislative branches, such as a line-item veto for the president.

13.2   The Role of Government Budgeting

The government's *federal budget* is the major tool for fiscal policy. *Government expenditures* (*G*) directly affect the economy's aggregate demand, while *personal and corporate taxation* (*T*) has an impact on consumption, saving, and investment. The federal budget policy regarding deficits is another important part of fiscal policy. For example, the government's willingness to stimulate the economy will directly affect the budget balance toward deficits (i.e., a smaller surplus or a larger deficit). The government is required to borrow money if it is running a deficit. If the deficit becomes persistent, government debt itself becomes a significant cost in the federal budget as a result of interest payments.

The federal budget is the annual statement of government expenditures and tax revenues. The president proposes the federal budget to Congress, which reviews and amends the budget and passes budget acts that the president can either sign or veto.

Government expenditures include the government's transfer payments, purchases of goods and services, and interest payments on government debt. The largest government expenditure is transfer payments, or grants or other payments not made in return for a product or service (e.g., pensions and unemployment benefits). Transfer payments are a form of income redistribution and are not a return to factors of production (e.g., labor).

Government's revenues result from taxation, a compulsory transfer of money from private individuals, institutions, or groups to the government. Typically, *tax revenues* (*T*) are received from four sources: personal income taxes, social security taxes, corporate income taxes, and indirect taxes. The largest source of revenue is the personal income tax, followed by social security taxes. Taxes may be levied on income or wealth (a direct tax), or through a surcharge (e.g., a value-added tax) on prices (an indirect tax).

A *budget surplus* occurs when tax revenues exceed expenditures ($T > G$); a *budget deficit* is the reverse ($T < G$). A *balanced budget* means that tax revenues equal expenditures ($T = G$). *Government debt* is the total amount that the government has borrowed.

The role of government differs among countries. Historically, the U.S. government has played a more limited role than the governments of other countries. Government expenditures as a percentage of GDP are about 30 percent in the United States. In Japan, Canada, and the United Kingdom, the percentage is between 36 and 40 percent, while in western European countries such as Italy, Germany, and France, the percentage is between 45 and 50 percent (e.g., France's government expenditures are about 49 percent of GDP).

13.3   Fiscal Policy and Macroeconomic Goals

Fiscal policy is the use of government spending (G) and taxation (T) to achieve macroeconomic objectives such as economic growth, full employment, and price-level stability. During a recession, fiscal policy to stimulate the economy may consist of increasing government spending and/or decreasing taxation (so-called deficit stimulus). The result of this expansionary policy may be a government budget deficit. In times of economic expansion, an anti-inflationary, "tightening" fiscal policy consists of decreased government spending and increased taxes. This contractionary policy may contribute to a government surplus or diminish a budget deficit.

There are important limitations to the short-term effectiveness of taxation as a form of fiscal policy. Tax law changes may take too long to be effective measures for fine-tuning the economy, and tax rate changes can upset the timing of economic decisions.

The amount of time it takes policy makers to determine which fiscal policy is required and to pass appropriate laws is called the *inside lag*. The time frame from the new policy taking effect to its impact on GDP is called the *outside lag*. The inside lag of fiscal policy is long, but the outside lag may be very short. Because of fiscal policy's long inside lag, monetary policy is usually employed to influence the economy in the short run.

Changes in taxation have various impacts on economic factors. An increase in the tax rate decreases the supply of labor (i.e., there is less incentive to work), so the higher tax rate has a negative impact on the equilibrium employment and GDP.

The economy's investment is financed by private saving (S), government saving ($T-G$), and foreign borrowing ($M-X$), or

$$I = S + (T - G) + (M - X)$$

A tax on interest income decreases private saving and shifts the saving supply to the left. The tax drives a wedge between the posttax interest rate received by savers and the interest rate paid by borrowers, decreasing the equilibrium quantity of investment. By decreasing investment, the tax lowers the economic growth rate.

Out-of-balance government budgets can have an immediate impact on the economy. A government budget surplus ($T > G$) adds to overall saving. This shifts the saving supply to the right, and the real interest rate drops. This increases the equilibrium quantity of investment, hiking the rate of economic growth. A government budget deficit ($T < G$) creates the need to borrow money. If this increases the interest rate, it will lower private spending because investors scale down their plans.

The displacement of private spending by government borrowing is called the *crowding-out* effect. If government borrowing does not affect the interest rate, there will be no reduction in private spending and aggregate demand will rise by the full amount of the government spending increase.

A modern approach to fiscal (and monetary) policy is to deemphasize demand-side policies (because of their inflationary effect) and focus on the factors influencing supply. *Supply-side economics* relies on the direct use of incentives (e.g., reduction in taxation) to encourage people to work, save, and invest, with the ultimate objective being to stimulate aggregate supply (instead of aggregate demand). Usually, supply-side policies are combined with tightly controlled monetary policies.

NOTE N13.3

The Federal Budget Deficit

In 2004, the U.S. budget deficit reached $412 billion, or 3.6 percent of GDP. The administration's policy is to reduce the deficit, possibly to an estimated 2.5 percent of GDP in 2008.

The prospect of long-term government budget deficits will tend to put upward pressure on interest rates because the government will have an ongoing need to borrow funds.

13.4   The Long-Range Impact of Fiscal Policy

The long-range balance of taxes and benefits involves the immediate and long-term needs for funding permanent benefits available through government (e.g., social security).

Generational accounting is an accounting system that measures the lifetime tax burden and benefits for subsequent generations. Present values, resulting from a discount method that values future amounts in current ("present") dollars, are used to compare the future values of taxes paid and benefits received.

Fiscal imbalance is the present value of the government's commitments to pay benefits minus the present value of its tax revenues. In 2003, the U.S. government's fiscal imbalance was estimated at $45 trillion. *Generational imbalance* is the division of the fiscal imbalance between current and future generations, assuming that the current generation will enjoy the current levels of taxes and benefits. The current generation is expected to pay about 40 percent of the fiscal imbalance, while future generations will pay about 60 percent.

NOTE N13.4

Social Security

Government and Congress are studying new financing arrangements for social security as the large baby boom generation prepares to retire. A 2004 report by the *Congressional Budget Office (CBO)* stated that social security benefits under the current system will require between 5 and 8 percent of GDP in the long term. Rising costs of the benefits are expected to outpace federal revenue from social security taxes in 2019, according to the CBO.

13.5   Discretionary Fiscal Policy

Discretionary fiscal policy is a specific policy passed as a law by Congress. Examples of such policies are increases in government spending for job education and higher tax rates on personal income. The impact of these programs on aggregate demand is as follows:

• Increases in government expenditure will increase aggregate demand income by

$$\text{Increase in government expenditure} \times \text{government expenditure multiplier} =$$
$$\text{increase in government expenditure} \times 1/\text{MPS}$$

For example, if MPS = 0.05, the government expenditure multiplier = 1/0.05 = 20, or a $1 billion increase in expenditures will increase aggregate demand by $20 billion.

- An increase in taxes will decrease aggregate demand by

$$\text{Increase in taxes} \times \text{tax multiplier} = \text{increase in taxes} \times -(1 - \text{MPS})/\text{MPS}$$

For example, if MPS = 0.05, the tax multiplier is −0.95/0.05 = −19, or a $1 billion increase in taxes will decrease aggregate demand by $19 billion.

An equal increase in government expenditures and tax revenues balances the budget and will increase aggregate demand by exactly the increase in government expenditures. This happens because the effects of both increases are exactly opposite.

Equal changes in expenditures and taxes—in order to balance the budget—have the following impact on aggregate demand:

$$\text{Change in government expenditures} \times \text{balanced budget multiplier} =$$
$$\text{change in government expenditures} \times 1$$

For example, if government expenditures increase by $1 billion, aggregate demand will also increase by $1 billion.

Because economic growth is a major macroeconomic objective, fiscal policy is used to guide real GDP toward the economy's potential (full-employment) GDP. In a recessionary gap, when real GDP is below potential GDP, expansionary fiscal policy, such as an increase in government purchases or a decrease in tax revenues, will shift the aggregate demand (AD) curve to the right. The multiplier effect moves aggregate demand by an amount larger than the expansionary fiscal policy. Figure 13-1 demonstrates how fiscal policy can eliminate a recessionary gap.

In an inflationary gap, when real GDP exceeds potential GDP, a contractionary fiscal policy, such as a decrease in government purchases or an increase in tax revenues, should be considered.

13.6 Automatic Fiscal Policy

Automatic fiscal policy is the result of changes in the government's tax revenues caused by the business cycle, since tax revenues fluctuate with changes in GDP.

Automatic stabilizers help to stabilize GDP without the need for discretionary action. Personal and corporate income taxes rise and fall with personal and business

Expansionary fiscal policy shifts the aggregate demand curve to the right (AD_0 to AD_1), removing the recessionary gap (Y_1-Y_0) and reestablishing GDP at its potential level Y_1.

LAS = long-run aggregate supply
SAS = short-run aggregate supply

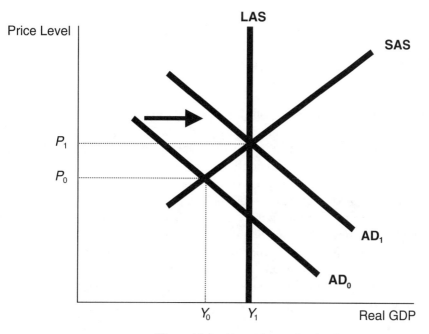

Figure 13-1. Expansionary fiscal policy.

income and thus slow down rapid expansions through higher taxes and stimulate a sagging economy through lower taxes. (*Induced taxes* are the taxes that change when GDP changes.) Other stabilizers are unemployment compensation (and similar transfer payments), which counteract recessions by paying the jobless. Also, farm support programs act as stabilizers by dampening fluctuations in farm prices. Stabilizers such as induced taxes decrease multipliers and dampen the swings of expansions and recessions, improving stability.

The *structural budget balance* (or *cyclically adjusted balance*) is a measure of government borrowing after the impact of the business cycle is removed. It is the level of borrowing during a year without expansion or recession. This is not a precise measure because it requires an estimate of the output gap (i.e., real GDP minus potential GDP). For example, if the economy's actual deficit is 2.5 percent during a severe recession, the structural budget balance may be considered practically zero. The *cyclical budget balance,* which is the result of business cycle fluctuations, is the actual budget balance minus the structural balance. The cyclical budget balance shows the impact of the business cycle on the government's budget balance.

NOTE N13.6

Prescott and Kydland, Part 2

One of Prescott and Kydland's (2004 Nobel Prize in Economics winners) lasting contributions was to demonstrate the importance of the credibility of economic policy.

The credibility of economic policy originates with the *policy ineffectiveness theorem,* which says that if prices and wages are flexible and if people hold rational expectations, then any government policy to stimulate demand will have no impact on GDP (or employment) unless the policy is *unanticipated.* For example, suppose a government promises that it will keep taxes low in the future to encourage saving today. However, government has an incentive to tax heavily in the future. Anticipating confiscatory taxes, people will refrain from saving now and instead consume to prevent the government from getting their money later.

This major incentive issue shifted the focus from discretionary policies by central bankers to transparent rules. The increased independence of central banks and their adoption of *transparent policy rules* has greatly contributed to lower global rates of inflation.

13.7   Global Economics and Fiscal Policy

The major impact of fiscal policy is the extent to which government finances its own expenditures or borrows money to cover budget deficits. The low U.S. average saving rate implies a reliance on foreign funds in the case of a government deficit. This means that foreign investors view the United States as an investment target, but may require attractive (i.e., high) interest rates. The investment decision will also be influenced by expectations about foreign exchange rates. In general, a stable U.S. exchange rate will be beneficial for the government's financing needs, but large government deficits may cause instability in foreign exchange markets. Therefore, the global repercussions of federal deficits are significant.

A *balance of payments* deficit during a recession triggers a dilemma. To correct the balance of payments problem, the country's price of imports needs to go up, together with a decrease in the price of exports (and a rise in interest rates). However, currency depreciation may start inflation, requiring a contractionary monetary policy that is inconsistent with recession (see hint H7.2.)

13.8   Hints

H13.1   Surprisingly, it is not always fully clear what a *tax* really is. For example, is an individual's compulsory saving to purchase a pension a "tax"? What if government applies high prices to the output of nationalized industries to raise revenues? And what about special duties, such as airline industry duties?

H13.2   The crowding-out effect may be offset when changes in private saving offset the changes in government saving (*Ricardo-Barro effect*). This effect says that deficits decrease government saving but mean higher taxes in the future, so taxpayers increase their private saving to pay the higher future taxes.

H13.3   The *Laffer curve* is the hypothetical relationship between the tax rate and the amount of tax revenue collected. It states that an optimum tax rate exists (somewhere between 0 and 100 percent) that yields the maximum tax revenue. Rates below the optimum are considered normal because hiking the tax rate can increase tax revenues. Rates above the optimum are prohibitive because they reduce economic incentives for individuals and businesses, and lead to lower tax revenues (the Laffer effect). U.S. tax rates are relatively low, so the Laffer effect is not likely to occur in the United States. There is no firm empirical evidence to back up the Laffer curve.

H13.4   A trade deficit is the value of imports minus the value of exports $(M-X)$, which requires foreign borrowing and implies that the United States owes an international debt. The *U.S. international debt* is currently approximately $4 trillion.

H13.5   The *tax multiplier* is always less than the spending multiplier because a $1 change in taxes is going to lead to a $1 change in *disposable income,* but not to a $1 change in *aggregate demand*. The reason is that part of the change in disposable income "leaks" into savings. The formula for the tax multiplier is

$$\text{Tax multiplier} = -\text{MPC} \times 1/\text{MPS} = -\text{MPC} \times 1/(1-\text{MPC})$$

H13.6   The *balanced budget multiplier* is the sum of the government expenditure multiplier and the tax multiplier:

$$\text{Government expenditure multiplier} + \text{tax multiplier} =$$
$$1/\text{MPS} - \text{MPC}/\text{MPS} = (1-\text{MPC})/\text{MPS} = \text{MPS}/\text{MPS} = 1$$

Quiz

Choose the one best answer for each question.

Q13.1 Which of the following statements describes a contractionary fiscal policy?
(a) Lower government spending and higher taxes
(b) Higher government spending and lower taxes
(c) Decreased money supply and a higher discount rate
(d) Higher government spending and higher taxes
(e) Lower government spending and lower taxes

Q13.2 The inside lag is the time it takes
(a) to change government expenditures.
(b) for fiscal policy, after its adoption, to affect GDP.
(c) to determine fiscal policy and pass it into law.
(d) for automatic fiscal stabilizers to take effect.
(e) to neutralize the "crowding-out" effect.

Q13.3 Which country has the lowest government expenditure as a percent of GDP?
(a) France
(b) United States
(c) United Kingdom
(d) Canada
(e) Japan

Q13.4 Most economists believe that, in the United States, an increase in the tax rate
(a) leaves total tax revenue unchanged.
(b) decreases total tax revenue.
(c) changes total tax revenue, but it's unclear if it's a decrease or an increase.
(d) most likely decreases total tax revenue.
(e) increases total tax revenue.

Q13.5 Fiscal policy's inside lag is _____, and its outside lag is _____.
(a) long; long
(b) zero; long
(c) long; short
(d) short; long
(e) short; short

Q13.6   Generational accounting demonstrates that the value of the
government's commitments to pay benefits is _____ the present value
of its taxes.
(a) equal to
(b) about 60 percent of
(c) about 25 percent of
(d) greater than
(e) not comparable to

Q13.7   Future generations, as opposed to the current generation, are expected to
pay approximately _____ percent of the government's fiscal imbalance.
(a) 10
(b) 30
(c) 60
(d) 85
(e) 95

Q13.8   What happens automatically if the economy goes into recession?
(a) A budget surplus decreases.
(b) Government purchases increase.
(c) Corporate investment goes up.
(d) Income taxes rise.
(e) A budget deficit decreases.

Q13.9   If the federal budget is in deficit when the economy is at full employment, the deficit is said to be
(a) cyclical.
(b) automatic.
(c) discretionary.
(d) persisting.
(e) structural.

Q13.10   An increase in the rate of income taxes is an example of
(a) automatic fiscal policy.
(b) the impact of the balanced budget multiplier.
(c) discretionary fiscal policy.
(d) expansionary fiscal policy.
(e) increased government spending.

Q13.11   What kind of policy rules do modern central banks follow?
(a) Discretionary
(b) Surprise
(c) Unanticipated

(d) Transparent

(e) Random

Q13.12 Which of the following is a true statement about automatic stabilizers?

(a) Inside lag is long.

(b) Outside lag is short.

(c) No discretionary measures are needed.

(d) They have the same impact as lump-sum taxes.

(e) They require significant discussion in Congress.

Quiz Answers

Q13.1 (a). A contractionary fiscal policy means that government spends less, decreasing aggregate demand, and increases taxes to slow down consumption, which also decreases aggregate demand. Please note that (b) is an expansionary monetary policy.

Q13.2 (c). The inside lag is the time it takes for policy to be decided and to be passed into law by Congress. The outside lag is the time it takes for the adopted fiscal policy to affect GDP.

Q13.3 (b). In 2001, U.S. government expenditures (as a percentage of GDP) were 30.4 percent, while those of the other countries named were substantially higher: Japan, 36.1 percent; Canada, 38.2 percent; United Kingdom, 38.3 percent; and France, 48.6 percent.

Q13.4 (e). Most experts believe that U.S. tax rates are low enough to cause an increase in overall tax revenue if tax rates are increased. In other words, the so-called Laffer effect is unlikely to happen in the United States. The hypothetical Laffer effect occurs at so-called prohibitively high tax rates when increases in rates cause a decrease in overall tax revenues.

Q13.5 (c). Because of the time it takes to recognize the problem and pass the appropriate fiscal legislation, the inside lag of fiscal policy will be long. However, once the new policy takes effect, its impact will be felt very shortly.

Q13.6 (d). Currently, the present value of commitments is estimated to exceed the present value of taxes by about $45 trillion.

Q13.7 (c). Future generations are expected to pay about 60 percent of the government's fiscal imbalance, leaving about 40 percent for the current generation.

Q13.8 (a). In a recession, tax revenues will typically go down because GDP declines. In addition, the government's transfer payments go up during a recession. This means that a government surplus would decline (and an existing deficit would widen).

Q13.9 (e). A deficit is called structural if it exists even when the economy is at full employment, as opposed to a cyclical deficit caused by changes in the business cycle.

Q13.10 (c). An increase in the income tax rate is not automatic, but would have to be passed into law. Therefore, it is called a discretionary fiscal policy. Note the difference from induced (automatic) tax revenue changes (under fixed tax rates) as GDP fluctuates.

Q13.11 (d). Modern central banks follow transparent rules to enhance the credibility of their policies. For that reason, discretionary rules are being used less.

Q13.12 (c). The advantage of automatic stabilizers is that they have a dampening influence on the business cycle without requiring specific discretionary measures.

CHAPTER 14

Monetary Policy

What are the main goals of monetary policy? What rules are required for effective monetary policy?
Who conducts policy in the absence of a rule? Should monetary control be in the hands of politicians or of an independent central bank?
What are modern views of the role of monetary policy? What is the critical importance of credible policy? Why?

14.1   Introduction

The *Federal Reserve System* is the *central bank* of the United States and functions as lender of last resort for U.S. banks. The Federal Reserve is an independent, federally chartered institution that has the day-to-day responsibility for implementing U.S. monetary policy. The Federal Reserve's primary goal is to ensure price stability. It has various secondary goals, such as, to support the stability of the international

value of the dollar. This latter function establishes a link between U.S. monetary policy and global economics.

14.2 The Goals of Monetary Policy

Monetary policy is the Federal Reserve's policy directed at causing changes in the availability of money in the economy in order to achieve price stability. The Federal Reserve aims to control the overall money supply, credit availability, and the level of interest rates by making changes in the banks' required reserve ratio, making changes in the discount rate, and engaging in open market operations involving government securities.

In developed economies, monetary policy is mostly implemented by the central bank's open market operations to produce short-term interest rates that will encourage banks to let deposits grow at a rate consistent with the central bank's policy objectives. The Federal Reserve System has the primary responsibility for U.S. monetary policy.

Because the economy works best with predictable prices (see the discussion of inflation), the *stability of the price level* is the primary goal of monetary policy. A low-single-digit price-level growth (between 0 and 3 percent) is considered the practical equivalent of price-level stability. Note that a modest positive rate of price-level growth is acceptable because of the positive measurement bias of certain price indices; for example, the Consumer Price Index (CPI) overestimates inflation by approximately 1 percent. See H14.1.

Monetary policy may also involve the secondary goals of GDP growth and of maintaining GDP close to potential (or full-employment) GDP. Intermediate-term targets of monetary policy include growth rates of monetary aggregates (e.g., M1 or M2) and goals for the federal funds rate.

Although monetary policy can help to limit fluctuations in GDP, some experts, especially monetarists, argue that monetary policies actually cause GDP fluctuations. They prefer that the Federal Reserve take a hands-off approach, similar to the Classical School's beliefs in noninterference by government. Economists have various reasons to disagree over monetary policy. First, the relationship between the money supply and short-term interest rates may change, and the same may be true of reserves and the money supply. Second, the velocity of money is not fully stable, and the impact of a change in money supply is therefore unclear. Third, available monetary data can be imperfect, and it is sometimes unclear which definition of the money supply (e.g., M_1, M_2, or M_3) is the appropriate one. Finally, economic relationships are dynamic, and any action taken now may not be the most effective under future conditions (e.g., because of inside and outside lags in fiscal policy).

14.3   Monetary Policy Rules

Monetary policy can be implemented by using different kinds of policy rules. The types of rules depend on whether their application is triggered by events or not. If the Federal Reserve acts as it sees fit, this is called a *discretionary rule* because the Federal Reserve acts entirely at its own discretion (e.g., it sometimes responds to recession, but not always). This has the advantage of giving the Federal Reserve a broad range of options, but it increases the uncertainty for the market as a whole. If the rule specifies that an action is to be pursued, independent of economic events, this is called a *fixed rule*. (A Classical School fixed rule would be to do nothing, irrespective of events.) A rule that indicates how the policy should respond to specific events is called a *feedback rule* (e.g., if the economy is in recession, implement an expansionary monetary policy).

What kind of rules should be used for the implementation of monetary policy? Fixed rules may be too simple to respond to complex events, while the effectiveness of feedback rules depends on how quickly the adopted policies can take effect. Discretionary rules may be too ad hoc and create economic uncertainty.

A decrease in aggregate demand would not cause a monetarist to do anything. Monetarists apply the fixed rule of passivity (no matter what kind of economic events happen). They believe that the quantity of money is a cause of GDP fluctuations. The short-run aggregate demand fluctuations will ultimately dissipate, and GDP will return to its original level, potential GDP.

Keynesians believe that demand fluctuations combined with inflexible wages cause economic fluctuations. The Keynesian feedback rule would be to apply expansionary monetary policy if aggregate demand goes down. This policy leads to increases in the quantity of money and a lowering of the interest rate, encouraging consumption and investment. Keynesians believe that if this kind of monetary policy is applied, aggregate demand will increase and GDP will return to potential GDP.

In Fig. 14-1 we assume that, because of a loss in productivity, the long-term aggregate supply (LAS) curve moves to the left (LAS_0 to LAS_1), decreasing GDP from Y_0 to Y_1 and increasing the price level from P_0 to P_1. The feedback rule (to stabilize GDP) kicks in, providing a boost in aggregate demand AD to increase GDP (AD_0 to AD_1). However GDP stays at Y_1 because of LAS_1, and the effect is that the price level goes up even more (from P_1 to P_2). The feedback rule therefore doesn't stabilize GDP and has an inflationary impact.

The decrease in LAS raises the price level. A feedback rule to stabilize the price level triggers a decrease in aggregate demand. This decrease has no impact on real GDP but can offset the rise in the price level so that price remains constant. Apparently, this kind of feedback rule works (in contrast to the first one).

The feedback rule (AD_0 to AD_1) fails to stabilize GDP and leads to a higher price level P_2.

LAS = long-run aggregate supply
AD = aggregate demand

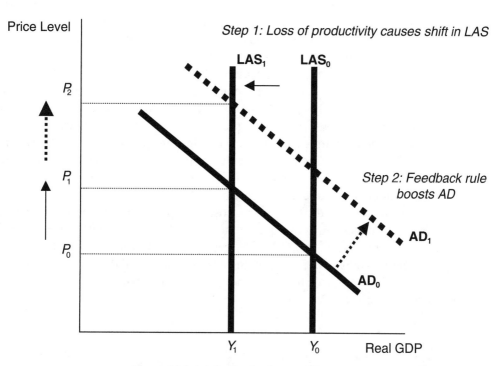

Figure 14-1.   A feedback rule to stabilize GDP.

Assume that the short-run aggregate supply (SAS) curve changes as a result of cost increases (i.e., wages). If the Federal Reserve pursues a policy that focuses on stabilizing GDP while allowing price hikes, no incentives will be in place to prevent groups from pushing up costs, leading to a cost-push inflation. A feedback rule that focuses on price-level changes (instead of GDP) may be more effective in limiting inflation.

14.4   Effective Policy

The challenge is to implement policies in such a way that the intended goal is reached. This is more difficult than it may sound. For example, if inflation reaches a significant level, a policy that aims at decreasing the growth in aggregate demand ("cooling down" the economy) is required. The negative impact of a surprise decrease in aggregate demand will be to decrease real GDP and increase unemployment. Instead of a surprise policy, a credible, widely announced policy aimed at slowing down the rate of inflation might be able to reduce inflation without reducing GDP and raising unemployment. In practice, many anti-inflationary policies lead to recessions because people do not believe that the announced anti-inflation measures will be fully carried out.

Prescott and Kydland (see Chapters 12 and 13) showed that a government's inability to demonstrate sincerity in achieving low inflation could lead to inflation as a self-fulfilling prophecy. For example, if individuals expect the government to follow inflationary policies (e.g., a preelection expansionary policy), they will bid up wages and accelerate the inflation. This insight was particularly relevant during the high-inflation 1970s and led central banks to follow *transparent* rules rather than discretionary ones. It appears that this new direction in policy has avoided severe inflation during the last two decades.

A monetarist fixed rule prevents cost-push pressure from becoming cost-push inflation, but it achieves this goal at the cost of lower real GDP. A Keynesian feedback rule that targets real GDP may cause inflation. A feedback rule targeting the price level avoids inflation, but at the cost of lost real GDP.

A special policy rule has been devised to respond to both the price level and real GDP. See hint H14.2.

14.5   The Mix of Monetary and Fiscal Policy

The U.S. government, through fiscal policy, and the Federal Reserve, through monetary policy, are the two main institutions that direct economic policy. Monetary policy can be implemented more quickly than fiscal policy (i.e., there is a short inside lag). This makes it more difficult to coordinate an effective mix of monetary and fiscal policy. The coordination is further complicated by the long and variable outside lag of monetary policy, compared to the very short outside lag for fiscal policy.

Historically, the Federal Reserve's policies have accommodated the government's fiscal policy decisions, but in the last two decades the Federal Reserve has adopted an increasingly independent role. Factors that have contributed to the Federal Reserve's independence are the increasingly influential theoretical views of the monetarists, combined with the need for credible central bank policies. In addition, Paul Volcker's strongly independent management as chairman of the Federal Reserve during the 1980s set the stage for the Federal Reserve's independent role.

NOTE N14.5A

U.S. Fiscal and Monetary Policy, 1960 to 2000

In the first half of the 1960s, extensive tax cuts stimulated the economy, leading to some of the highest U.S. growth rates in the post-World War II era. The Federal Reserve supported this policy by expanding the money supply, while keeping interest rates low.

In the late 1960s, taxes were not raised to pay for the Vietnam War, and this deficit-stimulus approach triggered the overheated economy of the inflationary era of the 1970s. Administration policies further pursued fiscal stimulus, supported by the Federal Reserve's expansionary monetary policies. These policies failed to address the inflationary problems.

When significant tax cuts were proposed in 1981, Federal Reserve Chairman Paul Volcker rejected the fiscal stimulus and pushed up interest rates to minimize the inflationary impact. The combination of the two policies caused the most severe recession since World War II, creating a high level of debt for the U.S. economy.

The 1990s administration policies included tax increases and interest rate reductions, leading to a unique 10-year period of expansion.

Apparently, the interplay between fiscal and monetary policy is critical. In the late 1970s, the U.S. economy experienced stagflation as a result of the negative supply shock from the OPEC oil embargo and the rising price of oil. The fiscal stimulus by government to increase GDP was amplified by the Federal Reserve's expansionary monetary policy. This led to extreme inflation because neither policy addressed the fundamental issue of providing incentives to increase supply (after the AS curve had shifted leftward because of the oil shock). Because AS was essentially constant, the aggregate demand stimulus by government raised price levels, aggravated by increased money supplies provided by the Federal Reserve. It took significant interest rate hikes in the early 1980s to cool down the overheating economy.

The current independent functioning of the Federal Reserve, combined with transparent, straightforward monetarist policy rules, has contributed significantly to economic stability.

NOTE N14.5B

Organization of Petroleum Exporting Countries (OPEC)

OPEC is a multinational organization established to coordinate the petroleum policies of its members and also to provide technical and economic aid.

Formally established in 1961, OPEC originally consisted of five countries: Saudi Arabia, Iran, Iraq, Kuwait, and Venezuela. Other countries that have been admitted to OPEC are Qatar (1961), Indonesia and Libya (1962), United Arab Emirates (1967), Algeria (1969), and Nigeria (1971). Ecuador (1973 to 1992) and Gabon (1975 to 1994) have withdrawn from OPEC. OPEC collectively owns 80 percent of the world's proven petroleum reserves, while accounting for 40 percent of its production.

In October 1973, OPEC raised oil prices by 70 percent. In December, prices were raised an additional 130 percent, with Arab countries curtailing production and placing an embargo on shipments to the United States because of its support of Israel in the 1973 Yom Kippur War. The oil-importing nations eventually found non-OPEC sources (e.g., Norway, Mexico, and the United Kingdom) and developed alternative energy sources (coal, gas, and nuclear). OPEC once again reduced production in the early 1980s but was not able to hold prices.

During the 1990s OPEC continued to use production quotas, and it recently has demonstrated greater internal unity as well as improved coordination with non-members (e.g., Mexico, Norway, Oman, and Russia).

International efforts to reduce the burning of fossil fuels are significant, and the long-term expectation is that demand for oil will decline at some point. Recently, OPEC has become more involved in environmental issues.

14.6 Global Economics and Monetary Policy

The Federal Reserve can intervene in the foreign exchange market by selling (or buying) dollars, driving the exchange rate down (or up). Central banks intervene frequently in the *currency market*. This is essentially a short-term policy (to move exchange rates) because the central bank can buy one currency only if it has another currency to sell.

The stability of the dollar's exchange rate is a potential goal of U.S. monetary policy. However, it is impossible to set goals separately for the money supply and the exchange rate because they are determined simultaneously: an increase in the supply of money will prompt a decrease in the exchange rate (because of the higher supply of dollars) unless interest rates are changed (creating a higher demand for dollars).

The benefit of exchange rate targets is that they reduce risky rate fluctuations (facilitating trade and lessening the impact of rate changes on the global earnings of U.S. companies), while money supply targets reduce the risk of inflation and may reflect the needs of the domestic economy. This raises the issue of conflicts between domestic and international policies. Conflicts between internal and external policies develop when a country has a balance of payments deficit during a recession. To correct the deficit requires a rise in the country's price of imports, a decrease in the price of exports, and a rise in interest rates. However, currency depreciation has an inflationary effect and may require contractionary monetary policy, which is inconsistent with a recessionary situation.

NOTE N14.6

European Monetary Union

Under the Maastricht Treaty (1992), members of the European Union agreed to establish a single currency, the *euro*, for those members who satisfied the *economic convergence criteria*:

- Government deficit below 3 percent of GDP
- Government debt not to exceed 60 percent of GDP
- Rate of inflation within 1.5 percent of the three best-performing (inflation) nations
- Long-term interest rates within 2 percent of the three-best performing (inflation) nations
- Exchange rate within European Exchange Rate standards over the last two years (i.e., "normal" rate fluctuations)

Twelve of the fifteen EU members joined: Austria, Belgium, Finland, France, Germany, Greece, Ireland, Italy, Luxembourg, the Netherlands, Portugal, and Spain. Three members (Denmark, Sweden, and the United Kingdom) did not join.

Member nations are not able to follow an independent monetary policy, and a specific interest rate level is set for all euro-zone members. If members experience different economic performance, the only available adjustment mechanism will be domestic prices and unemployment. For example, a country may be forced into recession in order to improve demand for its products and achieve GDP growth.

Based on classical economic thinking (neutrality of money), monetary union does not fundamentally change the policies of nations. Keynesians, in contrast, would consider a union of this nature extremely risky.

The *European Central Bank (ECB)* is responsible for the monetary policy of the 12 euro-zone countries at the supra-national level. It is based in Frankfurt, Germany, and it functions independently of the national governments. The European Central Bank has the exclusive right to issue euro banknotes. The ECB's main objectives, as stated in the 1992 Maastricht Treaty, are to maintain price stability (less than 2 percent annual increase in the harmonized consumer price index) and, subject to price stability, to support the economic policies of the members of the EMU.

EXAMPLE: Convergence "Price Developments"*

The *European Central Bank* (ECB) closely monitors the degree of *sustainable convergence* of non-euro EU-member states to assess compliance of requirements by national central banks (NCBs) to become an integral part of the euro system. Potential candidates for joining the system are the Czech Republic, Estonia, Cyprus, Latvia, Lithuania, Hungary, Malta, Poland, Slovenia, Slovakia, and Sweden. Countries are specifically urged to put a high priority on the integrity and quality of government finance statistics and ensure that those statistics are not vulnerable to political and electoral cycles:

> [The objective] is the achievement of a high degree of price stability; this will be apparent from a rate of inflation which is close to that of, at most, the three best-performing Member States in terms of price stability. [. . .] The criterion shall mean that a Member State has a price performance that is sustainable and an average rate of inflation, observed over a period of one year before the examination, that does not exceed 1½ percentage points that of, at most, the three best performing Member States in terms of price stability. Inflation shall be measured by means of the consumer price index on a comparable basis, taking into account differences in national definitions. (From: European Community Treaty provisions)

The 2004 Convergence report states that the reference value for price stability is the unweighted average of the following three countries: Finland (0.4 percent), Denmark (1.0 percent), and Sweden (1.3 percent). [The result for Lithuania (− 0.2 percent) is considered an outlier and is therefore not taken into account for the reference value.] The average rate is 0.9 percent and, adding 1.5 percent, the reference value is 2.4 percent. The Czech Republic, Estonia, Cyprus, Lithuania, and Sweden had inflation rates below the reference value, while Poland (2.5 percent) and Malta (2.6 percent) were just above the reference value. Other countries were

*Source: ECB Convergence report, 2004

considerably above the reference value: Slovenia (4.1 percent), Latvia (4.9 percent), Hungary (6.5 percent), and Slovakia (8.4 percent).

14.7   Hints

H14.1   The *Consumer Price Index (CPI)*, an important indicator of inflation, is estimated to overstate the rate of inflation by about 1 percentage point. This is caused by various positive price biases. Among them are the inclusion of new products (replacing older ones) in the CPI's basket of products and failing to take note of changed spending patterns, such as a move to lower-priced substitutes and people switching to lower-cost discount stores. (See also Chapter 3.)

H14.2   The *Taylor rule* is a simple rule for setting the short-term interest rate with the objective of keeping inflation stable. The rule states that

$$\text{Short-term interest} = 2.0 + \text{inflation} + \text{inflation deviation}$$
$$\text{from target} + \text{``output gap''}$$

The number 2.0 is the historical real interest rate, to which today's inflation is added to yield the long-term real average. If inflation is above its target, the deviation from the target is added, and if the economy is operating above its long-term capacity, then the "output gap" is added. Taylor wrote about this rule both as an approximate description of what central banks actually do when they set rates and as a possible prescription for monetary policy. Central banks follow some kind of Taylor rule, and the rule is a benchmark for judging actual policies.

The Taylor rule is a neo-Keynesian rule, focusing on price stability and stabilizing the business cycle. It targets the interest rate while letting the monetary base fluctuate. Although the Federal Reserve has not formally endorsed the Taylor rule, it is a close description of the Federal Reserve's policies.

H14.3   Monetary policy is considered to be a primary tool to control aggregate demand, and consequently to manage the rate of inflation. This demonstrates the increased importance of modern monetary policy over the Keynesian approach, which favored fiscal policy, with monetary policy relegated to a supporting role.

H14.4   The *prime rate* is the rate of interest charged for short-term loans by U.S. commercial banks to their best corporate customers. This rate forms the basis for U.S. commercial interest rates. The prime rate began to increase—after the relatively stable 1950s and early 1960s—during

the buildup of the Vietnam War in the late 1960s. The next spike (over 10 percent) was caused by the first OPEC oil embargo in 1973, followed by the 19 percent spike caused by the second oil embargo and exacerbated by the Federal Reserve's tight money policy. With some ups and downs, the prime rate essentially declined from 1990 until 2003. Rates in 2003 were similar to rates in the late 1950s. Recently, the prime rate has been rising again.

Quiz

Choose the one best answer for each question.

Q14.1   Which of the following statements about price stability is true?
   (a) Price stability is a secondary goal of the Federal Reserve's policy.
   (b) Price stability means that price-level changes must equal zero.
   (c) Price stability means that wage rates are locked in because of long-term contracts.
   (d) Price stability is reached when changes in the Consumer Price Index are between 0 and 3 percent.
   (e) Price stability is only a goal for the government's fiscal policy.

Q14.2   The primary responsibility for U.S. monetary policy lies with
   (a) the Federal Reserve System.
   (b) Congress.
   (c) the president.
   (d) the House of Representatives and the Federal Reserve System.
   (e) the U.S. Senate and the Federal Reserve System.

Q14.3   A policy that uniquely responds to economic events is
   (a) a contractionary policy.
   (b) a fixed-rule policy.
   (c) a feedback-rule policy.
   (d) a discretionary policy.
   (e) an expansionary policy.

Q14.4   If the government's anti-inflationary policy is not viewed as credible, it results in

(a) self-fulfilling inflation.
(b) deflation.
(c) disinflation.
(d) reflation.
(e) stable prices.

Q14.5 "Increase the quantity of money in a recession" is a
(a) monetarist fixed rule.
(b) monetarist feedback rule.
(c) monetarist discretionary rule.
(d) Keynesian fixed rule.
(e) Keynesian feedback rule.

Q14.6 A fixed-rule policy that fixes the growth rate of the money supply at 3 percent per year
(a) ensures that cost-push inflation does not occur.
(b) counteracts temporary increases in aggregate demand.
(c) counteracts temporary decreases in real output.
(d) offsets aggregate supply fluctuations.
(e) has no impact on GDP.

Q14.7 The inside lag of fiscal policy is _____, and the inside lag of monetary policy is _____.
(a) short; short
(b) long; short
(c) short; long
(d) variable; short
(e) long; long

Q14.8 How can the government reduce inflation and not increase unemployment at the same time?
(a) By having a Federal Reserve anti-inflation policy that is considered credible by people
(b) By a surprise reduction in the discount rate
(c) In no way
(d) By having a Federal Reserve anti-inflation policy that is not considered credible by people
(e) By having a Federal Reserve increase in the discount rate that is not anticipated

Q14.9 The prime rate is
(a) the basic interest rate on consumer mortgages.
(b) the rate the Federal Reserve charges banks.

(c) the rate banks charge their best commercial customers for short-term loans.

    (d) the rate banks charge each other for short-term loans.

    (e) the basic rate on consumer savings accounts.

Q14.10 The 1970s was a period of stagflation (inflation and recession) in the
U.S. economy. What policy mix by the government and the Federal Reserve contributed to the high inflation?

    (a) Expansionary fiscal; contractionary monetary

    (b) Expansionary fiscal; expansionary monetary

    (c) Contractionary fiscal; no monetary policy

    (d) Contractionary fiscal; contractionary monetary

    (e) Contractionary fiscal; expansionary monetary

Q14.11 Which of the following would lead the dollar to depreciate against
the yen?

    (a) The Fed buying dollars

    (b) An increase in American interest rates

    (c) A decrease in interest rates in Japan

    (d) The expectation that the dollar will depreciate against
the yen

    (e) A decrease in American interest rates

Q14.12 If the Fed buys U.S. dollars, the exchange rate

    (a) rises.

    (b) does not change.

    (c) falls.

    (d) falls or does not change, depending on the impact of
Fed's actions on the demand for and supply of
dollars.

    (e) changes, depending on the impact of Fed's actions on
the demand for and supply of dollars.

Quiz Answers

Q14.1 (d). Because the CPI has a positive bias of about + 1.0 percent (i.e., the CPI
overestimates inflation) and because very minor inflation is acceptable, any number for the CPI between 0 and 3 percent is considered to represent price stability.

Q14.2 (a). The Federal Reserve System, an independent federal institution, has
the sole responsibility for U.S. monetary policy. The Federal Reserve reports

regularly to Congress (i.e., the legislative branch) and stays in close touch with the administration (i.e., the executive branch).

Q14.3 (d). Policies responding in unique ways to events are discretionary in nature.

Q14.4 (a). If anti-inflation policy is not credible, people believe that inflation will persist and bid up wage rates, causing a self-fulfilling inflation. Note that *reflation* refers to a Keynesian policy of increasing aggregate demand, such as in deflationary economies.

Q14.5 (e). The quantity of money depends on the state of the economy (a feedback rule), and it represents a Keynesian policy. Monetarists believe that economies will return to potential without interference (similar to the Classical School) and believe that increasing the money supply to move aggregate demand will cause increasing instability.

Q14.6 (a). Fixed rules specifying low rates of monetary growth have the major benefit of eliminating persistent high rates of inflation. This is a basic monetarist rule that doesn't seek to influence aggregate demand or supply.

Q14.7 (b). The Federal Reserve can implement monetary policy quickly (e.g., through daily open market operations) with a short inside lag; fiscal policy requires Congress to pass new tax laws, a time-consuming process causing a long inside lag. The difference in inside lags complicates the coordination of monetary and fiscal policy.

Q14.8 (a). A credible, announced policy to reduce inflation is required for this policy to be effective. Otherwise people will bid up wages and self-fulfilling inflation will start.

Q14.9 (c). The prime rate is the rate that banks charge their best commercial clients for short-term loans. Please note that (b) refers to the Federal Reserve's discount rate, while (d) is the federal funds rate.

Q14.10 (b). At a time of limited output (a rigid AS curve that was below potential GDP after the oil shock), the combination of expansionary fiscal and expansionary monetary policy greatly contributed to price-level increases.

Q14.11 (d). This situation actually occurred in the mid-1990s when the expectation of depreciation led to actual depreciation.

Q14.12 (a). When the Fed buys dollars, it increases the demand for dollars, raising the exchange rate.

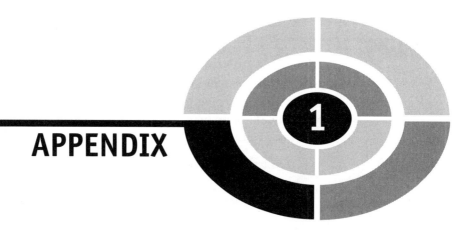

1

The Elasticity of Demand and Supply

The Law of Demand states that quantity demanded goes down as price increases. A supplier wants to know more precisely what happens to revenues if the price goes down (or up). For example, if demand is very sensitive to price, then the quantity demanded decreases "a lot" if price changes "just a bit." More specifically, a price hike of 10 percent may decrease quantity demanded by 30 percent, and the producer's change in revenue (price × quantity) would be −20 percent (i.e., 10 percent–30 percent). In other words, the producer needs to be careful about price increases when quantity demanded is very price-sensitive. (Quiz: What about the impact of price decreases if demand is very price sensitive?) To measure this sensitivity, critical for pricing goods and services, we use price elasticities.

Strategic and Tactical Pricing by Firms

A practical example of the use of price elasticities is strategic (and tactical) pricing by firms. For a fixed cost function, profit maximization involves finding the price that maximizes revenues, that is, at what point on the demand curve is demand unit-elastic?

The formula for elasticity (where Δ means "change of") is

$$\text{Elasticity } (y \text{ relative to } x) = \% \text{ change } y/\% \text{ change } x$$
$$= (\Delta y/y)/(\Delta x/x)$$
$$= (\Delta y/\Delta x) \times (x/y)$$

Assume the demand curve is Quantity (Q) = 110 − Price (P),
Then: Elasticity = $(\Delta Q/\Delta P) \times (P/Q) = -1 \times (P/Q)$ or:

$$\text{Elasticity} \begin{cases} > -1, \text{ if } P < Q \\ = -1, \text{ if } P = Q \\ < -1, \text{ if } P > Q \end{cases}$$

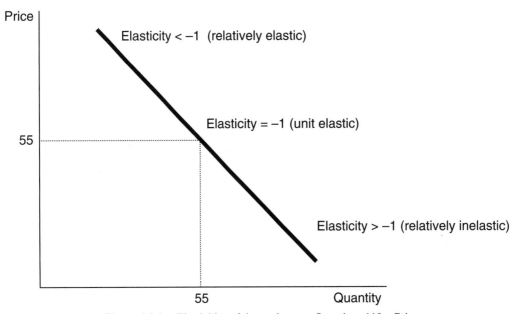

Figure A1-1. Elasticities of demand curve: Quantity = 110 − Price.

Elasticity measures the percent change responsiveness to a percent change, for example, the percent change of quantity demanded resulting from a percent change in price. Because elasticities are percent change comparisons, they are always relative to a base point on the curve, (x_1, y_1). This could be the midpoint of the curve or somewhere else.

Demand (supply) is *relatively elastic** when the percent change in quantity demanded (supplied) exceeds the percent change in price. Demand (supply) is *relatively inelastic* when the percent change in quantity demanded (supplied) is smaller than the percent change in price. Demand (supply) is *unit elastic* when the percent change in quantity demanded (supplied) is equal to the percent change in price.

Along a linear demand curve, there are price ranges over which demand is elastic, unit elastic, and inelastic (see Fig. A1-1 for an example).

Example (Price-Elastic and Price-Inelastic Demand)

The demand for necessity items (e.g., food staples, basic utilities) is relatively inelastic, because we need to buy a minimum quantity, irrespective of the price. Demand for luxuries (e.g., dining in an exclusive restaurant, international airline travel) will be relatively elastic because we are likely to give up some discretionary expenses if prices increase.

Other types of elasticities are labor demand elasticity to wages and demand elasticity to income.

Elasticity is *not* the same as the *slope* of the demand (supply) curve $Q = Q(P)$.

$$\text{Elasticity} = (\% \text{ change in } y)/(\% \text{ change in } x)$$

$$= (\Delta y/y)/(\Delta x/x) = (\Delta y/\Delta x) \times (x/y)$$

Therefore, the elasticity is equal to the slope $\Delta y/\Delta x$ only if $x = y$. The slope of a linear demand curve is constant, but its elasticities are not.

---

*Note: For ease of notation, we ignore the negative sign on the demand curve, so we are actually considering the so-called absolute value of the changes.

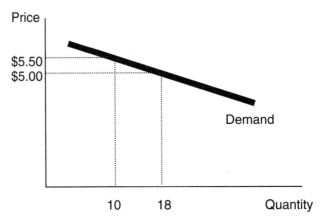

Figure A1-2. The price elasticity of demand.

Quiz

Please choose one best answer.

QA1.1   With a relatively elastic demand curve, if price increases by 20 percent,
the quantity will most likely
(a) decrease by less than 20 percent.
(b) decrease by exactly 20 percent.
(c) decrease by more than 20 percent.
(d) increase by less than 20 percent.
(e) increase by more than 20 percent.

QA1.2   Assume a linear demand curve $Q=200-P$, with $Q=$ quantity demanded and $P=$ price. The demand curve is _____ when
$P=Q=100$.
(a) unit elastic
(b) relatively inelastic
(c) perfectly inelastic
(d) perfectly elastic
(e) relatively elastic

See Fig. A1-2.

QA1.3   Assume a profit-maximizing company is considering raising the price
of its single product by 10 percent (from $5.00 to $5.50). If total costs
are constant at $30, this price change will

(a) increase the company's profits but not to their maximum.
(b) maximize profits.
(c) leave profits unchanged.
(d) decrease profits.
(e) show that the negative of the percent change in demand is smaller than the percent change in price.

Quiz Answers

QA1.1 (c). The demand curve is relatively elastic when the percent change in demand is larger than the (negative of the) percent change in price.

QA1.2 (a).

$$\text{Elasticity} = (\Delta Q/\Delta P) \times (P/Q) \text{ (from the definition of elasticity)}$$

The demand curve is $P = 200 - Q$, which can be written as $Q = 200 - P$. That means that $\Delta Q/\Delta P = -1$, the slope of the curve $Q = 200 - P$. Next, we plug $\Delta Q/\Delta P = -1$ into the elasticity formula.

$$\text{Elasticity} = -1 \times (P/Q) = -1 \quad \text{if } P = Q = 100$$

The demand curve is therefore unit elastic if $P = Q = 100$.

QA1.3 (d). The new revenue will be $10 \times \$5.50 = \$55$, with profits $\$55 - \$30 = \$25$. The revenue at a price of $\$5$ is $18 \times \$5 = \$90$, with profits $\$90 - \$30 = \$60$. Profits decrease by $\$35$ when price is increased from $\$5.00$ to $\$5.50$.

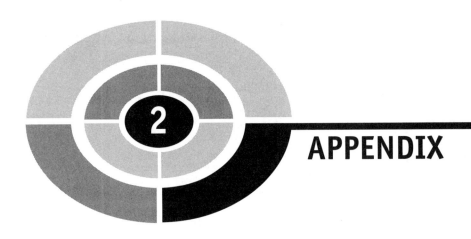

Measuring GDP, the Expenditure and the Income Methods

National income accounting is used to estimate the economy's output or income. The nation's output and income are identical because the value of the economy's output and the income earned producing this output are equivalent (see the sections about the circular flow). Therefore, there are two ways to calculate GDP.

The Expenditure Method

GDP consists of four major expenditure groups:

- Consumption expenditures (C)
- Gross private domestic investment (I_G)

- Government purchases (G)
- Net exports (X_N)

These expenditures are transformed into income when they are paid out in employee compensation, rents, interest, and so on.

In national income accounting, the amount expended on this year's output is equal to the money income derived from production of this year's output.

The Income Method

Measuring GDP by using the income method consists of adding income from domestic production and sale of final goods and services. The income items are

- Compensation of employees (the sum of the wages and salaries and the wage and salary supplements)
- Rents
- Interest (interest payments by businesses, excluding interest payments by government)
- Proprietors' income (profits of unincorporated firms)
- Corporate profits, consisting of
  - Corporate income taxes
  - Dividends
  - Undistributed profits
- Additions to balance expenditures with income
  - Indirect taxes (initial income, redistributed to the government)
  - Depreciation (initial income, deducted when accounting for profits)
  - Net foreign factor income (reflects income from domestic output, irrespective of domestic ownwership)

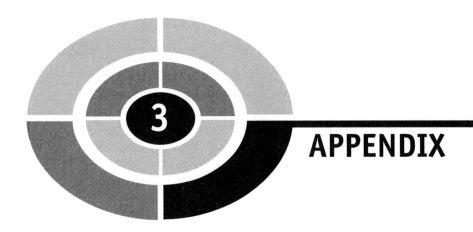

A Brief History of Economic Models

First There Were the French

A group of eighteenth-century French economists called the Physiocrats believed in the *natural order of society* and viewed the state's role as simply that of preserving property and upholding this natural order. The Physiocrats, led by François Quesnay, coined the phrase *laissez-faire, laissez-passer* ("let it work, let it go") to condemn any interference with industry, except in breaking up private monopolies. This belief greatly influenced contemporary Anglo-Saxon economic thinking, in particular Adam Smith, who considered dedicating his famous 1776 *Inquiry* to Quesnay, who died just two years before its publication.

Ever since Smith's book, classical economists have supported the principle of government's nonintervention in economic affairs. Interestingly, there are indications in Smith's writing that he was not convinced that perfect markets would produce perfect results.

Adam Smith's Unposed Question

Smith believed that the economy was harmonious and required a minimum of government interference. Although each individual was motivated by self-interest, all individuals acted for the good of the whole, guided by a "hidden" (or "invisible") hand made possible by free competition. However, Smith was aware of the forces that were at work to limit competition:

> People of the same trade seldom meet together for merriment and diversion, but the conversation ends in a conspiracy against the public, or on some contrivance to raise prices. It is impossible indeed to prevent such meetings by any law which either could be executed, or would be consistent with liberty and justice. But though the law cannot hinder people of the same trade from sometimes assembling together, it ought to do nothing to facilitate such assemblies, much less render them necessary.

This fragment suggests Adam Smith's "unposed question": what *are* the appropriate rules and institutions that secure the benefits of competition? Some of the triumphs of macroeconomics in the last century are the institutions (e.g., Federal Reserve, SEC, WTO) and their rules that govern today's economy.

Although Smith saw the early signs of the Industrial Revolution in his native Scotland, he did not grasp its significance for capital accumulation (and technology development). Also, Smith discussed the concept of opportunity cost but did not develop a theory of comparative advantage for international trade, which was still in its infancy in the eighteenth century.

Keynes Emphasizes the Short Run

During the 1930s Great Depression, U.K. policy to increase the growth of GDP and employment initially relied on classical economic thinking and involved asking the labor unions for wage concessions to improve the prospects of higher production. Keynes pointed out that in the short run, output prices (and some input prices) were essentially fixed, and therefore output itself was price-inflexible. As a result, the impulse to grow GDP had to come from aggregate demand, which could be provided by stimulating government expenditures. Because of the extreme deflation of the Great Depression era (low interest rates, low prices, and low expectations for growth), Keynes had prescribed a potential solution that classical economics could not provide in the short run. Keynes was quoted as saying,

"In the long run we're all dead." His 1930s prescription has become less relevant in the last 50 years, as the extreme nature of the Great Depression has not been repeated.

Milton Friedman Revives the Classics

Among his many contributions to economic theory, Friedman's main work has been the theoretical and empirical development of the quantity theory of money. Extending the $MV = PY$ quantity equation, Friedman's monetarist approach advocates strict control of the money supply. This implies a simple rule for yearly money growth to limit inflation. Objecting to stabilization policies aimed at dampening the business cycle, he became an early pioneer of policy effectiveness theories.

Theories Based on Rational Expectations

Most of Friedman's views have now been generally accepted, but recent theories have found more compelling foundations of classical theories in rational expectations (and microeconomics). *New classical economics* argues that governments can expect to have an influence on the economy only if their actions are unanticipated. Therefore, government demand intervention is ineffective, even in the short run. Growth can be enhanced only by influencing supply. The new classical theory has become an influential doctrine in macroeconomics.

New Keynesianism, like new classical theory, is based on rational expectations. It stresses the existence of institutions that may quite rationally lead to price rigidity. The New Keynesians do not believe that money is neutral, but believe that it can have an impact on real economic outcomes, as well as nominal ones. The business cycle can be partially explained by changes in aggregate demand, so that even anticipated changes can have an impact.

Supply-Side Economics

Demand-side economics, such as Keynesian policies, focuses on regulating aggregate demand and the supporting fiscal and monetary policies. In contrast, *supply-side economics* aims at policies and measures to stimulate production.

Supply-side economics developed as a complement to monetarism. It addresses the factors affecting the supply of goods and the supply of labor. Supply-side economists deny the role of stabilization policies but focus on incentive policies instead, including tax cuts, antimonopoly regulations, antiunion measures to ensure wage flexibility, limiting the growth of money to limit inflation, increasing the mobility of labor, and cutting benefits to those out of work.

Supply-side economic policies rely on the direct use of incentives. This could be a reduction in tax rates to provide incentives to work, save, and invest, stimulating aggregate supply. Tight monetary control to limit inflation is another hallmark of supply-side economics.

Summary

Many interpretations of macroeconomics have developed since the days of Quesnay and Smith. See Fig. A3-1 for a summary of major economic theories.

Despite many variations, most of these models stayed close to classical economics. Even Keynes did not disagree with classical price dynamics, as he pointed out that the special case of the Great Depression's extreme deflation and price rigidity hampered classical price adjustment. Recent economic theories have incorporated microeconomics and rational expectations theory, and it appears that new classical theory and supply-side economics (theories that put major emphasis on the supply factors in the economy) are alive and well.

What would Jean-Baptiste Say ("supply determines demand") have to say about this?

Figure A3-1. A summary of macroeconomic models.

Theory	Key Ideas	Fiscal Policy	Monetary Policy
Neoclassical	Pure competition in markets and price mechanism ensure that economy reaches full-employment potential. Economy is fairly stable and adjusts naturally; fine-tuning is not needed and may be detrimental to growth and stability. Restates classical *laissez-faire, laissez-passer* arguments.	Hands-off approach. If GDP is not at its potential, it will be a temporary deviation, and the flexibility of the price mechanism will ensure that potential GDP will ultimately be reached.	Money will influence only nominal values, not any real values (classical dichotomy). Monetary policy ineffective (i.e., does not affect real GDP) but may be detrimental by changing price level and causing inflation.
Keynesian	Economy is inherently unstable and may stagnate below full employment when savings are insufficient and/or not absorbed by investment. Short-term price rigidity (product prices, wages) prevents neoclassical price adjustment to full employment. Aggregate supply is constant in the short run because of fixed prices; therefore, aggregate demand will determine GDP. The expectations (e.g., pessimism) of consumers and producers play a role in economic decisions.	Government should follow deficit-stimulus policy to get out of recessions because stimulating aggregate demand is the key to achieving higher GDP. Increased government expenditures provide a stronger multiplier impact on GDP than tax decreases. Fiscal policy is the primary tool, with monetary policy in a supporting role.	Money is not neutral: its expansion supports the increase in aggregate demand needed to reach full employment. In addition, money has an indirect impact on GDP growth: the increased money supply lowers the interest rate and increases investment, fueling aggregate demand and therefore GDP.
Monetarist	Money, rather than aggregate demand, matters, and the supply of money is the primary tool to achieve economic stability.	"Do nothing!" Monetarists view fiscal policy as ineffective and potentially destabilizing. Increases in government spending will "crowd out" private spending, leaving no impact on real GDP.	The steady increase of the money supply should parallel the average growth of real GDP. Any activist monetary policy that deviates from this rule may create instability and fuel inflation.

Continued on next page . . .

Continued . . .

Theory	Key Ideas	Fiscal Policy	Monetary Policy
New classical	Accepts rational expectations theory. In addition, accepts policy effectiveness theorem: if prices are flexible and people have rational expectations, only unanticipated ("surprise") policy will have an impact,	Anticipated fiscal policies will be ineffective; policies designed to increase aggregate demand are not going to affect real GDP.	Anticipated expansionary money supply policies will be inflationary because people expect changes and take them into account. Anti-inflationary monetary policy must be credible to be effective.
New Keynesian	Accepts rational expectations theory. In the short run, conditions for policy effectiveness theorem do not apply because there are rational reasons for price rigidity, e.g., contracts, menu costs, labor unions. Because policy effectiveness theorem doesn't apply, anticipated policies can have an impact. Agrees with new classical theory that ultimately, in the long run, prices are flexible and GDP will tend to potential GDP.	Increasing aggregate demand can be partially effective in increasing GDP, because of price inflexibility	Monetary policy supports fiscal policy to increase aggregate demand.
Supply-side	In contrast to Keynesian demand-side policies, this theory focuses on supply-side policies, including incentives to supply goods and services and to supply labor. Supply-side economics complements monetarism.	Rejects need for stabilization policies. Tax reductions to increase supply of products (lower corporate taxes) and labor (lower income tax). Supply-side economics may also include extra government spending for job education and subsidies for technology innovation.	See monetarism.

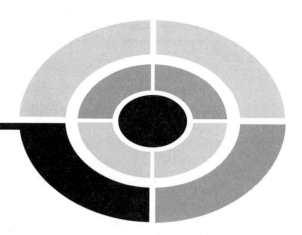

Final Test 1
Questions

Choose the one best answer for each question.

01T01.　Which of the following is a typical macroeconomic topic?
    (a) The impact of the price of crude oil on wholesale gasoline prices
    (b) The pricing decisions of a company
    (c) The rate of inflation
    (d) The consumption and saving behavior of households
    (e) The growth of the computer industry

01T02.　What is the primary goal of an economic system?
    (a) The organization of the production, distribution, exchange, and consumption of goods and services
    (b) To maximize profits for producers
    (c) To determine the flow and distribution of money
    (d) To produce, distribute, and exchange goods and services in the fastest possible way
    (e) To maximize trade with foreign countries

01T03.　What causes the production possibilities curve (see Fig. T1-1) to shift outward?

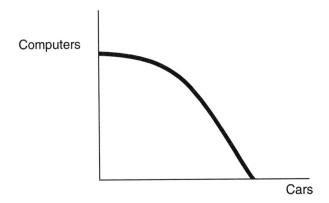

Figure T1-1. Production possibilities curve.

(a) Reopening computer plants
(b) Using machinery for making computers instead of making cars
(c) Improving manufacturing efficiency for computers
(d) Rehiring workers in the computer or car industry
(e) Using machinery for making cars instead of making computers

01T04. Which of the following is included in the circular flow of the economy?
(a) Firms buy outputs from households.
(b) Firms sell factor services to households.
(c) Households sell outputs to firms.
(d) Households buy factor services from firms.
(e) Households sell factor services to firms.

01T05. Which of the following is required for the mutual benefit of trade between two countries?
(a) Decreasing marginal returns in production
(b) Absolute advantage in the production of a good or service
(c) Each country being able to produce more of one product than the other country
(d) Comparative advantage in the production of a good or service
(e) Absolute and comparative advantage in the production of a good or service

01T06. Say's Law states that
    (a) demand goes down when price goes up.
    (b) supply goes up when price goes up.
    (c) supply creates its own demand.
    (d) demand creates its own supply.
    (e) supply and demand are always independent of each other.

01T07. If nominal GDP grew by 16 percent and real GDP grew by 5 percent in the same year, inflation would be
    (a) 7 percent.
    (b) 8 percent.
    (c) 11 percent.
    (d) 15 percent.
    (e) −11 percent.

01T08. The Consumer Price Index (CPI) measures which of the following?
    (a) The economy's price level
    (b) The gross domestic product deflator
    (c) Changes in the real gross domestic product
    (d) Weighted prices of a selection of consumer goods and services
    (e) Changes in the economy's cost level

01T09. A tariff on foreign cars imported into the United States will
    (a) benefit consumers.
    (b) benefit domestic producers.
    (c) benefit both consumers and domestic producers.
    (d) lead to a higher quantity of domestic and imported cars.
    (e) lower the price of domestic cars.

01T10. Which of the following transactions would represent an addition to a nation's current gross domestic product?
    (a) Mr. Jones purchases government bonds.
    (b) A father sells his computer to his son.
    (c) A retailer buys imported clothes.
    (d) A corporation sells trucks from last year's inventory.
    (e) A U.S. defense contractor manufactures a satellite for the government.

01T11. Which of the following does *not* cause a shift in aggregate demand?
    (a) Consumption
    (b) Imports

(c) Prices

(d) Investment

(e) Exports

01T12. A decrease in the labor force participation rate will
(a) increase government spending.
(b) decrease government spending
(c) have no impact on the rate of unemployment.
(d) make it easier to reduce the rate of unemployment.
(e) make it harder to reduce the rate of unemployment.

01T13. The aggregate demand curve is
(a) the (horizontal) summation of factor demand for all firms.
(b) the (horizontal) summation of all households' demand curves.
(c) not found by adding product demand curves.
(d) the aggregate of demand curves for intermediate goods and services.
(e) the (vertical) summation of all households' demand curves.

01T14. What causes the aggregate demand (AD) curve to shift to the right?
(a) An increase in personal income tax
(b) A decrease in government defense purchases
(c) Expectations of future shortages of goods
(d) A decrease in exports
(e) Expectations of future deflation

01T15. Assume that imports increased and, at the same time, new technology has increased labor productivity. What will certainly result?
(a) The price level goes up.
(b) The price level goes down.
(c) The price level doesn't change.
(d) Real GDP decreases.
(e) Real GDP increases.

01T16. Classical economists do *not* believe that
(a) Say's Law is true.
(b) wages are flexible in the short run.
(c) government needs to stimulate aggregate demand.
(d) input and output prices stay in line, fluctuating quickly.
(e) money affects nominal values only, not real values.

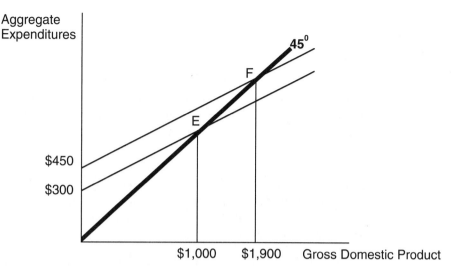

Figure T1-2. A Keynesian cross.

01T17. Long-run AS/AD equilibrium occurs when
(a) the AS curve is horizontal.
(b) GDP is at full-employment level.
(c) GDP is at full physical capacity level.
(d) Unemployment equals 0 percent.
(e) Structural unemployment equals 0 percent.

01T18. (See Fig. T1-2.) Equilibrium at *E* occurs for a closed economy with no government spending. If government spending results in equilibrium at *F*, which of the following is true?
(a) Government spending is $900, and the spending multiplier is 1.
(b) Government spending is $150, and the spending multiplier is 6.
(c) Government spending and GDP increase by $900 each.
(d) Consumption and GDP increase by $900 each.
(e) Consumption increases by $900, and government spending is $150.

01T19. What causes the largest increase in aggregate demand (AD)?
(a) A $1,000 increase in government expenditures
(b) A $1,000 increase in taxes
(c) A $1,000 decrease in taxes

(d) A $1,000 increase in government expenditures, together with a $1,000 decrease in taxes

(e) A $1,000 increase in government expenditures, together with a $1,000 increase in taxes

01T20. The economy's potential output equals $3,000,000. If current equilibrium output equals $2,500,000 and the marginal propensity to consume equals 0.5, what would a Keynesian economist be expected to recommend?

(a) Increase government spending by $250,000.

(b) Increase government spending by $1,000,000.

(c) Increase government spending by $500,000.

(d) Decrease taxes by $250,000.

(e) Decrease taxes by $500,000.

01T21. If exports increase and the economy is operating in the intermediate (upward-sloping) range of the aggregate supply (AS) curve, what happens to the price level, output, and the unemployment rate?

	Price Level	Output	Unemployment Rate
(a)	Increase	Decrease	Increase
(b)	Increase	Decrease	Decrease
(c)	Decrease	Decrease	Increase
(d)	Increase	Increase	Increase
(e)	Increase	Increase	Decrease

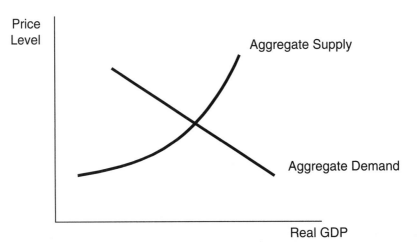

Figure T1-3. Aggregate supply and demand.

01T22. Which of the following most likely causes stagflation?
  (a) The aggregate demand (AD) curve shifts to the left
      when the economy is in the classical range of the
      aggregate supply (AS) curve.
  (b) The aggregate demand (AD) curve shifts to the
      right when the economy is in the classical range of
      the aggregate supply (AS) curve.
  (c) The aggregate demand (AD) curve shifts to the right
      when the economy is in the Keynesian range of the
      aggregate supply (AS) curve.
  (d) The aggregate supply (AS) curve shifts to the left.
  (e) The aggregate supply (AS) curve shifts to the right.

01T23. Based on Fig. T1-3, what is the likely impact of a decrease in world oil
        supplies on real GDP and the price level?

	Real GDP	**Price Level**
(a)	Decrease	Increase
(b)	Decrease	Decrease
(c)	Increase	Decrease
(d)	No change	Increase
(e)	Increase	Increase

01T24. A fractional reserve banking system means that
  (a) no loan by the bank can exceed 10 percent of bank
      deposits.
  (b) bank loans over $1 million require authorization by
      the Federal Reserve.
  (c) a bank is not allowed to lend all of its deposits.
  (d) the Federal Reserve has the right to audit U.S. banks.
  (e) the Federal Reserve is required to keep a fraction of
      the money supply in reserve.

01T25. Which of the following groups will *not* be hurt by inflation?
  (a) Individuals on fixed incomes
  (b) Borrowers at fixed interest rates
  (c) Individuals with savings earning fixed interest rates
  (d) Retail store owners
  (e) Lenders at fixed interest rates

01T26. If the excess reserves in the banking system are $1,000 and the reserve
        requirement is 25 percent, what is the maximum expansion of the
        money supply?

    (a) $250
    (b) $1,000
    (c) $2,500
    (d) $4,000
    (e) $5,000

01T27. If people decide to hold more money as currency (i.e., cash), banks will be
    (a) less able to expand credit.
    (b) unaffected.
    (c) more able to expand credit.
    (d) more able to decrease aggregate supply.
    (e) less able to decrease aggregate supply.

01T28. The Federal Reserve's monetary policy supports fiscal policy when
    (a) the money supply is increased when government spending goes down.
    (b) the money supply is decreased when government spending goes up.
    (c) the discount rate is increased when government spending goes up.
    (d) the discount rate is decreased when government spending goes down.
    (e) the money supply is increased when government spending goes up.

01T29. In a fractional banking system, if people increase their holdings of currency (i.e., cash), what is likely to go up?
    (a) The price level
    (b) The rate of interest
    (c) Disposable income
    (d) Employment
    (e) The discount rate

01T30. When consumers hold extra money (cash) rather than bonds because they expect interest rates to increase in the future, for what purpose are they holding money?
    (a) Medium of exchange
    (b) Unexpected expenditures
    (c) Illiquidity
    (d) Speculation
    (e) Transaction requirements

01T31. What is likely to happen if the Federal Reserve lowers the reserve requirement?

(a) Firms purchase more plants and equipment.
(b) The value of the dollar increases.
(c) There is an increased capital inflow from abroad.
(d) The rate of saving increases.
(e) Unemployment increases.

01T32. The intermediate (upward-sloping) section of the short-run aggregate supply (SAS) curve is the result of which of the following?
(a) Input prices being less flexible than output prices
(b) Full capacity of production output
(c) Excess capacity of production output
(d) Highly responsive aggregate demand (AD)
(e) Highly unresponsive aggregate demand (AD)

01T33. The long-run classical aggregate supply (LAS) curve is
(a) negatively sloped.
(b) positively sloped.
(c) vertical at the physical limit for output.
(d) horizontal at market price.
(e) vertical at full-employment output.

01T34. What best explains how an economy could have high inflation and high unemployment at the same time?
(a) Government increases spending but doesn't increase taxes.
(b) Supply shocks cause factor prices to increase.
(c) Government increases taxes but doesn't increase spending.
(d) Inflationary expectations decline.
(e) A high number of discouraged workers leave the labor force.

01T35. The short-run aggregate supply (SAS) curve shifts to the left with an increase in
(a) labor productivity.
(b) technology innovation.
(c) purchases of U.S. securities by the Federal Reserve.
(d) the cost of production inputs.
(e) the money multiplier.

01T36. An increase in aggregate supply is caused by an increase in
(a) government spending.
(b) consumer spending.

(c) interest rates.

(d) wage rates.

(e) labor productivity.

01T37. What best explains a decline in potential GDP?

(a) The discovery of new oil fields

(b) Negative net investment

(c) An increase in population growth

(d) A decrease in wage rates

(e) Deflation

01T38. Which of the following is most likely to improve the standard of living?

(a) An increase in the number of depository institutions

(b) Higher taxes

(c) Higher productivity of labor

(d) A decrease in the money supply

(e) An increase in the labor force

01T39. A trade surplus must be offset elsewhere in the

(a) current account balance or capital account balance only.

(b) capital account balance only.

(c) current account balance only.

(d) merchandise balance of trade only.

(e) merchandise balance of trade or current account balance only.

01T40. Which of the following will shift the demand for the Chinese currency, the yuan, to the left?

(a) Expectations that the yuan will increase in value

(b) A relative increase in China's interest rates vs. those of other countries

(c) A relatively lower rate of inflation in China vs. that of other countries

(d) An increase in income elsewhere relative to China

(e) A decrease in foreign demand for furniture made in China

01T41. Two countries, originally producing two commodities for domestic consumption, now specialize production according to comparative advantage and trade with each other. What is the result?

(a) Production will be more efficient in one country but less efficient in the other.

(b) The two countries will become more self-sufficient.

(c) Unemployment increases in at least one country.

(d) Both countries will be better off.

(e) Both countries will be producing inefficiently.

01T42. Which of the following creates the trade-off described by the Phillips Curve?

(a) The AS curve moves to the right.

(b) Input costs go up, together with increased unemployment.

(c) The AD curve moves to the right.

(d) GDP increases, while price levels go up.

(e) The AS curve moves to the left.

01T43. If the Federal Reserve's policy is to decrease interest rates, how will international capital flows be affected?

(a) Short-run capital outflows from the United States will decrease.

(b) Short-run capital inflows to the United States will decrease.

(c) Short-run capital inflows to the United States will not change.

(d) Long-run capital outflows from the United States will decrease.

(e) Long-run capital inflows to the United States will increase.

01T44. In the short run, what happens to the demand for U.S. dollars and the international value of the dollar if worldwide investors purchase U.S. securities?

	Demand for Dollars	International Value of the Dollar
(a)	Decrease	Decrease
(b)	Increase	Increase
(c)	Decrease	Increase
(d)	Decrease	No change
(e)	Increase	Decrease

01T45. Open market bond sales by the Federal Reserve are likely to change the money supply, interest rate, and value of the U.S. dollar in which of the following ways?

	Money Supply	**Interest Rate**	**International Value of the Dollar**
(a)	Decrease	Increase	Increase
(b)	Decrease	Increase	Decrease
(c)	Increase	Decrease	Decrease
(d)	Increase	Decrease	Increase
(e)	Decrease	Decrease	Decrease

01T46. Expansionary fiscal policy is appropriate to
(a) decrease the interest rate.
(b) decrease the rate of inflation.
(c) prevent the crowding-out effect of increased government spending.
(d) remove a recessionary gap.
(e) remove an inflationary gap.

01T47. To limit crowding-out effects, expansionary fiscal policy should be combined with

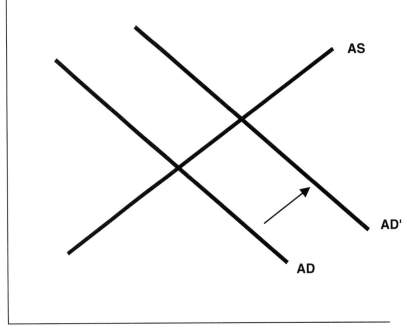

Figure T1-4. Aggregate demand (AD) curve and aggregate supply (AS) curve.

(a) increases in government spending.
(b) decreases in investment.
(c) contractionary monetary policy.
(d) increases in the rate of interest.
(e) expansionary monetary policy.

01T48. What does the theory of rational expectations predict after an anticipated increase in government spending increases aggregate demand
from AD to AD′, as indicated in Fig. T1-4?
(a) The AD curve will shift to the left.
(b) The AS curve will shift to the left.
(c) The AD curve will shift to the right.
(d) The AS curve will shift to the right.
(e) Nothing will happen.

01T49. Which of the following policy combinations is most likely to eliminate
a recession?

	Open Market Operations	Taxes	Government Spending
(a)	Buy securities	Increase	Decrease
(b)	Buy securities	Decrease	Increase
(c)	Sell securities	Increase	Increase
(d)	Buy securities	Decrease	Decrease
(e)	Sell securities	Decrease	Decrease

01T50. An inflationary gap can be reduced by
(a) increasing personal income taxes.
(b) increasing government expenditures.
(c) decreasing reserve requirements for banks.
(d) decreasing the discount rate.
(e) increasing the purchases of securities by the Federal
Reserve.

01T51. Facing a budget deficit, government decreases expenditures and tax revenues by the same amount. How will this affect output and interest rates?

	Output	Interest Rates
(a)	Increase	Increase
(b)	Increase	Decrease
(c)	Decrease	Decrease
(d)	No change	Decrease
(e)	Decrease	Increase

01T52. Automatic stabilizers in fiscal policy are helpful because they
   (a) reduce the public debt.
   (b) increase the possibility of a balanced budget.
   (c) stabilize the unemployment rate.
   (d) automatically reduce the inflation rate.
   (e) go into effect without passage of new legislation.

01T53. Monetarist policy makers emphasize long-run growth and stability during a mild recession. Which policy actions are they most likely to recommend?

	Monetary Policy	**Fiscal Policy**
(a)	Sell bonds	Reduce taxes
(b)	Sell bonds	Raise taxes
(c)	Buy bonds	No change
(d)	No change	Raise taxes
(e)	Buy bonds	Reduce spending

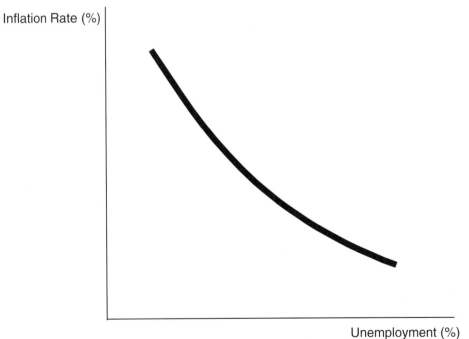

Figure T1-5.

01T54. Compared to expansionary monetary policy to resolve a recession, the immediate impact of expansionary fiscal policy is likely to be
(a) lower inflation.
(b) less public spending.
(c) higher interest rates.
(d) a lower GDP growth rate.
(e) GDP decreasing to a level below potential GDP.

01T55. If the government simultaneously employs expansionary monetary and fiscal policies, what will be the likely effect on interest rates and unemployment?

	Interest Rates	**Unemployment**
(a)	Decrease	Decrease
(b)	Might either increase or decrease	Decrease
(c)	Might either increase or decrease	Increase
(d)	Increase	Might either increase or decrease
(e)	Increase	Decrease

01T56. Figure T1-5 illustrates the
(a) production possibilities frontier.
(b) aggregate demand (AD) curve.
(c) Phillips Curve.
(d) short-run aggregate supply (SAS) curve.
(e) long-run aggregate supply (LAS) curve.

01T57. China's increased demand for U.S. products causes the value of the dollar to
(a) depreciate because of increased U.S. selling of dollars to China.
(b) depreciate because of the increased U.S. money supply.
(c) appreciate because of increased buying of U.S. dollars by China.
(d) appreciate because of increased selling of U.S. dollars by China.
(e) depreciate because of U.S. inflation.

01T58. Which of the following results from stagflation?
(a) Unemployment goes down.
(b) The price level goes down.
(c) The aggregate supply (AS) curve shifts rightward.

(d) The Phillips Curve shifts rightward.

(e) Real GDP increases.

01T59. If the U.S. dollar appreciates relative to foreign currencies, which one of the following most likely occurs?

(a) U.S. exports will increase.

(b) U.S. residents will increasingly vacation abroad.

(c) U.S. imports will decrease.

(d) Investments in U.S. securities will increase.

(e) Foreign tourism in the United States will increase.

01T60. Which of the following is designed to restrict trade?

(a) European Union

(b) GATT

(c) Import quotas

(d) NAFTA

(e) Global corporations

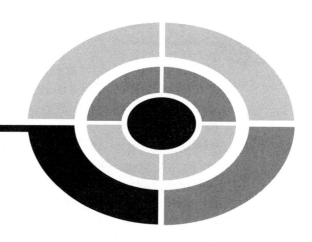

Final Test 1
Answers

01T01. (c). Macroeconomics deals with the economy as a whole (e.g., a national economy), while the behavior of smaller elements of the economy (e.g., consumers, firms, or industry sectors) is covered by microeconomics. Therefore, pricing decisions by firms, the behavior of households, and the growth of the computer industry are typical microeconomic topics. Although the price of crude oil could have an impact on the economy as a whole, the study of its effect on wholesale prices is a sector-specific topic, and therefore part of microeconomics. The rate of inflation, the persistent increase of the economy's price level, is a typical macroeconomic topic.

01T02. (a). The primary function of an economic system is to determine what, how, and for whom to produce scarce goods and services; in other words, the organization of production, distribution, exchange, and consumption. It does *not* necessarily involve producers' profit maximization, ruling out (b), or trade maximization, eliminating (e). In addition, traditional societies may rely on barter and not use money, ruling out (c). The speed with which the system functions is not a primary goal; for example, fast production may lead to low-quality or useless products, ruling out answer (d).

01T03. (c). The production possibilities curve (PPC) shifts outward if new productive capacity (potential) is added. Answers (b) and (e) represent movements

along the curve, exchanging one product for the other [this eliminates (b) and (e)]. The reopening of plants (a) does not add new capacity, and neither does the rehiring of workers (d). The improvement of efficiency moves the curve up (right shift, upward) because it provides higher computer production potential.

01T04. (e). In the circular flow of economic activity between consumers and producers, firms sell outputs to consumers, who can buy products and services because they earn a wage income by selling factor services to producers, allowing them to produce the goods and services bought by consumers.

01T05. (d). Marginal returns in production are *not* critical for mutual beneficial trade [ruling out (a)]. It's not required for beneficial trade that one country be able to produce more of the product, ruling out (c). Beneficial trade does *not* depend on absolute advantage, so (b) and (e) are incorrect, because it's the relative advantage that counts. Therefore, the benefits from trade are determined by the comparative advantage, which allows countries to obtain products at a relatively lower price (opportunity cost) than they could produce the products themselves. Pooling the productive resources of the two countries through trade allows them to achieve a point outside of their own production possibilities curve (i.e., gains from trade).

01T06. (c). Say's Law states that supply creates its own demand. Through the supply of goods, workers earn wages, which they either spend (= demand) or save. The savings will be used to borrow money and will finally also be spent (= demand). Say's Law is an important part of classical and neoclassical economic thinking. The short-run version of Say's Law was rejected by John Maynard Keynes when he launched his demand-side theories in the 1930s.

01T07. (c). Inflation is equal to *nominal* GDP growth minus *real* GDP growth $= 16\% - 5\% = 11\%$.

01T08. (d). The Consumer Price Index (CPI) measures estimated price changes in total consumers' expenditures by using a selection of key consumer goods and services (a so-called product basket). The CPI does *not* measure the overall price level (which would also include producer prices), nor does it measure the economy's cost level, ruling out answers (a) and (e). The GDP deflator measures overall national price changes (i.e., not just consumer prices), eliminating (b). Changes in *real* GDP are found after GDP price changes have been taken into account (i.e., real GDP growth = nominal GDP growth minus inflation), ruling out answer (c).

01T09. (b). There's only a domestic production benefit from the tariff. Domestic producers will produce and sell cars at higher prices. Domestic consumption is diminished because of higher prices, so (a) and (c) can be ruled out. The opposite of (e) is actually happening, so (e) can be eliminated. Higher prices will lead to fewer cars being sold, so answer (d) can be eliminated.

01T10. (e). The purchase of U.S. bonds is a redistribution of money and does not count in GDP, eliminating (a). A family transaction is not the production of a good, but a redistribution, ruling out (b). Imports are excluded from U.S. GDP (they are produced outside the United States), which eliminates answer (c). Because we're measuring current GDP, last year's inventory would have been counted already in previous GDP and must be excluded to avoid double-counting, ruling out answer (d). The U.S.-based manufacturing of the satellite is part of current GDP.

01T11. (c). *Shifts* in the aggregate demand (AD) curve are caused by changes in expenditures, that is, consumption, investment, government expenditure, or net exports (exports minus imports). A change in price causes a movement *along* the AD curve, *ceteris paribus*.

01T12. (d). Government spending may or may not change as a result of change in labor force, but there is no direct relationship, eliminating (a) and (b). The rate of unemployment is the number of unemployed persons divided by the size of the labor force. This eliminates answer (c). The unemployment rate is often criticized as a measure of employment because it does not reflect so-called discouraged workers who stop looking for work and drop out of the labor force. Because the labor force decreases, the rate of unemployment becomes smaller, signaling an "improvement."

For example, assume that the rate of unemployment is total unemployment/labor force $= 5,000/100,000 = 5\%$. If 1,000 so-called discouraged workers stop looking for work and leave the labor force, the new rate of unemployment equals $4,000/99,000 = 4\%$, a *decrease* of one percentage point in the rate of unemployment.

01T13. (c). The aggregate demand (AD) is macroeconomic demand, constructed from the quantity of output that the macroeconomic sectors (households, firms, government, and foreign) are willing to purchase at various price levels (i.e., the economy's aggregate price level). Aggregate demand (AD) = aggregate expenditures (AE) = consumption + investment + government expenditures + net exports (value of exports minus imports). Unlike microeconomic demand curves (e.g., market demand), macroeconomic demand curves are not the result of either horizontal or vertical summation of individual demand curves, eliminating answers (a), (b), (d), and (e).

01T14. (c). Aggregate demand (AD) = aggregate expenditures = consumption + investment + government expenditures + exports − imports. A shift to the right

of the AD curve occurs when AD increases. Answer (a) implies that consumption will go down (a decrease in AD, moving the curve to the left); this eliminates (a). Answers (b) and (c) contribute to a decline in AD and can also be eliminated. Expectations of future deflation (e) mean that people expect price levels to go down, prompting less current and more future consumption, investment, and so on, causing current AD to go down. In contrast, if future shortages are expected, people will be more inclined to purchase now and less in the future, increasing AD and moving the AD curve to the right.

01T15. (b). The increase of imports will decrease aggregate demand (AD), shifting the AD curve to the left, which decreases GDP and also decreases the price level. The new technology will cause a rightward shift in the aggregate supply (AS) curve, increasing GDP and decreasing the price level. The impact on GDP of the two events together is not clear, but they will lead to a decrease in the price level.

01T16. (c). Classical School thinking supports Say's Law ("supply creates its own demand"), eliminating (a). Classical economists also believe that flexible prices will resolve temporary deviations from full-employment GDP, ruling out answers (b) and (d). The so-called classical dichotomy states that money will have an impact only on nominal values and will not affect real values, ruling out (e). Classical economists do *not* believe that government should interfere by stimulating demand because the price mechanism will take care of recessions through lower wages. This ultimately results in new hiring, restoring GDP to its potential (full-employment) level.

01T17. (b). Full-employment GDP is the highest level of GDP that doesn't cause inflation (unemployment is at the natural rate of unemployment). A higher GDP would require expensive overtime and other high-cost production inputs. This would naturally lead to lower profits, lower productive volume, and a return to potential GDP, the long-run equilibrium volume.

01T18. (b). The chart shows that aggregate expenditures go up from $300 to $450 as the economy moves from point E to point F. This is due to government spending (which, as given, causes the change from E to F) of $150. As a result, GDP goes from $1,000 to $1,900, an increase of $900. This is the result of the spending multiplier effect from government spending of $150. The multiplier is 6, because 6 multiplied by $150 equals $900.

01T19. (d). An increase in government expenditures contributes to an increase in aggregate demand (AD). Also, a decrease in taxes contributes to an increase in AD as a result of higher consumption (lower personal income taxes) and/or investment (lower corporate taxes). This eliminates (b) and (e). Answers (a) and

(b) lead to higher AD, but the greatest increase is caused by the combination of the two, answer (d).

Note that (d) is an example of a significant deficit stimulus: It decreases the federal budget balance $(T - G)$ in a "double" fashion by decreasing T (lowering tax revenue) and increasing G (= more government expenditures). In contrast, answer (e) reflects a "balanced budget" stimulus, raising taxes by the amount of extra expenditures.

01T20. (a). There's a recessionary gap in GDP of $500,000 (i.e., potential GDP – actual GDP = \$3,000,000 – \$2,500,000). A Keynesian would propose to stimulate aggregate spending. The impact of government spending is more immediate than the impact of tax decreases (because part of the tax decrease "leaks" into saving) and is equal to the spending multiplier $1/(1 - MPC) = 1/0.5 = 2$. Therefore, the required GDP increase of $500,000 can be accomplished by increasing government spending by $250,000.

01T21. (e). The intermediate-range AS curve (neither Keynesian nor classical, in the range between a relatively low GDP and potential GDP) is positively sloped. If exports increase, the AD curve shifts to the right, causing a price-level increase [ruling out answer (c)], an increase in GDP [ruling out (a) and (b)], and a decrease in the rate of unemployment because the intermediate-range AS occurs below potential GDP. This eliminates (d).

01T22. (d). Stagflation occurs when the aggregate supply (AS) curve moves to the left (e.g., because of higher input costs for producers). This causes lower real GDP (stagnation) and also higher price levels (inflation). Stagflation occurred during the oil crisis of the 1970s, when the price of oil increased very significantly.

01T23. (a). The aggregate supply (AS) curve moves to the left because of fewer oil supplies and the resulting higher input costs for producers ("supply shock"). This means that real GDP decreases and price levels increase.

01T24. (c). Fractional reserve banking means that banks (and other depository institutions) are required to hold a fraction of their total deposits on reserve, while the rest can be lent to customers. The fact that banks can never lend all of their deposits lowers the risk of illiquid banks, that is, banks that run out of money when depositors request their money. This was a major issue in the early 1930s when many U.S. banks collapsed during the beginning of the Great Depression.

01T25. (b). Individuals on fixed incomes or those with savings at fixed interest rates are hurt by inflation because, as the value of money goes down over time, the purchasing power of their income or savings decreases. This eliminates

answers (a) and (c). Retail store owners have to update (and pay for) prices on products regularly (so-called menu costs), ruling out (d). Lenders at fixed interest rates are ultimately hurt because persistent price increases will lower the value of the money borrowers will pay back. This eliminates (e). Borrowers with fixed interest rates are actually helped by inflation because the value they need to pay back the loan goes down.

01T26. (d). The money multiplier (= 1/required reserve ratio) times excess reserves is the maximum expansion of the money supply. In this case, the money multiplier equals $1/0.25 = 4$. Therefore, $4 \times \$1,000 = \$4,000$ is the maximum expansion of the money supply.

01T27. (a). More money being held as currency by individuals (i.e., "under the mattress") means withdrawals from banks, lowering bank deposits. This decreases the ability of banks to create money (because of the Fed's reserve requirements) and therefore decreases the money supply.

01T28. (e). The Federal Reserve supports expansionary (contractionary) fiscal policy by following an expansionary (contractionary) monetary policy. Answers (b) and (c) are combinations of contractionary monetary policy and expansionary fiscal policy. This rules out answers (b) and (c). Expansionary monetary policy consists of either increasing the money supply or decreasing the discount rate. Answers (a), (d), and (e) reflect expansionary monetary policy, but (a) and (d) include a contractionary fiscal policy (i.e., government spending is down). This eliminates (a) and (d). Increasing the money supply (expansionary monetary policy) supports the expansionary fiscal policy of higher government expenditures.

01T29. (b). If people increase their cash holdings, they decrease the money supply because banks are less able to provide credit as a result of lower deposit totals and the Fed's reserve requirements. The lower supply of money causes interest rates to go up.

01T30. (d). The reason people are holding cash is the expectation that interest rates will be up in the future. This is a speculative reason to hold cash—the expectation of earning high future income from increased interest rates.

01T31. (a). The immediate impact of the lowering of reserve requirements by the Fed is to expand the credit that can be offered by banks. This lowers the rate of interest and makes it more attractive to invest in plant and equipment.

01T32. (a). Answer (b) describes the vertical (or classical) section of the short-run aggregate supply (SAS) curve, when GDP is at potential (i.e., full-employment level). Answer (c) describes the horizontal (or Keynesian) section of the SAS curve, when output can be increased without inflationary pressure because of excess capacity. Answers (d) and (e) have no immediate impact on the shape of the SAS curve because they refer to demand instead of supply. In the short run, input prices are considered relatively inflexible (e.g., wages fixed by long-term labor contracts), which provides an incentive for producers to increase output at higher price levels because they will earn higher profits.

01T33. (e). The classical long-run aggregate supply (LAS) curve is vertical at full-employment level because this is the highest possible output level that doesn't cause upward pressure on wages, taking away the incentive to produce more in the long run. An inflationary gap (i.e., GDP above the full-employment level) can exist in the short run as a result of overtime and other such practices and because, typically, there is physical capacity left beyond full-employment GDP. This inflationary gap will be a temporary deviation before GDP returns to its potential level: Higher input prices decrease profitability and take away the incentive for producers to move beyond potential GDP.

01T34. (b). High inflation combined with high unemployment (i.e., relatively low GDP) is an example of stagflation. This is the result of a leftward shift of the AS curve, perhaps because of a negative supply shock from input resources, increasing the input price. The 1970s oil crisis, with a negative oil shock, is an example of this situation.

01T35. (d). The shift in the short-run aggregate supply (SAS) curve to the left implies that AD decreases. A higher level of technology innovation will cause a rightward shift of the AS curve, ruling out (b). Expansionary monetary policy, increasing the money supply with downward pressure on interest rates, will not cause the SAS curve to move to the left, ruling out answers (c) and (e). An increase in labor productivity causes a rightward shift of the SAS curve, ruling out (a). The shift to the left implies that less quantity is supplied at the same price level (because an increase in the cost of production causes lower profits), so the answer is (d).

01T36. (e). Changes in government and consumer spending cause an immediate shift in aggregate demand, not aggregate supply. This eliminates (a) and (b). Higher interest rates affect investments negatively, causing a decrease in AS [this eliminates answer (c)]. An increase in wage rates implies that the cost of production goes up; this shifts the AS curve to the left, ruling out (d). An increase in labor productivity means that more can be produced with the same labor resources, increasing profitability, which moves the AS curve rightward.

01T37. (b). Potential GDP declines when the economy's productive capacity at full employment goes down. Changes in wages and price levels do not affect this capacity, ruling out (d) and (e). The discovery of new productive resources and increases in population will tend to increase the potential GDP. This eliminates answers (a) and (c). If net investments are negative, it means that existing plants and equipment are not being fully replaced by new investments, decreasing the productive capacity and therefore potential GDP.

01T38. (c). A basic measure of the standard of living is GDP per capita. A higher number of depository institutions increases competition in the financial industry but does not imply a higher standard of living, ruling out (a). Higher taxes may lead to a lower supply of labor (i.e., there's a disincentive to work) and lower corporate profits (decreased investments), offsetting potential benefits from increased government tax revenues; this eliminates (b). Increases in population will tend to lower GDP per capita, ruling out (d). Increases in the labor force in themselves do not improve the standard of living because such an improvement depends on the additional labor productivity, ruling out (e). A higher productivity of labor will lift GDP for the same amount of labor, and so will increase GDP per capita and the standard of living.

01T39. (a). The trade surplus occurs in the merchandise balance of trade, part of the current account balance. This surplus must be offset elsewhere in either the current account balance or the capital account balance because the current account balance, capital account balance, and official settlements balance (e.g., official reserves transactions by nations) must add up to zero. (*Note:* The official settlements account is not relevant to this particular question).

01T40. (e). The shift to the left means less demand for Chinese yuan in the foreign exchange markets. If the expectations are that the yuan's value will increase, it will lead to more demand now, ruling out (a). Higher Chinese interest rates will lead investors to demand more yuan, eliminating answer (b). Low inflation will lead to additional demand for Chinese products. This rules out answer (c). Increased foreign income leads to increased foreign demand for Chinese products and increased demand for yuan, ruling out (d). A decrease in demand for Chinese furniture products will decrease demand for yuan and shift the demand curve to the left.

01T41. (d). By specializing according to comparative advantage, the two countries will efficiently produce the commodity with the lowest opportunity cost. This rules out (a), (c), and (e). By pooling their productive activities (specializing and trading), the countries become more interdependent, eliminating (b). Because by trading they can obtain the other product at a lower opportunity cost than if they produced only for domestic consumption, both countries benefit. This benefit is also called *gains from trade,* and it allows a solution outside the original production possibilities curve (PPC) for each country.

01T42. (c). The Phillips Curve's trade-off is between unemployment and inflation. Shifts in AS curves cause both inflation and unemployment to either decrease or increase. This rules out (a) and (e). Changes in input costs cause the AS curve to shift, ruling out (b). When GDP increases, unemployment goes down and inflation goes up, so there's no trade-off in this case, eliminating answer (d). When the AD curve moves to the right, it increases the price level (inflation) while decreasing unemployment. This shift demonstrates the trade-off of the Phillips Curve.

01T43. (b). The decrease in U.S. interest rates will have a short-term impact [this rules out (d) and (e)] on planned international capital inflows into the United States. The immediate effect is that lower U.S. interest rates make investment in the United States less attractive, which decreases the demand for dollars, so there are decreased short-run capital inflows.

01T44. (b). Worldwide demand for U.S. securities will increase the demand for dollars and lead to a currency appreciation of the dollar (i.e., a higher international value of the dollar) in the short term.

01T45. (a). Open market sales by the Fed limit money creation by banks and therefore the supply of money. The money supply decrease triggers an increase in interest rates, which will attract foreign capital to the United States, increasing the demand for U.S. dollars and increasing the value of the dollar. Also, foreign demand for bonds offered by the Fed will increase demand for dollars, also contributing to an increase in the dollar.

01T46. (d). Expansionary fiscal policy involves higher government expenditures and/or reduced taxes (deficit stimulus), increasing aggregate demand (AD), with the ultimate goal of increasing GDP. This rules out (a), (b), and (e). Because expansionary fiscal policies can cause crowding out, this eliminates answer (c). The policy is appropriate for a recessionary gap, when GDP is below potential GDP and increased AD can have a positive impact on GDP. This policy has inflationary risks, while also increasing budget deficits; it is a typical Keynesian policy.

01T47. (e). Increased government expenditures as a result of an expansionary fiscal policy cause an increase in interest rates and will tend to decrease investments (the crowding-out effect). Therefore, (a), (b), and (d) can be ruled out. Answer (c) can be ruled out because contractionary monetary policy will

increase the interest rate. The best way to limit the impact of crowding out is to have an expansionary monetary policy that eases upward interest rate pressures, allowing the level of private investment to remain the same.

01T48. (b). According to the rational expectations theory, people take *anticipated* policy into account in their wage demands. Anticipating the shift from AD to AD′ and the resulting higher price level, people will demand higher wages. This will lead to a shift of AS to the left (i.e., a decrease in aggregate supply). The ultimate result of the policy will be to lead to inflation (price levels will be higher than before), with no increase in GDP.

01T49. (b). A recession (i.e., GDP below potential GDP) can be eliminated by expansionary fiscal policy (higher government expenditures or lower taxes) to increase AD, and ultimately GDP. To prevent interest rates from increasing (because of higher expenditures) and discouraging investment, a supporting expansionary monetary policy is required. This can be achieved through the Fed's open market operations, in this case by buying securities to expand the money supply.

01T50. (a). An inflationary gap (i.e., GDP exceeds potential GDP) can be reduced by limiting aggregate demand and the supply of money, that is, by contractionary fiscal and monetary policies. Answers (c), (d), and (e) can be ruled out because they are expansionary monetary policies. Answer (b) can be eliminated because it is an expansionary fiscal policy. Increasing the income tax rate will limit households' consumption expenditures and decrease aggregate demand.

01T51. (c). In fiscal policy, the negative impact of the decrease in government expenditures on GDP is larger than the positive impact of decreased tax revenues (by the same amount) because the expenditure multiplier $[1/(1 - MPC)]$ is larger than the (negative) tax multiplier $[-MPC/(1 - MPC)]$. This means that GDP will decrease; this rules out (a), (b), and (d). The decreased government expenditures will cause demand for money to go down, decreasing the interest rate. This eliminates (e).

01T52. (e). Automatic stabilizers dampen fluctuations in GDP because they are tied to GDP and move the opposite way. For example, when GDP decreases, income taxes go down, softening the blow to aggregate demand. In contrast, when GDP goes up, income taxes increase, acting as a brake on aggregate demand. Because income taxes are tied to GDP, they are called induced taxes. These stabilizers are helpful because they work automatically, without the need for new legislation.

01T53. (c). Long-run growth and stability are best served by modest growth in the money supply, according to the Monetarist School. In a recession, fiscal policy may lead to increased instability, upsetting long-run growth. Therefore, open market policy by the Fed (buying bonds) to increase the money supply without fiscal stimulus is a likely recommendation.

01T54. (c). Expansionary fiscal policy is aimed at increasing aggregate demand, eliminating answer (b). Expansionary fiscal policy will, all other things held the same, lead to higher price levels and higher GDP. This rules out (a) and (e). Expansionary fiscal policy is likely to increase GDP growth during a recession, ruling out (d).

   Because government spending increases, it will increase money demand and increase interest rates [answer (c)].

01T55. (b). Expansionary monetary policy will increase the supply of money, decreasing interest rates and probably increasing GDP (higher investments and consumption). Expansionary fiscal policy will increase aggregate demand, increasing the price level and interest rates, while also probably increasing GDP. Therefore, it's unclear what will happen to interest rates. Because GDP is likely to increase, employment will also increase, that is, unemployment will go down.

01T56. (c). The relationship between inflation and unemployment was first explored theoretically and empirically by New Zealand economist A. W. Phillips. The Phillips Curve demonstrates the challenge of simultaneously achieving low inflation and low unemployment. This is due to increasing upward wage and price pressures as unemployment reaches its minimum natural rate.

01T57. (c). Increased demand for U.S. products by China leads to increased demand for U.S. dollars to finance the U.S. products. This causes the value of the dollar to increase, that is, the U.S. dollar appreciates.

01T58. (d). Stagflation results from the leftward shift of the AS curve, ruling out (c). As a result of the shift to the left, the price level increases (inflation) and GDP declines (stagnation), eliminating answers (b) and (e). Because GDP declines, unemployment will increase, ruling out (a). The Phillips Curve shifts to the right because of higher inflation and a higher rate of unemployment.

01T59. (c). If the dollar appreciates, its value increases relative to foreign currencies. This makes U.S. exports less attractive to foreign markets, while making U.S. imports relatively cheap. This eliminates (a) and (b). The higher value of the dollar will discourage investment and tourism by foreigners, ruling out (d) and (e). The higher value of the dollar makes it cheaper for U.S. tourists to vacation abroad.

01T60. (c). Global corporations are not designed to restrict trade; in general, they are beneficiaries of increased, unrestricted international trade. GATT (General Agreement of Tariffs and Trade) is an organization dedicated to removing trade barriers. The European Union and NAFTA (North American Free Trade Agreement) are multinational organizations whose goal is the removal of internal trade barriers. Import quotas set limits on imports and therefore restrict international trade.

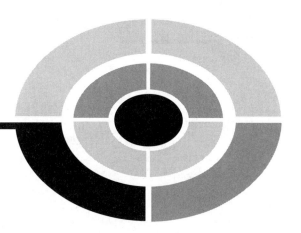

Final Test 2
Questions

Choose the one best answer for each question.

02T01. Which of the following are true for the production possibilities curve drawn in Fig. T2-1?

  I. The opportunity cost of moving from point A to point C is 100 cars.

  II. The opportunity cost of moving from point B to point C is 100 cars.

  III. The opportunity cost of moving from point C to point A is 5 houses.

  (a) I only

  (b) III only

  (c) I and III only

  (d) II and III only

  (e) I, II, and III

02T02. In the circular flow model, government provides goods and services, while receiving tax revenue from

  (a) businesses.

  (b) charities.

  (c) households.

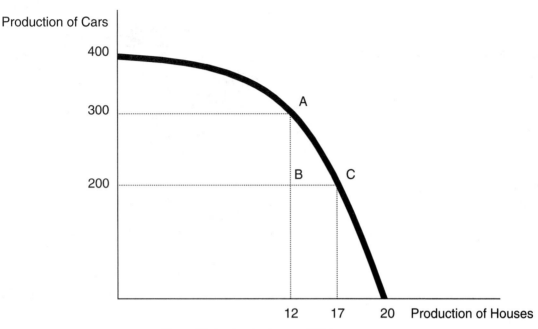

Figure T2-1. Production possibilities curve.

    (d) businesses and households.
    (e) foreign nations.

02T03.   Production equipment belongs to what factor of production?
    (a) Entrepreneurship
    (b) Manufacturing
    (c) Capital
    (d) Money
    (e) Land

02T04.   For Country A to have a comparative advantage over another country in producing Good X, it must be true that Country A has
    (a) a lower opportunity cost in producing Good X.
    (b) a better way to use Good X.
    (c) a higher opportunity cost in producing Good X.
    (d) the absolute advantage in producing Good X.
    (e) no need for products other than Good X.

02T05.   Which statement describes the circular flow correctly?
    (a) Firms pay revenue for factors of production in the product markets.
    (b) Income is exchanged for wages in the product markets.

(c) Households' expenditures are the revenues for companies in the product markets.

(d) Households' income are the revenues for companies in the factor markets.

(e) Goods and services are inputs in the factor markets.

02T06. Which of the following is included in the U.S. GDP?
(a) A U.S. citizen paying for a meal in Canada
(b) A Dutch tourist staying in a U.S. hotel
(c) A feature movie made by U.S. citizens in Australia
(d) The value of French-made cheese, exported to and sold in the United States
(e) The U.S. production of windshield wipers, to be assembled into U.S. cars

02T07. What is an example of structural unemployment?
(a) A factory worker replaced by an automatic production system
(b) A landscape designer who doesn't work during the winter
(c) An office worker who doesn't have anything to do
(d) A doctor who moves his practice from Michigan to Florida
(e) A factory worker laid off during a temporary plant closing in a recession

02T08. If the economy is producing at the full-employment level of output, then
(a) the government's budget is balanced.
(b) the balance of trade is in equilibrium.
(c) the unemployment rate is zero.
(d) no person is receiving unemployment compensation from the government.
(e) there is frictional unemployment.

02T09. If the Consumer Price Index (CPI) rises from 100 to 300, then
(a) the average price of a consumer's market basket has tripled.
(b) consumer disposable incomes have tripled.
(c) all consumer goods' prices have tripled.
(d) each person's disposable income has been cut by two-thirds.
(e) all prices in the economy have tripled.

02T10.   If real GDP increases at 5 percent per year and nominal GDP increases
          at 8 percent per year, which statement is necessarily true?
          (a) Unemployment has gone up.
          (b) The price level is increasing.
          (c) The economy is in a recession.
          (d) The economy has a foreign trade deficit.
          (e) The government is running a budget surplus.

02T11.   If nominal GDP fell while real GDP went up, which statement is neces-
          sarily true?
          (a) Unemployment decreased.
          (b) Exports were bigger than imports.
          (c) The average of stock prices fell.
          (d) The growth of nominal interest rates was below the
               rate of inflation.
          (e) The change in price level was negative.

02T12.   A Keynesian economist believes that
          (a) Say's Law always holds.
          (b) fiscal policy is more effective than monetary policy.
          (c) economies are stable in the short run.
          (d) aggregate supply causes recessions.
          (e) flexible prices will always lift the economy out of
               recessions.

02T13.   What is illustrated in Fig. T2-2?
          (a) Deflation
          (b) Cost-push inflation
          (c) Demand-pull inflation
          (d) Supply-side inflation
          (e) Stagflation

02T14.   The marginal propensity to save is
          (a) the tendency to save more than to consume.
          (b) the cost of saving one extra item.
          (c) the percentage change in saving divided by the per-
               centage change in the interest rate.
          (d) the change in saving divided by the change in income.
          (e) The change in saving divided by the change in inter-
               est rate.

02T15.   A large increase in labor productivity would _____ real GDP and _____
          the price level.

AS = aggregate supply
AD = aggregate demand

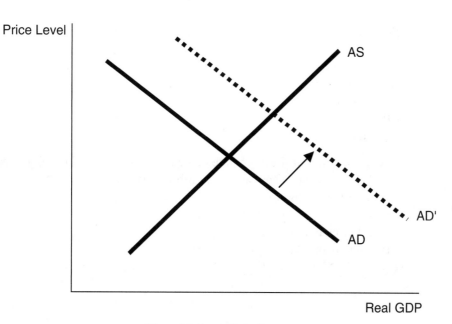

Figure T2-2. AS/AD diagram.

(a) Not change	Increase
(b) Decrease	Increase
(c) Decrease	Not change
(d) Increase	Increase
(e) Increase	Decrease

02T16. According to the Keynesian model, which would directly increase aggregate demand?
(a) An increase in the discount rate
(b) An increase in autonomous investment
(c) A decrease in autonomous consumption
(d) Open market sales by the Federal Reserve
(e) A decrease in government expenditures

02T17. What would most likely result from an increase in government spending?
(a) An increase in aggregate demand (AD)
(b) An increase in aggregate supply (AS)

(c) An increase in unemployment
(d) A decrease in GDP
(e) A decrease in price level

02T18. Suppose taxes decrease by $50 billion. If the marginal propensity to consume (MPC) is 0.8, the value of equilibrium output increases by
(a) $40 billion.
(b) $50 billion.
(c) $160 billion.
(d) $200 billion.
(e) $400 billion.

02T19. The intersection of the aggregate demand (AD) curve and the aggregate supply (AS) curve occurs at the equilibrium values of
(a) exports and imports.
(b) government expenditures and taxes.
(c) inflation and unemployment.
(d) investment and the interest rate.
(e) real GDP and the price level.

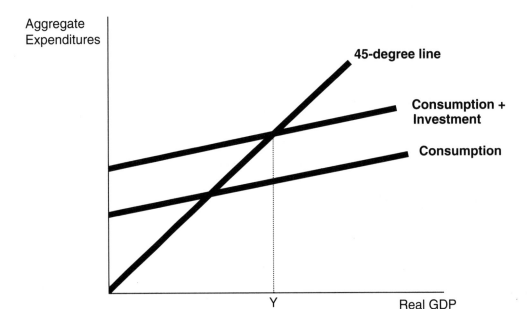

Figure T2-3. Aggregate expenditures.

02T20. If government expenditures G increase, while taxation T increases by the same amount (such that $T-G=0$), which of the following will happen?
(a) The money supply increases.
(b) The money supply decreases.
(c) Aggregate demand doesn't change.
(d) Aggregate demand increases.
(e) Interest rates go down.

02T21. In Fig. T2-3, at income level Y, an economy without government or international sectors is
(a) in equilibrium but not necessarily at full employment.
(b) in equilibrium with some unemployment.
(c) in equilibrium at full employment.
(d) not in equilibrium, but at full employment.
(e) neither in equilibrium nor at full employment.

02T22. The money supply will decrease as a result of which of the following?
(a) A decrease in the discount rate
(b) The buying of bonds by the Federal Reserve
(c) An increase in the required reserve ratio
(d) A decrease in the fraction of deposits that must be held by banks
(e) Open market activities by the Federal Reserve that involve the buying of government securities

02T23. Commercial banks can create money by
(a) transferring client deposits at the Federal Reserve for cash.
(b) lending excess reserves to bank customers.
(c) buying U.S. Treasury bills from the Federal Reserve.
(d) sending vault cash to the Federal Reserve.
(e) maintaining a 100 percent reserve requirement.

02T24. If the money supply decreases while nominal GDP remains constant, which of the following occurred?
(a) Real GDP went up.
(b) The price level went down.
(c) The price level went up.
(d) The velocity of money went up.
(e) The velocity of money went down.

02T25. The demand for money increases when national income goes up because
(a) the interest rate goes up.
(b) the budget deficit increases.

(c) the trade deficit increases.

(d) the money supply increases.

(e) spending on goods and services increases.

02T26. Assume that the required reserve ratio is 10 percent and a single bank (with no excess reserves) receives a $1,000 deposit from a customer. What is the value of the bank's excess reserves?

(a) $100

(b) $900

(c) $1,000

(d) $9,000

(e) $10,000

02T27. In an economy, if more money is demanded than is supplied, what is most likely to happen?

(a) Capital inflows from abroad decrease.

(b) The money demand curve shifts leftward.

(c) The money demand curve shifts rightward.

(d) Interest rates go up.

(e) Interest rates go down.

02T28. Which of the following lessens the impact of the money multiplier?

(a) People increase their cash holdings.

(b) Banks increase loans.

(c) Banks sell U.S. securities to the Federal Reserve.

(d) Households pay less taxes.

(e) Interest rates drop.

02T29. To fight a recession, the Federal Reserve should

(a) increase the discount rate and the reserve requirement.

(b) lower the discount rate and buy securities on the open market.

(c) increase the discount rate and buy securities on the open market.

(d) lower the discount rate and sell securities on the open market.

(e) increase the discount rate and sell securities on the open market.

02T30. When do bond purchases by the Federal Reserve have the greatest impact on real GDP?

(a) There is a high required reserve ratio, and the interest rate has a large effect on investment spending.

(b) There is a high required reserve ratio, and the interest rate has a small effect on investment spending.

(c) There is a low required reserve ratio, and the interest rate has a large effect on investment spending.

(d) There is a low required reserve ratio, and the marginal propensity to consume is low.

(e) There is a high marginal propensity to consume, and the interest rate has a small effect on investment spending.

02T31. What happens if the Federal Reserve sells a significant amount of government securities on the open market?

(a) Commercial bank loans will decrease.

(b) Commercial bank loans will increase.

(c) The money supply will increase.

(d) Rates of interest will decrease.

(e) Rates of interest and commercial bank loans will remain unchanged.

02T32. The aggregate supply (AS) curve shifts rightward if

(a) the opportunity for education decreases.

(b) corporate taxes go up.

(c) natural disasters occur.

(d) labor supply goes down.

(e) investment in plant and equipment increases.

02T33. Natural disasters that restrict a nation's economic resources lead to

(a) disinflation

(b) a leftward shift of the aggregate supply curve.

(c) a downward shift of the Phillips Curve.

(d) structural demand shocks.

(e) deflation.

02T34. The long-run aggregate supply curve shifts to the right when there is

(a) an increase in the cost of productive resources.

(b) an increase in productivity.

(c) an increase in the federal budget deficit.

(d) a decrease in the money supply.

(e) a decrease in the population.

02T35. A rightward shift in the aggregate supply curve is caused by
(a) new laws requiring less air pollution.
(b) a tariff on exported products.
(c) higher interest rates.
(d) a gasoline tax increase.
(e) a wage rate decrease in manufacturing.

02T36. From one year to another, unemployment fell from 6.4 to 5.7 percent, while inflation decreased from 4.3 to 1.9 percent. An explanation for this might be that the
(a) aggregate supply curve shifted to the right.
(b) short-run Phillips curve shifted to the right.
(c) aggregate demand curve shifted to the left.
(d) aggregate demand curve shifted to the right.
(e) aggregate supply curve shifted to the left.

02T37. What most likely supports the long-run growth rate of real per capita income?
(a) High population growth
(b) High level of consumption in the economy
(c) High supply of money in circulation
(d) High levels of education of the population
(e) High level of personal income taxes

02T38. What is the most likely to affect economic growth negatively?
(a) Higher expenditures on research
(b) Increased capital investment
(c) Increased interest rates
(d) Increased utilization of plants
(e) Higher spending on education

02T39. Which of the following is true of supply shocks?
(a) They change the price level as well as relative prices.
(b) They change the price level only.
(c) They can be anticipated and offset with appropriate fiscal policy.
(d) They can be anticipated and offset with appropriate monetary policy.
(e) They make the aggregate supply curve vertical.

02T40. To protect high-cost domestic producers, a country imposes a tariff on an imported commodity *Y*. Which of the following is most likely to occur in the short run?

I. Domestic production of *Y* will increase.

II. Domestic production of *Y* will decrease.

III. Foreign output of *Y* will increase.

(a) I only

(b) II only

(c) III only

(d) I and III only

(e) II and III only

02T41. Who will benefit from inflation that is *not* anticipated?

I. Savers

II. Lender

III. Borrowers

(a) I only

(b) II only

(c) III only

(d) II and III only

(e) I and III only

02T42. Higher U.S. interest rates lead to increased foreign demand for the U.S. dollar. What is likely to happen to the value of the dollar and U.S. exports?

	Value of the Dollar	**U.S. Exports**
(a)	Decrease	Decrease
(b)	Increase	No change
(c)	Decrease	Increase
(d)	Increase	Increase
(e)	Increase	Decrease

02T43. What relationship does the short-run Phillips Curve depict?

(a) A decrease in inflation combined with an increase in GDP growth

(b) An increase in inflation combined with a decrease in GDP growth

(c) An increase in inflation combined with an increase in the unemployment rate

(d) A decrease in GDP growth combined with a decrease in the unemployment rate

(e) A decrease in inflation combined with an increase in the unemployment rate

02T44. What would most likely occur if the United States placed tariffs on imported goods?

(a) The U.S. economy would become less efficient.
(b) U.S. exports would increase.
(c) Long-run U.S. employment would increase.
(d) U.S. GDP would equal potential GDP.
(e) The U.S. standard of living would increase.

02T45. What causes an increase in the value of the U.S. dollar?
(a) Lower U.S. government expenditures
(b) Higher interest rates abroad
(c) Expansionary U.S. monetary policy
(d) Higher U.S. interest rates
(e) Reduced inflation abroad

02T46. What is the likely monetarist point of view?
(a) Use monetary policy to stabilize the economy.
(b) There should be a steadily increasing supply of money.
(c) Crowding out is never an issue.
(d) Money velocity is not stable.
(e) Economies are unstable.

02T47. A government budget deficit exists when
(a) the amount of government debt is positive.
(b) the value of imports exceeds the value of exports.
(c) there is a generational imbalance.
(d) over 50 percent of social security is funded by future generations.
(e) government spending exceeds tax revenues in a given period.

02T48. The government's balanced budget multiplier is
(a) −1.
(b) 0.
(c) 0.5.
(d) 1.
(e) 10.

02T49. If the economy is in a severe recession, which of the following is the most effective fiscal policy to stimulate production?
(a) Government spending is increased.
(b) The discount rate is decreased.
(c) Corporate taxes are increased.

(d) The Federal Reserve sells U.S. securities on the open market.

(e) The Federal Reserve buys U.S. securities on the open market.

02T50. If policy makers want to reduce unemployment by increasing investment during a recession, what is the best policy?
(a) Increase government expenditure and taxes equally.
(b) Increase government expenditure only.
(c) Pursue the purchase of bonds by the Federal Reserve.
(d) Increase government transfer payments.
(e) Increase the banks' reserve requirements.

02T51. What combination of monetary and fiscal policy is most likely to result in a decrease in aggregate demand?

Discount Rate	Open Market Operations	Government Spending
(a) Raise	Sell bonds	Increase
(b) Raise	Buy bonds	Increase
(c) Lower	Buy bonds	Increase
(d) Raise	Sell bonds	Decrease
(e) Lower	Buy bonds	Decrease

02T52. The crowding-out effect occurs when government borrowing causes
(a) a smaller money supply, increasing private-sector investment.
(b) a smaller money supply, decreasing private-sector investment.
(c) lower interest rates, increasing private-sector investment.
(d) lower interest rates, decreasing private-sector investment.
(e) higher interest rates, decreasing private-sector investment.

02T53. The government wants to increase its spending by $10 billion without increasing inflation in the short run. If GDP is at its potential level, what should the government do?
(a) Raise taxes by $10 billion.
(b) Raise taxes by more than $10 billion.
(c) Raise taxes by less than $10 billion.

(d) Lower taxes by $10 billion.

(e) Lower taxes by less than $10 billion.

02T54. What is the monetarists' view of expansionary fiscal policy?

(a) Don't use policy as long as there is no national debt.

(b) Use policy only when there is unemployment and inflation is low.

(c) Use policy only if it will decrease aggregate income.

(d) Don't use policy because it will lead to increased interest rates and crowd out private investment.

(e) Policy will increase aggregate income, provided the money supply is decreased at a slow, steady rate.

02T55. An expansionary fiscal policy together with a contractionary monetary policy most likely causes

(a) increases in interest rates.

(b) GDP to go up.

(c) GDP to go down.

(d) decreases in interest rates.

(e) decreased budget deficits.

02T56. A long-run constant level of output at full employment leads to what kind of Phillips Curve?

(a) "Bowed out" (concave) relative to the origin

(b) "Bowed in" (convex) relative to the origin

(c) Linear, but not vertical or horizontal

(d) Vertical

(e) Horizontal

02T57. An increase in U.S. imports is likely to lead to

(a) dollar depreciation, as the supply of dollars goes up.

(b) dollar depreciation, as the demand for dollars goes up.

(c) dollar appreciation, as the supply of dollars goes up.

(d) dollar appreciation, as the demand for dollars goes up.

(e) no impact on the dollar's exchange rate.

02T58. If a bottle of shampoo costs $4 in the United States and 800 yen in Japan, and assuming that transaction costs are zero, the exchange rate will be

(a) 2 yen per dollar.

(b) 20 yen per dollar.

(c) 200 yen per dollar.

(d) $5 per yen.

(e) $10 per yen.

02T59. An aggregate supply (AS) curve is horizontal because

(a) employment is constant as a result of fixed factor prices.

(b) resources are underemployed and an increase in demand does not cause pressure on the price level.

(c) a higher price level leads to higher interest rates, which reduces the money supply.

(d) there is an inflationary gap because GDP exceeds potential GDP.

(e) output can only be increased unless prices increase.

02T60. A contractionary supply shock most likely results in

(a) increased aggregate demand (AD).

(b) decreased employment.

(c) increased potential GDP.

(d) increased GDP.

(e) a decreased price level.

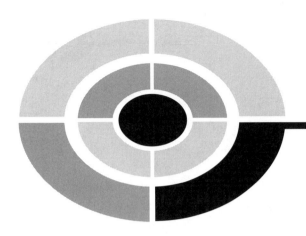

Final Test 2 Answers

02T01. (c). The opportunity cost is the quantity of one product that is given up by producing extra units of the other product. Going from point A to point C, the extra production of 5 houses comes at the expense of producing 100 cars fewer than before (300 cars vs. 200 cars), and that is the opportunity cost of moving from A to C. Moving from point C to point A, we produce an extra 100 cars (300 vs. 200) at the expense of 5 fewer houses (12 vs. 17), so the opportunity cost is 5 houses. Moving from the (inside) point B to point C, we do not need to give up any car production (it remains at 200 units) in order to produce 5 more houses (17 vs. 12), so the opportunity cost is zero (i.e., statement II is incorrect).

Anytime we move from an inside point to the boundary, the opportunity cost is zero. The main reason is that points inside the curve are not efficient, so we can do better by producing more of one product *without* having to give up on the other.

02T02. (d). In the circular flow model, government tax revenue comes from both corporate and personal taxation on income and wealth. Foreign companies with U.S. subsidiaries may pay U.S. taxes, but foreign nations never do.

02T03. (c). Capital consists of equipment, plants, office buildings, machinery, and human skill required for production of goods and services. Please note that manufacturing [answer (b)] and money [answer (d)] are *not* factors of production.

02T04. (a). Comparative advantage in Good X means that a country has the lowest opportunity cost. The country does *not* need to have the absolute advantage [ruling out (d)]. Answers (b) and (e) can be ruled out because they have nothing to do with the opportunity costs of producing Good X, while (c) implies that the *other* country has the comparative advantage.

02T05. (c). In the economy's circular flow, wages are exchanged for inputs in factor markets, and goods and services are exchanged for revenue dollars in the product markets. The income that households earn leads to expenditures in the product markets, resulting in revenue for companies. This rules out (a), (b), (d), and (e).

02T06. (b). U.S. GDP is the value of all final goods and services produced in the United States. Answers (a), (c), and (d) can be ruled out because they involve production outside the United States. Answer (e) involves U.S. production, but it's not a final good (it's intermediary, to be assembled into a final product, i.e., automobile). This leaves answer (b), the U.S. production of a final service (hotel accommodations).

02T07. (a). Answer (d) is not considered unemployment, but a change of work location. Answer (b) is seasonal unemployment, while answer (c) is so-called hidden unemployment. Answer (e) is cyclical unemployment (i.e., caused by the business cycle). Answer (a) is the immediate result of technological advances causing unemployment, or structural unemployment.

02T08. (e). The full-employment level of GDP relates to employment but not to government budgets or trade balance, excluding (a) and (b). Full employment is the sum of frictional and structural unemployment (with zero *cyclical* unemployment). Full employment therefore does *not* mean zero unemployment. This excludes answers (c) and (d).

02T09. (a). The Consumer Price Index (CPI) measures the changes in prices of a selected basket of consumer products. The index does not involve consumer disposable income [ruling out answers (b) and (d)]. The index does not cover all consumer goods [eliminating answer (c)] and certainly does not cover all prices in the economy [ruling out (e)].

02T10. (b). The only thing we know is that nominal GDP increased faster than real GDP, at, 8 percent vs. 5 percent, meaning that the economy's price level must have increased. Although the other answers [(a), (c), (d), and (e)] *may* be true, they are *not* necessarily true.

02T11. (e). The only thing we can conclude is that price levels went down because real GDP growth exceeded nominal GDP growth. Answers (a) through (d) are *not* necessarily true.

02T12. (b). A Keynesian believes in demand-side economics, or the effectiveness of stimulating aggregate demand to get the economy out of recession. The reason for this belief is that in the short run, prices are inflexible (rigid or "sticky" prices) as a result of long-term contracts and transaction costs requiring time and effort to change prices (e.g., producers' menu costs to change brochures). The price rigidity fixes aggregate supply (AS) and makes aggregate demand (AD) the key factor in increasing GDP in a recession. Say's Law states that "supply determines demand," contradicting the Keynesian short-run demand-side approach. This eliminates answer (a). Also, (c) can be eliminated because Keynesians believe that the economy is inherently unstable in the short run (though probably stable in the long run after full price flexibility applies). Answer (d) can be eliminated because Keynesians believe that lack of aggregate demand (not supply) is primarily responsible for recessions. Fiscal policy (increasing government expenditures and reducing taxes) is the primary Keynesian deficit-stimulus tool to combat recessions, with monetary policy in a secondary, supporting role. Please note that this Keynesian view is in sharp contrast to the monetarist perspective that fiscal policy will cause increased instability in the economy (e.g., inflation and interest rate fluctuations).

02T13. (c). By moving from the AD curve to AD', the price level increases (inflation), eliminating answer (a). Stagflation occurs when prices increase while GDP decreases, which rules out answer (e). Cost-push (also called supply-side) inflation happens when input prices rise (e.g., wages), moving the AS curve to the left. This eliminates (b) and (d). The shift to the right of the demand curve AD to AD' signals demand-pull inflation.

02T14. (d). The marginal propensity to save (MPS) is the change in saving divided by the change in income. Assuming no taxes, all income is either consumed or saved, and the marginal propensity to consume (MPC) plus the marginal propensity to save (MPS) equals 1, or, in shorthand, MPS = 1 − MPC. The (simple) Keynesian multiplier is equal to 1/MPS.

02T15. (e). A large increase in labor productivity would shift the aggregate supply (AS) curve to the right, decreasing the price level, but increasing real GDP.

02T16. (b). Aggregate demand (AD) = aggregate expenditures (AE) = consumption + investment + government expenditure + (exports − imports). Contractionary monetary policy (i.e., a decreasing money supply) will increase interest rates and lower consumption and investment, thereby lowering AD; this eliminates (a) and (d). Answers (c) and (e) are decreases in AD, while the increase in autonomous investment will increase AD.

02T17. (a). Increases in government expenditure will tend to increase GDP (and employment) as well as the price level because the increase in government spending results in an increase in aggregate demand$=C+I+G+(E-M)$, where G is government expenditures. This eliminates (b), (c), (d), and (e).

02T18. (d). The tax multiplier equals $-MPC/(1-MPC)=-0.8/0.2=-4$. The change in equilibrium is GDP$=-4$ multiplied by $-\$50$ billion, or $\$200$ billion.

02T19. (e). The intersection of the AS curve and the AD curve is the macroeconomic equilibrium that determines the economy's equilibrium real output (GDP) and equilibrium price level.

02T20. (d). The immediate impact of this fiscal policy will be on aggregate demand (AD)$=$aggregate expenditures (AE)$=$consumption$+$investment$+$government expenditure$+$(exports$-$imports). The negative impact of taxation on consumption (because of the leakage into savings) will be less than the increase in government expenditures. Therefore, AD will increase. Answers (a) and (b) refer to monetary policy, not fiscal policy. The increased expenditure by government, covered by increased taxes, will not decrease interest rates, ruling out answer (e).

02T21. (a). The economy depicted in the diagram is in equilibrium: AE$=$real GDP, or the economy's output equals aggregate demand $Y=C+I$ (and national income) when real GDP$=Y$. This rules out (d) and (e). We cannot tell from the diagram if at GDP$=Y$ the economy is at full employment or not. This eliminates (b) and (c).

02T22. (c). The buying of bonds and U.S. securities by the Fed will increase the opportunities for credit and money creation by banks, eliminating (b) and (e). A lower discount rate makes borrowing money from the Fed cheaper, increasing the money supply; this rules out (a). A decrease in the fraction of deposits to be held in reserve (i.e., the required reserve ratio) tends to expand the banks' excess reserves, eliminating (d). An increase in required reserves will limit credit and money creation by banks.

02T23. (b). Buying U.S. Treasury bills will limit banks' opportunities to extend credit (this transaction is equivalent to a restrictive open market operation by the Fed); this rules out answer (c). Sending cash to or converting deposits at the Fed will limit credit opportunities for banks, ruling out (a) and (d). If a 100 percent reserve requirement were to be maintained, the bank could never extend credit beyond its deposits, and it would be impossible to create money; this rules out (e). The banks' excess reserves are the source of money creation and increased money supply.

02T24. (d). The equation of exchange is $M \times V = P \times Y$. As stated, money supply M goes down while $P \times Y$ (nominal GDP) is constant. Therefore, velocity V must have increased.

02T25. (e). When national income goes up, aggregate expenditures (AE) also increase. This increases the demand for money, as increased consumption and investment represent higher spending on goods and services by households and firms.

02T26. (b). The bank is required to keep the required reserve ratio of 10 percent of the $1,000 deposit in reserve, so it can extend credit on $900, the excess reserves.

02T27. (d). The equilibrium in the money market is the balance of money demand and money supply, based on the equilibrium interest rate. The rate of interest goes up if money demanded exceeds money supplied.

02T28. (a). When people hold extra cash ("inactive" money), it means that the money is not available as a deposit at the bank; this limits the money creation by banks in a fractional banking system and therefore lessens the impact of the money multiplier (1/required reserve ratio).

02T29. (b). The Fed should combat a recession (GDP below potential) through an expansionary monetary policy. This involves buying securities on the open market and lowering the discount rate.

02T30. (c). By lowering the reserve ratio, the Fed pursues an expansionary monetary policy, increasing the supply of money. This will lead to a decrease in the interest rate. If investments are sensitive to changes in the interest rate, the decrease will have a large impact on GDP as investment I goes up significantly [GDP = AE = aggregate expenditures = $C + I + G + (X - M)$]. The open market operations have the greatest impact when the required reserve ratio is low, combined with a large impact of the interest rate on investment.

02T31. (a). The open market operation of selling government securities to banks (contractionary monetary policy by the Fed) limits the banks' ability to create money. Therefore, the amount of commercial bank loans will decrease.

02T32. (e). The AS curve shifts rightward when production inputs become cheaper, more productive, or increasingly available. This rules out (b), because it makes inputs relatively more expensive. Also, natural disasters will put extra limits on the availability of inputs, ruling out (c). A decreasing labor supply implies fewer labor inputs available, eliminating (d). An increase in training and education will make labor inputs more productive, causing a rightward shift of the AS curve. This rules out (a). With an investment in capital (plant, equipment, and so on), workers can be more productive, and the AS curve shifts to the right.

02T33. (b). The limitations on economic resources imply that the productive capabilities of the economy have diminished, which leads to a shift in the AS curve to the left. This is similar to the impact of the oil embargo in the 1970s. The change in the AS curve implies that inflation goes up [eliminating answers (a) and (e)] and GDP will be down [this rules out a downward shift of the Phillips Curve, i.e., answer (c)]. Natural disasters may disrupt and affect demand, but they will structurally affect supply, not demand. This eliminates answer (d).

02T34. (b). The long-run aggregate supply (LAS) curve shifts rightward when input resources' availability goes up, become cheaper, or become increasingly productive. This eliminates (a) and (e). Changes in the money supply or fiscal policy do not directly effect the LAS curve itself, ruling out (c) and (d). The general increase in productivity, defined by more output per productive input, shifts the LAS curve to the right.

02T35. (e). New laws requiring less pollution and a tax increase will increase the cost of production, shifting the AS curve to the left. This eliminates (a) and (d). Moving production to foreign locations (with domestic shutdowns) will decrease GDP and cause a leftward shift in the AS curve, ruling out (b). An increase in the rate of interest will discourage investment because it becomes more expensive to finance; this causes a leftward shift of the AS curve, eliminating (c). A sectorwide wage reduction makes inputs less expensive and moves the AS curve to the right.

02T36. (a). A rightward shift of the Phillips Curve occurs when both unemployment and inflation increase, ruling out (b). A leftward shift of the AS curve or a rightward shift of the AD curve will increase the price level, eliminating (d) and (e). A leftward shift of the AD curve decreases GDP, increasing unemployment. This rules out (c). The AS curve's shift to the right leads to lower price levels (decreased inflation) and higher GDP (lower unemployment).

02T37. (d). The long-run growth of real per capita income is supported by high labor productivity, or high output per unit of labor, and a sufficient level of investment in new capital (plant, equipment, and so on). High population growth tends to depress the overall productivity of labor, while also complicating training and education. This rules out (a). The higher consumption is as a percentage of GDP, the lower investment. To support growth, short-term consumption may need to take a back seat to net investment designed to increase the economy's productive capacity. This eliminates (b). A large supply of money may be inflationary, which will add instability to the economy, compromising its long-run growth prospects, ruling out (c). A high level of personal income taxes discourages workers from being part of the labor force, decreasing the supply of labor and diminishing the economy's growth potential, eliminating answer (e). The levels of education and training are critical to growth: they increase labor productivity, allowing for high-level productive capital investments.

02T38. (c). Higher spending and investments will improve labor productivity, enhancing economic growth; this rules out (a) and (e). Increased capital utilization implies that GDP is moving closer to potential GDP, improving economic growth. This rules out answer (d). Increased capital investment means the addition of productive capacity through plant, equipment, and so on that fosters growth; this rules out (b). Growth prospects are negatively affected by higher interest rates because it becomes more expensive to finance net investments in productive capacity.

02T39. (a). Supply shocks, such as unanticipated higher oil prices as a result of fewer resources, move the AS curve to the left, ruling out (c), (d), and (e). The shock changes price levels as well as relative prices as a result of increased input prices, eliminating (b).

02T40. (a). The tariff causes the cost of foreign production of Y to go up, making domestic production of Y relatively cheap and therefore increasing domestic production of Y. Foreign output of Y will decline.

02T41. (c). Savers cannot protect themselves from unanticipated inflation, ruling out (a) and (e). Lenders will get less value returned from borrowers than originally anticipated, eliminating answers (b) and (d). Borrowers will benefit because they end up paying back an amount that's worth less as a result of the unanticipated loss of the value of money.

02T42. (e). If foreign demand for the dollar increases, it implies dollar appreciation in the currency markets. U.S. exports will become relatively more expensive (they now need to be bought by purchasing higher-valued dollars) and will decrease.

02T43. (e). The short-run Phillips Curve demonstrates the negative relationship between the rate of inflation and the rate of unemployment; it therefore shows the challenge of achieving the major macroeconomic goals of low inflation and low unemployment simultaneously. This challenge is mostly due to increasing upward wage and price pressures as unemployment reaches its natural minimum rate.

02T44. (a). The U.S. tariffs add extra costs to foreign products and therefore limit competition for domestic producers. This allows the domestic producers to operate at less than efficient levels.

02T45. (d). Lower expenditures decrease demand, decreasing interest rates. This would decrease demand for U.S. securities and decrease demand for U.S. dollars.

This eliminates (a). Higher interest rates abroad imply relatively lower U.S. interest rates, ruling out (b). An expansionary monetary policy, aimed at expanding the money supply, causes interest rates to come down. This eliminates (c). A reduction in inflation abroad would improve the purchasing power of foreign currency, decreasing the value of U.S. dollar, ruling out (e). Higher U.S. interest rates will attract foreign capital and lead to U.S. dollar appreciation.

02T46. (b). Monetarists do not believe that policies to fine-tune or stabilize the economy are effective. In fact, they believe that such policies may add to instability. This rules out (a). One of the reasons that fiscal policy may be destabilizing is that increased demand triggers higher interest rates and causes the crowding out of investment. This eliminates (c). Monetarists adhere to the quantity theory of money and its equation of exchange $M \times V = P \times Y$; they believe that the velocity of money V is stable, which rules out (d). Monetarists believe, like the Neoclassical School, that the price mechanism will keep the economy inherently stable (therefore there is no need for special fiscal policy), eliminating (e). Because of their belief in the inherent stability of the economy and the constancy of V, monetarists prefer a steadily increasing supply of money M to support GDP growth.

02T47. (e). Government debt accumulates as a result of deficits in current and/or past periods. A positive government debt does not necessarily mean that government has a budget deficit in a given period, ruling out (a). Answer (b) refers to a trade deficit, not a budget deficit. A generational imbalance refers to the financing of current (and future) government benefits (e.g., social security) by the current generation vs. future generations. It does not imply a budget deficit. This rules out (c) and (d). A budget deficit in a given period is defined by $T - G < 0$, that is, government expenditures exceed tax revenues.

02T48. (d). The balanced budget multiplier applies when government's fiscal policy spending is combined with a similar increase in tax revenues to maintain a balanced budget, that is, $T - G = 0$. By adding the spending multiplier $1/(1 - MPC)$ and the tax multiplier $-MPC/(1 - MPC)$, we find the balanced budget multiplier: $1/(1 - MPC) + [-MPC/(1 - MPC)] = (1 - MPC)/(1 - MPC) = 1$.

02T49. (a). In a severe recession (i.e., GDP well below potential), stimulating aggregate demand with expansionary fiscal policy may be an appropriate policy. Answers (b), (d), and (e) are ruled out because they represent monetary policy (*not* fiscal policy). Increasing taxes and decreasing government spending are contractionary fiscal policies, which eliminates (c). Increasing government spending, which increases AD, is the most effective policy.

02T50. (c). In a mild recession, expansionary monetary policy may be an appropriate way to stimulate the economy. In this specific case, policy makers focus on encouraging investment. One way to achieve this is to increase the money supply and decrease interest rates. The purchase of government securities by the Fed accomplishes the goal of enlarging the money supply (through open market operations).

02T51. (d). Aggregate demand decreases as a result of contractionary monetary policy and fiscal policy. Contractionary fiscal policy involves a decrease in government spending, ruling out (a), (b), and (c). Contractionary monetary policy includes the selling of bonds by the Fed, eliminating (e). The raising of the discount rate is another element of contractionary monetary policy, which points to answer (d).

02T52. (e). The crowding-out effect occurs when increased government borrowing (e.g., expansionary fiscal policy, including increased government spending) leads to higher interest rates (more demand for money), which decreases private investment. Monetarists especially object to this potential destabilizing effect of fiscal policy.

02T53. (b). For the new fiscal policy to not cause inflation, it should leave GDP unchanged. Because the (government) spending multiplier $[1/(1-MPC)]$ is larger than the (negative) tax multiplier $[-MPC/(1-MPC)]$, the government must raise taxes by more than the increase in government spending ($10 billion).

02T54. (d). The Monetarist School's view of fiscal policy is to do nothing. They believe that expansionary fiscal policy can only contribute to instability in GDP because as interest rates go up, private investment is discouraged (the crowding-out effect).

02T55. (a). An expansionary fiscal policy leads to higher deficits, ruling out (e). The overall effect on GDP of expansionary fiscal and contractionary monetary policy is unclear, eliminating (b) and (c). Expansionary fiscal policy increases the demand for money and increases the interest rate; contractionary monetary policy is aimed at a smaller supply of money, also leading to increased interest rates. This eliminates (d). The higher expenditures from fiscal policy increase money demand, while a contractionary monetary policy leads to decreased money supply. Both policies lead to interest rate increases.

02T56. (d). The long-run Phillips Curve at full-employment GDP has a fixed rate of unemployment, equaling the natural rate of unemployment at long-run potential GDP. Therefore, the curve is vertical.

02T57. (a). The increase in U.S. imports needs to be paid for with foreign currency and increases the supply of U.S. dollars, leading to currency depreciation, other things held constant.

02T58. (c). Purchasing power parity, given that transaction costs are zero, requires that $4 = 800$ yen, or $1 = 200$ yen.

02T59. (b). Fixed factor prices imply that producers have an incentive to increase production at higher price levels (i.e., higher profits), which would increase employment. Constant employment is typical for full-employment, potential GDP (when AS is vertical, not horizontal). This rules out (a). The horizontal AS curve refers to constant price levels, ruling out (c) and (e). If GDP exceeds potential GDP, the inflationary gap will be due to an AD increase, ruling out (d). The aggregate supply (AS) curve is horizontal (or Keynesian) at relatively low levels of GDP, under excess-capacity conditions (overcapacity). Therefore, an increase in aggregate demand (AD) will not increase pressure on price levels.

02T60. (b). A contractionary supply shock shifts the AS curve to the left, decreasing GDP, thus eliminating (d). There is no increase in potential GDP from the shock, eliminating (c). The leftward shift also increases the price level, ruling out (e). The supply shock itself does not cause a shift in the AD curve, eliminating (a). The impact of the shock is lower GDP and, consequently, lower employment.

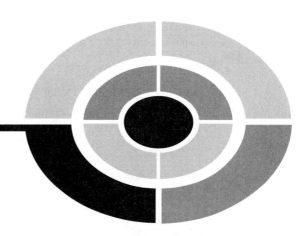

Sources

U.S. Government

Department of Commerce (www.commerce.gov)

- Economics and Statistics Administration (ESA) (www.esa.doc.gov)
  - Access to key economic indicators from the Bureau of Economic Analysis (BEA) and the U.S. Census Bureau (www.economicindicators.gov).
- Bureau of Economic Analysis (BEA) (www.bea.gov)
  - Extensive statistical information on the U.S. economy.
- Department of Commerce—Other
  - STAT-USA (www.stat-usa.gov) a subscription-based service providing Internet browsing for business, trade, and economic information.
  - State of the Nation, a special area for current and historical economic and financial releases and economic data.
  - GLOBUS and NTDB (National Trade Data Bank), current and historical trade-related releases, international market research, trade opportunities, country analysis, and so on.
  - USA Trade Online (U.S. foreign merchandise trade data).
  - Euro Trade Online (European Union merchandise trade data).

Bureau of the Census (www.census.gov)
Department of Labor, Bureau of Labor Statistics (www.bls.gov)
Federal Reserve System (www.federalreserve.gov)
Treasury Department (www.ustreas.gov)
Fedstats (www.fedstats.gov), Links to statistics and information from 70 federal government agencies.

International

OECD (www.oecd.org)
IMF (www.imf.org)
United Nations (www.un.org)
European Union—Eurostat (www.europa.ue.int/comm/dgs/eurostat/index_en.htm
European Central Bank (ECB) (www.ecb.int)
World Bank Group (www.worldbank.org)

General Reference

Graham Bannock, Ron Baxter, and Evan Davis, *The Economist: Dictionary of Economics,* 4th ed. Bloomberg Press: Princeton, N. J., 2003.
The Economist: Guide to Economic Indicators, 5th ed. Bloomberg Press: Princeton, N. J., 2003.

Charts and Figures (Public Domain Sources)

Federal Reserve Bank, St. Louis, Missouri, www.stlouisfed.org (Figs. 3-2, 3-4)
Federal Reserve System, Washington, D.C., www.federalreserve.org (Fig. 6-6)
World Bank, www.worldbank.org (Fig. 8-1)
U.S. Department of Labor, Bureau of Labor Statistics, www.bls.gov (Fig. 11-7)
U.S. Department of Commerce, Bureau of Economic Analysis, www.bea.doc.gov (Fig. 12-5)

GLOSSARY

Absolute advantage
Country A has the absolute advantage over Country B in Product X if A can produce X more efficiently than B.

Accelerator model
The model states that net investments depend on changes in GDP, accelerating growth.

Aggregate demand (AD)
The relationship between the quantity of real GDP demanded and the price level, i.e., the average price for goods and services in the economy.

Aggregate expenditures (AE)
The aggregate of consumption (C), investment (I), government expenditures (G), and net exports [i.e., exports (E) minus imports (M)].

Aggregate income (AI)
The total income earned in the economy; aggregate income equals GDP equals aggregate demand AD [i.e., aggregate expenditures (AE)].

Aggregate supply (AS)
The relationship between the quantity of real GDP supplied and the price level, i.e., the average price for goods and services in the economy.

AS/AD framework
The theory of macroeconomic supply (AS) and demand (AD) and macroeconomic equilibrium.

ASEAN
Association of South East Asian Nations (ASEAN) is a free-trade agreement among Asian nations.

Balance of payments
Keeps track of international transactions; it includes the current account, capital account, and official settlements account. The overall balance of these accounts must be zero.

Barter market
The acquisition of goods and services by exchanging other goods and services instead of money.

Bathtub theorem
The economy grows when injections are greater than leakages, and it shrinks if leakages exceed injections.

Bretton Woods Conference
Conference that designed the post-World War II foreign exchange system and led to the establishment of the IMF and the World Bank.

Business cycle
The up-and-down pattern of GDP growth over time, affecting employment and inflation, and consisting of expansions (recoveries) and contractions (recessions).

Business cycle, contraction
The downside phase of the business cycle (from peak to trough).

Business cycle, expansion
The upside phase of the business cycle (from trough to peak).

Capital (stock)
The aggregate value of plant, equipment, buildings, and inventories used to produce goods and services.

Capital account
Records foreign investment in the United States and U.S. investments abroad.

Capital depreciation
Decrease in capital because of wear and tear and obsolescence; also called *capital consumption*.

Capital market
The meeting of investment demand (ID) and savings supply (SS), resulting in the macroeconomic equilibrium real interest rate and investment.

Capital per hour of labor
Capital employed divided by aggregate labor hours; indicator of capital vs. labor intensity of production.

Cash holdings
Currency held by households (e.g., not in bank deposits), also called *inactive money*. This could be the result of very low interest rates or high levels of insecurity.

Central bank
See lender of last resort (Federal Reserve, ECB).

Ceteris paribus
Latin for "all other things held the same (constant)," the logical requirement to ensure that demand or supply curves are relationships between quantity and price only.

Glossary

China's economic policy
Interest rate and foreign exchange policies by China's central bank are critical aspects of the global economy. The growth rates of Australia's economy and major Asian economies (Japan, South Korea, Malaysia, the Philippines, and Taiwan) are increasingly reliant on trade with China. Changes in expectations about growth rates of the Chinese economy may have significant impact on worldwide commodity prices (e.g., steel, oil).

Circular flow
A model of the economy that describes the movement of resources and money across household, business, government, and foreign sectors.

Classical dichotomy (neutrality of money)
At full employment, because of the complete flexibility of prices, money will have no impact on real variables (e.g., real GDP), and will impact only nominal values, i.e., the forces that determine real variables are independent from the forces that determine nominal values ("dichotomy"). The neutrality of money is a cornerstone belief of the Classical School.

Classical School
Adherents of the theory that the economy is self-regulating and will normally operate at full employment. Any deviations from the potential GDP are temporary and will be corrected by the price mechanism. Money is neutral: it will not affect real quantities, only nominal values.

Classical School, "New"
Governments can expect to have an influence on the economy only if their actions are unanticipated. Therefore, government demand intervention is ineffective, even in the short run. Growth can be enhanced only by influencing supply.

Comparative advantage
Country A has the comparative advantage over country B in Product X if A can produce X at a lower opportunity cost than can B.

Concave ("bowed out")
The shape of the production possibilities curve or frontier, curving away ("bowing out") from the origin, indicating the rising opportunity costs of increasingly manufacturing one good over the other.

Consumer confidence
The perception of economic progress by households, expressed as "optimistic" verses "pessimistic."

Consumer Price Index (CPI)
Measures the cost of a typical consumer's basket of goods in order to estimate the average household's purchase cost and price level; collected monthly by the U.S. Bureau of Labor Statistics (BLS).

Consumption (C)
Total expenditures by households for goods and services.

Consumption, autonomous
The amount of consumption when disposable income is zero.

Consumption, induced
The amount of consumption that varies with disposable income.

Consumption function
The relationship between consumption expenditure and disposable income.

Cost of Living Adjustment (COLA)
Adjustment of income or benefits (e.g., social security) by the rate of inflation.

Crowding-out effect
Increased government borrowing usually causes increased interest rates and displaces private investment. This effect decreases the impact of fiscal policy.

Currency
Bills or coins in circulation.

Currency appreciation/depreciation
Currency appreciation (depreciation) occurs when one currency rises (drops) in value in terms of another currency; in the case of the United States, value of the dollar.

Current account
Records exports, imports, net interest, and net transfers. The balance equals net exports plus net interest plus net transfers.

Cyclical budget balance
Actual budget balance minus the structural budget balance.

Deflation
Negative inflation, i.e., persistently decreasing price levels.

Demand, Law of
The quantity demanded of a good or service decreases as the price goes up. This law holds provided everything else remains the same (*ceteris paribus*), i.e., income, price of substitutes, price of complementary goods, and consumer preferences. The Law of Demand determines the shape of the negatively sloped demand curve.

Demand curve
The graphic representation of price (y axis) and quantity demanded (x axis), based on a schedule of potential demand.

Demand curve, complementary goods
Good B is complementary to Good A if their consumption is interdependent (e.g., coffee and cream). An increase in the price of complementary Good B decreases its demand and, because of complementarity, also decreases the demand for Good A.

Demand curve, consumer expectations
Consumers' expectations about the future may influence current buying behavior, e.g., if the price of oranges is expected to go up, consumers will tend to buy more now.

Demand curve, income effect
An increase in income usually increases the quantity demanded (i.e., demand curve shifts to the right), the case of a so-called normal good. If the good is inferior, its quantity demanded decreases as income rises (e.g., hamburger meat).

Demand curve, inferior good
Good whose quantity demanded decreases as consumer income goes up.

Demand curve, normal good
Good whose quantity demanded increases as consumer income goes up. ·

Demand curve, number of consumers
The quantity demanded increases as the number of consumers goes up, e.g., increased immigration.

Demand curve, substitute goods
A substitute for Good A is a Good B that at least partly satisfies the same needs of consumers (e.g., commuting by train vs. commuting by car).

Demand curve, substitution effect
The quantity demanded of Good A increases as the price of a substitute Good B increases (i.e., demand curve shifts to the right). The demand for Good A increases because it becomes relatively cheaper.

Demand curve, tastes and preferences
The quantity demanded goes up as the desire for the product increases, e.g., cell phones entering the mainstream after early adoption.

Demand-side economics
Focuses on regulating aggregate demand and the supporting fiscal and monetary policies.

Depository institution
Any firm that takes deposits and uses the deposits to make loans, e.g., commercial banks, savings banks, and credit unions.

Depression, The Great
The period from 1929 to 1939, when GDP and international trade declined significantly across major Western nations, with unprecedented rates of unemployment.

Diminishing Returns, Law of
This law states that that as the quantity of labor increases, *ceteris paribus,* the marginal product of labor goes down.

Discount rate
The interest rate at which the Fed lends reserves to commercial banks. A decrease in the discount rate means that banks will borrow more from the Fed, increasing the money supply.

Discouraged workers
Unemployed people who have stopped looking for work and are not part of the labor force.

Disposable income
The household's income after taxes, consisting of consumption (C) and saving (S).

Dumping
Selling goods and services in a foreign market at a price below (marginal) cost.

eBay
Major online auction Web site; uses feedback scores to estimate "trust" in exchange.

Economic development
Study of national differences in economic growth and GDP per capita. It tries to answer the question of why developing nations consistently remain behind advanced countries.

Economic good
Any physical object, natural or artificial, or services rendered, that could command a price in a market.

Economic growth
The increase in a country's GDP (or per capita GDP).

Economic systems
The organization of the production, distribution, exchange, and consumption of goods and services (e.g., free market system).

Economic theory
Set of beliefs about how economies function and their corresponding policy implications.

Economics
The study of the production, distribution, and consumption of scarce goods.

Efficient production
Production of goods and services at the frontier (on the edge) of the production possibilities curve (PPC), as opposed to inefficient production which takes place inside the PPC.

Elasticity, price
The percentage-change responsiveness of the demand (supply) curve to a percentage change in price.

Employment-to-population ratio
The percentage of working-age people who have jobs.

Equation of Exchange
$M \times V = P \times Y$ (M = quantity of money; V = velocity of money, P = price level; Y = real GDP)

Equilibrium
The market outcome when the price is such that quantity demanded is equal to quantity supplied, and there is no incentive for buyers and sellers to change the result.

Equilibrium price
The price at which potential demand and supply are in stable balance.

Equilibrium quantity
The quantity at which potential demand and supply are in stable balance.

European Central Bank (ECB)
The central bank for the euro-currency zone (located in Frankfurt, Germany); the ECB operates as an independent central bank, issuing euro bank notes and setting the rate of interest.

European Monetary Union
The Treaty of Maastricht (1992) established the single currency, the euro, for members of the European Union. To join the common European currency, nations are required to satisfy economic convergence criteria, including limits on government deficit, government debt, rate of inflation, long-term interest rates, and stability of the national currency. Currently, 12 nations have adopted the euro (Austria, Belgium, Finland, France, Germany, Greece, Ireland, Italy, Luxemburg, the Netherlands, Portugal, and Spain). Three of the original 15 member states have not yet opted to join (Denmark, Sweden, and the United Kingdom).

European Union (EU)
Organization of 25 European nations with the objective of developing a common market with a common currency, the euro.

Excess reserves
The funds available to banks to lend under a system of fractional reserve banking.

Expenditures, autonomous
Expenditures (e.g., consumption, government) that are independent of GDP.

Exports (X)
The value of the economy's sales of goods and services abroad.

Factors of production
The economic resources (inputs) available to the economy for production of goods and services: land, labor, capital, and entrepreneurship.

Federal budget
The federal government's income (T) through taxation minus government expenditures (G) (i.e., $T - G$).

Federal funds rate
The interest rate at which financial institutions can borrow from other financial institutions (e.g., banks borrowing from banks). The Fed's discount rate (and its open market operations) will affect the federal funds rate.

Federal Reserve System
The central bank of the United States; it is responsible for monetary policy, adjusting the money in circulation and guiding interest rates.

Federal Reserve System, Board of Governors
Seven members appointed by the president and confirmed by the Senate for 14-year terms. This board oversees the operations of the Fed.

Federal Reserve System, Federal Open Market Committee
The main policy-making group of the Fed. The voting members are the Board of Governors, the president of the Federal Reserve Bank of New York and, on a rotating basis, the presidents of four other Federal Reserve banks.

Fiat money
Money established by law as a valid form of financial exchange (usually has no intrinsic value).

Financial innovation
Innovations lowering the cost of switching between money and other assets, e.g., banks offering savings accounts with higher flexibility for withdrawal.

Fiscal imbalance
The present value of the government's commitments to pay benefits minus the present value of its tax revenues.

Fiscal policy
The pursuit of macroeconomic goals by government by changing (personal and corporate) tax rates and the amount of government spending.

Fisher, Irving
Irving Fisher (1867–1947) designed the monetary equation of exchange ($MV=PY$). He also developed the theory of index numbers.

Foreign exchange markets
Markets where currencies of nations are traded. Their main functions are the transfer of purchasing power, the provision of credit, and the minimization of exchange risk.

Fractional reserve banking
A banking system in which only a fraction of total deposits is held on reserve, while the rest is lent out.

Free market system
An economic system based on private ownership, individual economic freedom, competition, the profit motive, and the market price system to achieve economic goals.

Friedman, Milton
Milton Friedman (b. 1912), winner of the 1976 Nobel Memorial Prize for economics. Friedman's major contribution has been the theoretical and empirical development of the quantity theory of money. He extended the equation of exchange ($MV=PY$) into

a monetarist theory, advocating strict control of the money supply, expressed in a basic rule for yearly money growth to limit inflation. Friedman also pioneered the theory of policy effectiveness.

Full employment
Full employment occurs when cyclical unemployment is zero and unemployment equals the natural rate of unemployment.

Gains from trade
Gains from trade are achieved when nations specialize and trade the products for which they hold the comparative advantage, i.e., the lowest opportunity cost.

GATT
The General Agreement on Tariffs and Trade (GATT) is an international economic policy agreement (1948) designed to reduce tariffs and increase international trade.

GDP, potential
The amount of goods and services that could be produced if all of the economy's factors are fully and efficiently employed; also, full-employment level of GDP.

GDP deflator
Nominal GDP divided by real GDP; measures the change in the economy's price level.

Generational imbalance
The division of the fiscal imbalance between current and future generations, assuming the current generation will enjoy the current levels of taxes and benefits.

Germany's hyperinflation
In the wake of World War I, Germany experienced an escalating inflation rooted in war debts. The hyperinflation of 1923 was triggered by industrial strikes after the French-Belgian occupation of the Ruhr Valley. On November 15, 1923, one U.S. dollar was worth 4.2 trillion German marks.

Global economics
The increasing worldwide import and export flows, enhanced by global financing flows, and the resulting interdependence of all economies in the world.

Gold standard
The fixing of exchange rates on the basis of gold; ultimately abandoned when the dollar was declared inconvertible in 1971.

Golden Rule of Capital Accumulation
The growth path that maximizes GDP per capita is equal to the one that maximizes consumption per worker over time.

Goods and services, final
The value of final goods and services (excluding intermediate goods and services) is the measure for GDP.

Government debt
The total amount that government has borrowed, usually as a result of persistent budget deficits.

Government expenditures (G)
Total expenditures by government for goods and services.

Government saving
Equals the excess of government income (T) over government expenditures (G), i.e., $T-G$.

Gross domestic product (GDP)
The market value of all final goods and services produced within a country in a given time period.

Growth accounting
The discipline that estimates the extent to which sources for growth contribute to GDP growth.

Human capital
The skills and knowledge embodied in the labor force, including entrepreneurship. Investment in human capital should increase labor productivity in the same way that investment in machinery does.

Hyperinflation
Inflation exceeding a rate of 50 percent per month.

Impact of money, long-run
The long-run impact of money (when GDP=potential GDP) is the change in aggregate demand leading to recessionary or inflationary gaps. The inflationary gap leads to higher price levels (inflation).

Impact of money, short-run
The short-run impact of money derives from interest rate changes (resulting from price rigidity) affecting consumption (saving), investment, and foreign capital flows.

Imports (M)
The value of the economy's purchases of foreign goods and services.

Income per capita
GDP divided by population. This number may be expressed in current dollars or purchasing power parity dollars.

Infant-industry protection
Protection of a relatively young industry to allow it to improve its productivity in order for it to ultimately compete in world markets.

Inflation
The sustained increase in the general level of prices in the economy.

Inflation, cost-push
Inflation caused by the increase in the cost of production of goods and services. Typically, rises in wage rates and raw materials costs move the SAS curve to the left, causing this kind of inflation when also supported by expansionary monetary policy.

Inflation, demand-pull
Inflation caused by persistent excess aggregate demand (AD) over aggregate supply (AS) when also supported by expansionary monetary policy.

Inflation target
The target is designed to provide a transparent trigger for monetary policy by the central bank.

Inflationary gap
An inflationary gap occurs when short-run real GDP exceeds potential GDP.

Injections
Expenditures by government (G), investment (I), or foreign sector (E).

Inside lag
Amount of time it takes policy makers to determine which fiscal policy is required and to pass appropriate fiscal policy laws.

Interest rate
The real interest rate is the opportunity cost of the funds required for investment; the nominal interest rate is the real interest rate plus inflation.

Interest rate parity
The adjustment of exchange rates so that the return from investing in assets in different nations is the same.

Intermediate goods and services
Goods and services used for the production of final goods and services; excluded from GDP to avoid double-counting.

International capital flow
Cross-country investment flow, often spurred by currency and interest rate fluctuations.

International debt
The accumulation of foreign borrowing ($M - X$).

Intrinsic value
The inherent value of currency being used (e.g., a coin's weight in gold); in modern economies, the intrinsic value of money is practically zero.

Investment (I)
Total expenditures by business for capital stock (i.e., plants, office buildings, equipment).

Investment, gross
The aggregate of all investments in capital (including depreciation).

Investment, net
Gross investment minus capital depreciation.

Investment demand (ID)
The relationship between the real interest rate and the amount of investment.

Invisible hand
Under free competition, individuals motivated by self-interest are guided by the invisible (or "hidden") hand to a result that is good for the whole.

Japan's deflation, 2001–2004
The extended period of decreases in Japan's extremely high price levels for food, clothes, and real estate, moving prices closer to those of other countries. This period coincides with Japan's central bank policy of near-zero interest rates, intended to spur demand and reverse price declines.

Jevons, Willam Stanley
Jevons (1835–1882) was a British economist who stated the "Law of One Price." He was one of the founders of econometrics by using mathematics and statistics in economics; he invented moving averages.

Keynes, John Maynard
John Maynard Keynes (1883–1946) is considered the founding father of modern macroeconomics. He published his major work, *The General Theory of Employment, Interest, and Money,* in 1936. Keynes played a leading role in the 1944 Bretton Woods Conference that established the post-World War II international financial organization, including the International Monetary Fund (IMF).

Keynesian cross
The equilibrium of aggregate expenditures and GDP at the intersection of the 45-degree line (AE = GDP) and the AE function $C + I + G + (X - M)$.

Keynesian School
Adherents to the theory that aggregate demand (AD) [i.e., aggregate expenditures (AE)] is a main driver of macroeconomic equilibrium, particularly in a recessionary gap.

Keynesianism, "New"
This theory stresses the existence of institutions that may rationally lead to price rigidity. It does not maintain that money is neutral and that it can affect real variables. The business cycle can be (partially) explained by changes in aggregate demand so that even anticipated changes can have an impact.

L
In addition to M3, includes liquid and near-liquid assets, e.g., short-term treasury notes.

Labor, demand for (LD)
The relationship between the real wage rate and the quantity of labor firms demand; as the real wage rate increases, the quantity of labor demanded decreases.

Labor, marginal product of
The additional real GDP produced by an additional hour of labor.

Labor, protection
Protection of domestic labor by tariffs in order to compete with cheap foreign labor.

Labor, supply of (LS)
The relationship between the real wage rate and the quantity of labor supplied; as the real wage increases, the quantity of labor supplied increases.

Labor force
The aggregate of employed workers and those actively looking for work.

Labor force participation rate
Labor force divided by the working-age population.

Labor market
Labor supply (LS) and labor demand (LD) determining the macroeconomic equilibrium real wage rate and quantity of labor.

Labor productivity
Real GDP divided by aggregate labor hours, i.e., real GDP per hour of labor. Increases when physical capital (plants and equipment) and/or human capital (training and education) goes up.

Laffer curve
Named after supply-side economist Arthur Laffer, this curve shows the relationship between the marginal tax rate and total tax revenues. The optimum tax rate is the one that maximizes total revenues. Rates below the optimum are "normal" because tax revenues increase as the tax rate increases. Rates above the optimum are "prohibitive": increasing tax rates will decrease total tax revenues. This relationship has not been empirically verified, and it remains hypothetical.

Laissez-faire, laissez-passer
The physiocrats' phrase ("let it work, let it go") to condemn any government interference in industry, except to break up monopolies.

Law of One Price
The neoclassical law that states that a single price prevails for commodities of uniform quality in a market.

Leading indicators
Those economic measures that signal the beginning of a swing in the business cycle.

Leakages
Uses of household income other than consumption (C), including taxes, savings, and imports (foreign purchases).

Lender of last resort
The essential function of the central bank, at all times being willing to lend money to the banks on its own terms.

Liquidity preference
The reasons for holding certain assets in liquid form; introduced by Keynes as one of the factors of influence for determining the rate of interest.

Long-run aggregate supply (LAS)
The relationship between the quantity of GDP supplied and the price level in the long run, when GDP equals potential GDP, i.e., the LAS curve is vertical.

Lucas Wedge
The accumulated loss of output due to the slowdown in productivity (or real GDP per capita).

M1
Currency held by the public, demand deposits and other checkable deposits, and traveler's checks (money used as a medium of exchange).

M2
In addition to M1, includes savings and money market deposits noninstitutional money market mutual funds, and other short-term money market accounts (money used as a store of value).

M3
In addition to M2, includes the financial assets and instruments of large businesses and financial institutions (money used as a unit of account).

Macroeconomic equilibrium, long-run
Long-run macroeconomic equilibrium occurs when aggregate demand (AD) equals long-run aggregate supply (LAS).

Macroeconomic equilibrium, short-run
Short-run macroeconomic equilibrium occurs when aggregate demand (AD) equals short-run aggregate supply (SAS).

Macroeconomic long run
Period of time long enough so that all prices are fully flexible, i.e., fully flexible price level.

Macroeconomic short run
Period of time during which at least some prices are inflexible.

Macroeconomics
The study of the economics of very large entities, e.g., a national economy.

Marginal propensity to consume (MPC)
The change in consumption expenditure caused by a change in disposable income.

Marginal propensity to save (MPS)
The change in savings caused by a change in disposable income.

Glossary

Market failure
Market failure occurs when free trade and self-interested behavior do not result in mutually beneficial results for buyers and sellers (e.g., selling a car that's a lemon, or selling an asset with an ambiguous legal title).

Markets
The meeting of potential sellers and buyers, with the means to exchange products and services.

Menu costs
The transaction costs of changing product prices (under inflation), e.g., update of price lists, retagging of items. In the short run, these transaction costs can slow down inflation.

Mercantilists
Sixteenth-century economic theory emphasizing national wealth by building export surplus and active intervention by the state.

Mercosur
The "Southern Common Market," a customs union of a group of South American countries.

Microeconomics
The study of the economic behavior of individual units, such as households, corporations, or industry sectors.

Misery index
A quick indicator of consumer confidence, consisting of the sum of inflation and unemployment (or interest rate).

Model
Simplified representation of a complex object (e.g., a geographic map); economists use models to derive insights about complex real-world economics.

Monetarist School
Adherents to the theory that the economy is self-regulating and will normally operate at full employment (similar to Classical School). Pace of money growth must be kept steady because changes in the quantity of money are the most significant source of fluctuations in aggregate demand (AD).

Monetary Control Act of 1980
This act made all U.S. banks part of the Federal Reserve System.

Monetary exchange
Trusted capability to exchange money for products and services, a key requirement for effective markets, which are critical for economic growth.

Monetary policy
The pursuit of macroeconomic goals by the Federal Reserve System, in particular

price stability, by changing the interest rate (charged to banks) and the supply of money in the economy.

Money
Any item or commodity generally accepted as a means of payment for goods and services or in repayment of debt, and serving as an asset to its holder.

Money, medium of exchange
The acceptability of money in exchange for goods and services.

Money, neutrality of
The independence between the economic forces determining real variables (real GDP, real wage rate) and nominal variables (nominal GDP, nominal wage rate). This is also called the *classical dichotomy*.

Money, store of value
The durability of money for exchange at a later date, requiring some form of price stability.

Money, unit of account
The usability of money for quoting prices.

Money creation
The ability of depository institutions to add to the money supply by making loans.

Money demand (MD) curve
The relationship between the real interest rate and the quantity of money demanded; if the interest rate is low, it is cheaper to borrow money and the quantity of money demanded goes up.

Money market
Money supply (MS) and money demand (MD) determining the macroequilibrium values of the real interest rate and quantity of money.

Money multiplier
The money multiplier equals 1 divided by the required reserve ratio.

Money supply (MS) curve
The relationship between the real interest rate and the quantity of money supplied; because the Federal Reserve guides the supply of money, we assume for simplicity that the MS curve is vertical.

Multiplier, balanced budget
The sum of spending multiplier and tax multiplier (under equal increase in autonomous government spending and taxation), i.e., $1/(1-MPC) - MPC(1-MPC) = 1$.

Multiplier, investment
The amount by which a change in investment is multiplied to determine the change in equilibrium values of aggregate expenditures (AE) and GDP; in an economy with no taxation or foreign sectors the multiplier equals $1/MPC = 1/(1-MPC)$.

Multiplier, spending
The amount by which a change in government expenditure is multiplied to determine the change in equilibrium values of aggregate expenditures (AE) and GDP; in an economy with no taxation or foreign sectors the multiplier equals $1/\text{MPC} = 1/(1 - \text{MPC})$.

Multiplier, tax
The amount by which a change in taxes (e.g., lump-sum taxes) is multiplied to determine the equilibrium value of GDP; equals $-\text{MPC}/(1 - \text{MPC})$.

Multiplier effect
The amount by which a change in autonomous expenditure is multiplied to determine the change in equilibrium values of aggregate expenditures (AE) and GDP; in an economy with no taxation or foreign sectors, the multiplier equals $1/\text{MPC} = 1/(1 - \text{MPC})$.

NAFTA
North American Free Trade Agreement (NAFTA), concluded in 1994, establishing a free trade area between Canada, the United States, and Mexico. The objective of NAFTA is to phase out quotas and other barriers to trade between the participating countries.

National income accounting
Estimation of the output or income for a nation as a whole using the income or expenditure method.

National saving
The aggregate of private saving (S) and government saving ($T - G$).

National security, protection of
Protection of industries necessary for the national defense.

Natural order of society
The eighteenth-century French physiocrats viewed the state's role as simply preserving property and upholding the natural order.

Net exports
The value of exports (X) minus imports (M) (i.e., $X - M$).

New Economy
IT-based economy expected to move economic growth to new levels by improving productivity and enlarging global trade.

Nontariff barriers
Any actions other than a tariff that restrict international trade.

Official Settlements Account
Changes in U.S. official reserves and the government holdings of foreign currency.

Okun's Law
The empirical finding that real GDP must grow at 2.5 percent above trend in order to decrease unemployment by 1 percent.

One Third Rule
On average, a 1 percent increase in capital per hour of labor yields 1/3 percent increase in labor productivity. This rule assists in estimating labor productivity increase from technology.

OPEC
The Organization of Petroleum Exporting Countries (OPEC) is a multinational organization established to coordinate the petroleum policies of its members and also to provide technical and economic aid. OPEC collectively owns 80 percent of the world's oil reserves and accounts for 40 percent of its production.

Open market operations
The purchase and sales of U.S. securities by the Fed in the open market. Banks' reserves increase when the Fed buys securities, which increases potential lending and the money supply.

Opportunity cost
The value of the next-best alternative that must be given up to acquire or achieve something.

Optimal growth theory
Theory of the level of growth that maximizes GDP per capita.

Output gap ("Okun gap")
The estimated difference between real GDP and potential GDP.

Outside lag
The time frame from a new policy taking effect to its impact on GDP.

Phillips, A. W. H.
Alban William Housego (A. W. H.) Phillips (1914–1975) developed the well-known Phillips curve, depicting the tradeoff between unemployment percentage and rate of inflation. This (hypothetical) curve reveals the potential inconsistency of pursuing low unemployment and low inflation simultaneously.

Phillips Curve, long-run
The relationship between the rate of unemployment and the rate of inflation when the rate of inflation equals the expected rate of inflation. The curve is vertical at the natural rate of unemployment.

Phillips Curve, short-run
The negatively sloped relationship between the rate of unemployment and the rate of inflation, assuming that the expected rate of inflation and natural rate of unemployment are constant.

Physiocrats
A group of eighteenth-century economists led by Francois Quesnay.

Policy, anticipated
Widely publicized policy, expected by rational economic agents.

Policy, unanticipated
Surprise policy, not expected by rational economic agents.

Policy Ineffectiveness Theorem
If prices and wages are flexible and people hold rational expectations, then any government policy to stimulate demand will have no impact on GDP (or employment) unless the policy is unanticipated.

Precautionary demand, money
Money demanded because of unanticipated payments.

Prescott, Edward, and Kydland, Finn
Economics Nobel Prize winners in 2004 for contributions to the theory of business cycles, in particular the impact of changes in technology and supply shocks.

Price level
The economy's aggregate level of prices (nominal GDP/real GDP).

Price mechanism
The mechanism that drives up the price when demand exceeds supply, and drives the price down when supply exceeds demand.

Price stability
The major goal of monetary policy, price stability is critical for effective economic growth.

Prime rate
The interest rate charged by commercial banks to their best customers.

Private saving (S)
The aggregate of saving by households and business (S).

Private sector
Economic activity outside government control.

Producer Price Index (PPI)
Based on the goods used in the production process, the PPI is viewed as an early inflation indicator through increased factor goods.

Production costs
The aggregate of the costs of the factors of production, i.e., factor inputs.

Production function
The relationship between real GDP and the quantity of labor employed, provided all other factors influencing production are held constant (*ceteris paribus*).

Production possibilities curve (PPC)
The graphical representation of the opportunity costs of using scarce resources to produce one good or service over another.

Productivity curve
The relationship between capital per hour of labor and real GDP per hour of labor (labor productivity).

Profit expectations
The profit rate expected from an investment; depends on the business cycle, technology, and taxes.

Property rights
Fully allocated property rights enable exchange of goods and services, a key requirement for effective markets and critical for economic growth.

Protection
General measures (e.g., tariffs, quotas) to protect domestic industries from the impact of foreign countries.

Public goods
Goods and services that are necessary but are not efficiently served by private markets (e.g., military).

Public policy
The policies (resulting from a society's social, economic, legal and political values and institutions) that determine the effectiveness of markets and the production of goods and services.

Public sector
Economic activity by government agencies for the benefit of the public.

Purchasing power parity
The adjustment of exchange rates so that currencies buy the same amount of goods and services.

Quantity theory of money
This theory, building on the equation of exchange ($M \times V = P \times Y$) states that changes in M will only cause changes in P.

Quesnay, Francois
Francois Quesnay (1694–1774) constructed the first macroeconomic input-output model of the economy. He was the leader of the physiocrats, a group of economists in France.

Quotas
Special protective quantity limits on imported goods.

Rational expectations theory
The theory that economic agents have an understanding of the economy and will be

able to construct expectations that take into account all relevant information. Ultimately, agents' expectations will be subject to random errors only.

Recession
A situation when GDP is below potential GDP; a mild recession is just below potential GDP for a brief period, while a severe recession is far below potential GDP for an extensive period.

Recessionary gap
A recessionary gap occurs when short-run real GDP is below potential GDP.

Required reserve ratio
The ratio of reserves to deposits required by regulation.

Ricardo, David
David Ricardo (1772–1823) published his major work, "The Principles of Political Economy and Taxation," in 1817. It identifies the economic laws regulating the distribution of income between the landowners, capitalists, and labor. Ricardo was the first economist to recognize the importance of comparative advantage in international trade.

Ricardo-Barro effect
Government budget deficits decrease government saving, implying higher future taxation. This increases private saving to pay for higher future taxes.

Saving (S)
Saving depends on the real interest rate: the higher the interest, the more saving.

Saving supply (SS)
The relationship between the real interest rate and the amount of saving.

Say, Jean-Baptiste
Jean-Baptiste Say (1767–1832) stated that "supply creates its own demand" (Say's Law). One of Keynes's major claims was that Say's Law may not hold in the short run, although it holds in the long run.

Say's Law
The law states that "supply creates its own demand," a key classical belief.

Scarcity
The situation in which the needs and wants of an individual or group of individuals exceed the resources available to them.

Securities and Exchange Commission (SEC)
Created in the aftermath of the Great Crash of 1929, the SEC's objective is to regulate U.S. securities transactions.

Short-run aggregate supply (SAS)
The relationship between the quantity of GDP supplied and the price level in the short run, i.e., the period in which GDP may not equal potential GDP.

Smith, Adam
Adam Smith (1723–1790) is considered the founding father of economic science. In 1776 he published "An Inquiry into the Nature and Causes of the Wealth of Nations," identifying the division of labor and accumulation of capital as major sources for wealth creation. He also introduced the concept of the "invisible hand"—made possible by free competition—which guided self-interested individual behavior to a result that was "good" for the whole of society.

Smithsonian Agreement
Agreement by the IMF Group of Ten in 1971 to establish a fixed-rate system for currencies with some degree of flexibility.

Social security
The Congressional Budget Office stated that social security benefits under the current system will require between 5 percent and 8 percent of GDP, in the long term. The rising costs of benefits will outpace revenue in 2019.

South Sea Bubble
A major stock speculation panic in England in 1720. It resulted in the so-called Bubble Act of 1721, which made the founding of joint-stock companies without royal approval unlawful.

Speculative demand, money
The decision to either hold money or deposit it based on expected interest rate fluctuations.

Stabilizers, automatic
Stabilization of GDP without the need for discretionary action; this occurs when tax revenues and expenditures are changed as GDP changes.

Stagflation
The combination of inflation and a recessionary gap, resulting from a leftward shift of the AS curve.

Standard of living
The quantity of goods and services consumed by an individual or household. A general, cross-country measure is GDP per capita.

Structural budget balance
The amount of government borrowing after the impact of the business cycle is removed.

Supply, Law of
The quantity supplied of a good or service increases as its price goes up. This law holds provided everything else remains the same (*ceteris paribus*), i.e., technology, the cost of inputs, and the price of other goods. The Law of Supply determines the shape of the positively sloped supply curve.

Supply curve
The graphic representation of price (y axis) and quantity supplied (x axis), based on a schedule of potential supply.

Supply curve, government policy
Government has an impact on quantity supplied by using taxation, subsidies, and quotas, e.g., increased corporate taxes increase the cost of production, and quantity supplied will go down.

Supply curve, input prices
An increase in the input price means that the unit cost of inputs goes up. This decreases profitability and shifts the supply curve to the left.

Supply curve, number of suppliers
The quantity supplied goes down if the number of suppliers decreases, e.g., corporate bankruptcies.

Supply curve, prices of other goods
A producer who manufactures Goods A and B will tend to shift production to Good A if its price goes up (e.g., because of increased demand).

Supply curve, producer expectations
Producers' expectations about the future may influence current production behavior, e.g., if producers expect the costs of inputs to increase, they will tend to accelerate production now, shifting the supply curve to the right.

Supply curve, technology
New technology increases labor productivity, decreasing the unit cost of production. This increases profitability and shifts the supply curve to the right.

Supply shocks
Unanticipated, sudden changes that cause the AS curve to shift (e.g., input shortages, input-price changes).

Supply-side economics
Focuses on stimulating aggregate supply by using incentives (e.g., tax relief) and support (e.g., subsidies).

Sustainable economic growth
The economic growth pace that conserves the environment and its depletable resources.

T-accounts
The accounts that list the debits and credits for the Fed, banks, and the public.

Tariffs
Special protective taxes on imported goods.

Tax revenues (T)
Compulsory transfer of money from private individuals, institutions, or groups to the government.

Taxes, induced
Taxes that change when GDP changes.

Taylor Rule
A simple rule for setting the short-term interest rates with the objective of keeping inflation stable.

Technology
The knowledge and know-how of the means and methods or producing goods and services. It encompasses basic and applied science and general production skills, consisting of knowledge ahead of science.

The Bank of the United States
Chartered by Congress in 1791, the Bank of the United States caused intense debate about its constitutionality (supported by the Federalists, led by Alexander Hamilton) and the purported violation of states' rights (argued by the Democratic-Republicans, led by Thomas Jefferson).

The European Union (EU)
A group of 25 countries in Europe dedicated to forming a free-trade area; the economies of 12 countries operate with a common currency, the euro.

The 45-degree line
The reference line through the origin used to indicate the equilibrium condition AE = real GDP in the Keynesian model.

The Glass-Steagal Act
Enacted during the Depression, the act disallowed commercial banks from participating in investment banking (and vice versa); act repealed in 2001.

The Great Crash
The collapse of the U.S. stock market in October 1929, triggered by speculation, the proliferation of debt-creating holding companies, and large illiquid bank loans. The Securities and Exchange Commission (SEC) was created in the aftermath of the Great Crash.

The Great Depression
The Great Depression (1929–1939) was the longest and most severe economic downturn ever experienced in the Western world. It is generally agreed that the complete business recovery in the United States after the Great Depression was not achieved until government began spending heavily for defense in the early 1940s.

The 1970s oil crisis
Oil-producing nations (OPEC) quadrupled the price of crude oil in 1973. This caused high rates of inflation (up to 25 percent).

The 2004 federal budget deficit
The 2004 U.S. budget deficit was $412B or 3.6 percent of GDP. The administration's policy is to reduce the deficit, possibly to an estimated 2.5 percent of GDP in 2008.

Trade balance
The difference between a nation's imports and exports of merchandise to and from all foreign countries in a given period.

Trade-off
The consequence of choosing one good or service over another. Trade-offs are the result of scarcity.

Trade restrictions
Regulations issued by national governments to restrict international trade, often to protect domestic industries; regulations include tariffs, quotas, and other trade barriers.

Transaction demand, money
Money demand for day-to-day payments through balances held by households and firms (instead of stocks, bonds, etc.).

Transfer payments, government
Payments by government not for goods and services (e.g., benefit payments), excluded from aggregate expenditure (AE) component *G*, i.e., spending by government on goods and services.

Unemployment
The aggregate of people who are (a) without a job and have made efforts to find a job in the past four weeks; or (b) waiting to be called back to work after a layoff; or (c) waiting to start a new job within 30 days.

Unemployment, cyclical
The fluctuating unemployment over the course of the business cycle; increases during recession and goes down during expansion.

Unemployment, frictional
Unemployment resulting from normal market turnover, such as people entering the labor force and businesses expanding and contracting. Frictionally unemployed workers are searching for good job matches.

Unemployment, natural rate of
The sum of frictional and structural unemployment.

Unemployment, rate of
Number of unemployed people divided by the labor force ($\times 100$).

Unemployment, structural
Unemployment that results from changes in technology or international competition, requiring new job skills and/or changing the location of jobs.

U.S. securities
Government-issued securities (U.S. Treasury bills and bonds), whose purchase or selling by the Federal Reserve forms the open market operations by which the Fed seeks to guide the money supply.

Velocity of money
The average number of times a unit of money is used during a year to purchase GDP's goods and services.

Voluntary export restraints
Agreements between governments in which the exporting country agrees to limit the volume of its exports.

Wage rate
The demand and supply of labor depend on the real wage rate; the money wage rate is the number of dollars an hour of labor earns.

Working-age population
People aged 16 years and over who are not in jail, hospitals, or other institutions.

World Trade Organization (WTO)
The World Trade Organization (WTO) is a group of nations dedicated to free global trade. Its members are expected to closely obey established GATT rules. The organization issues fines and penalties to nations who violate international free-trade rules.

INDEX

ABOUT THE AUTHOR

August Swanenberg graduated with an M.Sc. degree in Applied Mathematics and Econometrics from Tilburg University in the Netherlands, publishing articles about the testability of economic theories and equilibrium theory. He then received his MBA from Northwestern University's Kellogg School of Management and subsequently worked for McKinsey & Company and Dun & Bradstreet-ACNielsen before starting his own innovation consulting firm, IniQuest, Inc. He is a member of the Faculty of Business Professionals at Lake Forest Graduate School of Management in Lake Forest, Illinois.